Reforming Fictions

D0888976

Reforming Fictions

Native, African, and Jewish American Women's
Literature and Journalism in the Progressive Era

Carol J. Batker

Columbia University Press
NEW YORK

Columbia University Press

Publishers Since 1893

New York   Chichester, West Sussex

Copyright © 2000 Columbia University Press

Library of Congress Cataloging-in-Publication Data

Batker, Carol J.

Reforming fictions : Native, African, and Jewish American women's literature and
  journalism in the progressive era / Carol J. Batker.

  p. cm.

Includes bibliographical references and index.

ISBN 0-231-11850-3 (casebound : acid-free paper) — ISBN 0-231-11851-1 (pbk.)

1. American prose literature—Minority authors—History and criticism. 2. Social
  problems in literature. 3. Women and literature—United States—History—20th
  century. 4. Women in journalism—United States—History—20th century.
  5. Social problems—United States—History—20th century. 6. American fiction—Women authors—History and criticism. 7. American fiction—20th century—History and criticicm. 8. Journalism—United States—History—20th
  century. 9. Fauset, Jessie Redmon—Political and social views. 10. Women social
  reformers—United States. I. Title.

PS366.S62 B38 2000

818′.508099287′08693—dc21   99-089025

For Barry, Olivia, and Aaron

Contents

Acknowledgments

For their invaluable assistance, I would like to thank the American Jewish Archives, the Western History Collections at the University of Oklahoma Library, the Manuscripts, Archives, and Special Collections of the Holland Library at Washington State University, the Hadassah Archives, the Moorland-Spingarn Research Center at Howard University, the Tozzer Library at Harvard University, the American Native Press Archive at the University of Arkansas at Little Rock, the Special Collections Department of Brandeis University Libraries, the Department of Special Collections of Mugar Library at Boston University, and the American Jewish Historical Society.

Wendy Bergoffen's early editorial help and Dolores Lima's support are also gratefully acknowledged. I sincerely appreciate permission to reprint "'Overcoming All Obstacles': The Assimilation Debate in Native American Women's Journalism of the Dawes Era," *Early Native American Writing: New Critical Essays* (ed. Helen Jaskoski, Cambridge: Cambridge University Press, 1996), which appears here in a lengthier version as chapter 1 and "Literary Reformers: Crossing Class and Ethnic Boundaries in Jewish Women's Fiction of the 1920s," *MELUS*, forthcoming, which has become chapter 6. My heartfelt thanks go to the editors and staff at Columbia University Press, particularly Joan McQuary and Ann Miller.

For their guidance and intellectual stimulation throughout the early stages of this project, I would like to thank Ketu Katrak, Kathy Peiss, and especially Jules Chametzky. I am grateful to Christopher P. Wilson and Elizabeth Ammons for their scholarship and encouragement. A. LaVonne Brown Ruoff, Alanna Kathleen Brown, Helen Jaskoski, Shelley Fisher Fishkin, Nicholas Bromell, Valerie Traub, Judith E. Smith, Jonathan Sarna, and Joseph T. Skerrett Jr. all read parts of the manuscript with insight and provided extremely helpful criticism. The invaluable contributions of my colleagues Stacy Wolf, Terry Galloway, Donna Nudd, Delia Poey, and Jerrilyn McGregory improved the manuscript and challenged my thinking. Their friendship continues to sustain me. I am deeply indebted to Daniel F. Littlefield Jr. and Priscilla Wald for their generosity and belief in this project. For the remarkable care and acuity with which she read my manuscript, I would like particularly to thank Laura Doyle, friend and mentor. I also owe thanks to my family for inspiring and nurturing my work with their activism. In Barry Pritzker, I found my most delightful help. His intellect, humor, and compassion have had a profound effect on the imagining and writing of this book.

Reforming Fictions

Introduction

Women's political activism profoundly influenced their writing in the early twentieth century. *Reforming Fictions* recovers the enabling role reform work, in particular, played for women writers. I argue that political networks provided the inspiration and the opportunity for women's journalistic and literary publishing. Many women writers built their careers on the political-journalistic foundation reconstructed here. By considering these overlooked origins of women's writing, I develop a critical model that also makes visible cultural exchange among Native, African, and Jewish American women. A wide range of reform politics taken up in women's journalism shaped the preoccupations, language, and domestic form of women's fiction in these communities.

Often seen as having a direct and didactic impulse, journalism has been read apart from the self-conscious and literary preoccupations of the modernist period. An unfortunate consequence of this splitting of interests has been to oversimplify women's writing in the Progressive Era and to overlook affinities among women writers. Building on current criticism, which rejects the opposition between aesthetic and political concerns, *Reforming Fictions* takes up early periodical journalism as a dialogic and elaborately textured form that spoke to fiction in an intimate and influential exchange.[1] In the following pages I argue that we need radically to reread early twentieth-century fiction by

American women in the light of their political activism and journalism. My goal is to recreate the dialogue between journalism and fiction and recover the sophisticated conversation over reform politics among Native, African, and Jewish American women at its height in the 1910s and 1920s.

Meetings: Activism and Networks Among Women Writers

All of the writers treated here were political activists. Zitkala-Sa (Yankton Sioux) helped document corruption in Oklahoma, lobbied against peyote, worked with the General Federation of Women's Clubs Indian Welfare Committee in 1921, and founded the National Council of American Indians in 1926.[2] Mourning Dove (Okanogan Colville) advocated Native American employment in local companies, spoke to organizations such as the Women's Christian Temperance Union, and worked for fishing rights in 1930 (Miller, "Mourning Dove" 161–179; "Introduction" xxv). Active in racial uplift, Alice Dunbar-Nelson campaigned for women's suffrage in 1915, belonged to the National Federation of Colored Women's Clubs, organized African American women during the war, and headed the Anti-Lynching Crusaders in Delaware in 1922 (Hull, *Give Us Each Day* 468).[3] Jessie Fauset was active in the National Association for the Advancement of Colored People (NAACP) beginning in 1912 and belonged to a variety of women's clubs, as well (Sylvander, 40, 67). Having experienced immigrant aid firsthand, Anzia Yezierska worked for Hebrew Charities and conducted research for John Dewey among Polish immigrants in 1918 (Henriksen, 21, 71, 72, 94). As a journalist, Edna Ferber covered national party conventions, and she notes in her autobiography that she wrote "war propaganda" for the Red Cross, Young Men's Christian Association (YMCA), and Salvation Army and made speeches all over the country for Liberty Loan drives (*A Peculiar Treasure* 232, 240). Fannie Hurst supported the New York Urban League, Hadassah, the United Neighborhood Houses, the Federation of Jewish Philanthropies, and the campaign for the relief of Eastern European Jews in the 1920s ("Fannie Hurst" 29; Frederick,

360). She also chaired the Committee on Workman's Compensation for Household Employees in 1940 (Frederick, 360).[4]

Despite their impressive political record, literary women are not often read as activists or reformers. Their political contributions are generally underestimated or subsumed under aesthetic or literary concerns. Because of genre considerations and voice, for example, the overt politics in Mourning Dove's *Cogewea* have been attributed to her editor, Virgil McWhorter, and the "folk" content to her.[5] Similarly, although Jessie Fauset's column in *The Crisis* was often explicitly political, her contributions to the journal have been most often described in terms of her literary patronage and have not figured in interpretations of her novels.[6] Fannie Hurst and Edna Ferber's association with Hollywood likewise has influenced critics' decontextualized readings of their work.[7] Many of the authors discussed here have been judged by critics as accommodationist or aesthetically flawed, as reflected in critical comments on Yezierska's work.[8] While critics such as Hazel Carby, Carla L. Peterson, Claudia Tate, Diane Lichtenstein, and A. LaVonne Brown Ruoff have foregrounded the political activism of nineteenth- or turn-of-the-century works, the political writing and art of early twentieth-century women has been neglected.[9] The literary focus of modernism and writers' own declarations against propaganda in the context of World War I censorship and the Palmer raids of 1919 and 1920 continue to deter critical investigations of women's literary politicking during this period.

Yet, working for Pan-Indianism and off-reservation boarding schools, for racial uplift, and women's clubs, and for specific causes like antilynching or immigrant aid influenced women writers significantly. Women's political associations offered forums for debate and often made publication possible. The periodicals of the Society of American Indians (*The American Indian Magazine*), the National Association for the Advancement of Colored People (*The Crisis*), and the National Council of Jewish Women (*The Jewish Woman* and *The Immigrant*) published the fiction and journalism of their members. Editing these journals, Zitkala-Sa (from 1918 to 1919), Jessie Fauset (from 1919 to 1926), Estelle Sternberger and Cecilia Razovsky (from 1921 through the twenties) solicited literary contributions even as they defined and participated in public discourse (Fisher, "Zitkala-Sa" 235; Sylvander, 53, 95, 115; Rogow, 282). Not surprisingly, many women combined their literary writing with journalistic endeavor.[10]

However, very little attention has been paid to the periodical journalism of Native, African, and Jewish American women in the early twentieth century. Virtually no secondary material exists on Native American women's fairly abundant early journalism.[11] Although women's writing for the Yiddish press is a new and exciting field of inquiry, women's journalism in the Jewish English-language press has received attention only secondarily in studies of Jewish women's organizations.[12] Like acculturated Jewish women's early journalism, African American women's political journalism has primarily received attention through organizational studies.[13] Rodger Streitmatter's *Raising Her Voice: African-American Women Journalists Who Changed History* points out the lack of material on African American women's journalism but is itself primarily biographical in nature.

Not surprisingly, perhaps, reestablishing connections between women's literature and reform politics positions us to rethink relations among women writers. Indeed, literary and journalistic forums provide incontrovertible evidence of cultural exchange among prominent Native, African, and Jewish Americans. Since both African Americans and American Indians attended Hampton Institute, Hampton's journal, *The Southern Workman* (1872–1939), is one such source. Alice Dunbar-Nelson and Jessie Fauset both taught at Hampton, and Elizabeth G. Bender (Chippewa), who was active in the Society of American Indians (SAI), attended Hampton.[14] In *The Southern Workman*, the journalism of Arthur Parker (Seneca) mingles with essays written by Robert Moton and James Weldon Johnson. In addition, the journal included regular accounts of the National Association of Colored Women and foregrounded women like Laura Cornelius Kellogg (Oneida) and Angel DeCora Dietz (Winnebago) in articles on the SAI. Alice Dunbar-Nelson and Ella Cara Deloria (Yankton Sioux) published in this journal in 1922 and 1924, respectively.[15]

Collecting in its pages the writing of prominent intellectuals from Native, African, and Jewish American communities, *The Southern Workman* also featured articles by prominent Reform Rabbi Stephen Wise (Wise, 382–383). He is also mentioned as an acquaintance of

Charles Eastman (Santee Sioux), who is known for his autobiographical writing and his work on Sioux culture and history (*From the Deep Woods to Civilization* 192). In addition, Eastman attended the first Universal Races Congress with figures such as W. E. B. Du Bois in 1911 (*Warrior* xx). The roles played by Zitkala-Sa, Elizabeth Bender Roe Cloud (Chippewa), and Roberta Campbell Lawson (Delaware) in the General Federation of Women's Clubs also undoubtedly put them in touch with women of varied backgrounds and cultural affiliations.[16] According to Hazel Hertzberg, "Reform Pan-Indians sometimes spoke admiringly of the Jewish experience in preserving an identity in spite of persecutions" (311). Likewise, Jewish American writers were aware of issues affecting American Indians, even though their political interactions are difficult to document. Much of the evidence is piecemeal and local such as when, in her autobiography, Edna Ferber mentions a trip to Oklahoma in 1928 to research *Cimarron* (1930) or a visit to the Taos Pueblo in 1936 (*Peculiar Treasure* 326-331, 381).[17]

The significant relationships among African and Jewish Americans during the early twentieth century are already well-documented. Fannie Hurst's relationship as patron and employer of Zora Neale Hurston has been the focus of several articles, for example, as has the response of Harlem Renaissance writers to the 1934 film version of Hurst's novel *Imitation of Life* (1933).[18] The African American journal *Heebie Jeebies*, to which Hurston contributed, also featured Edna Ferber on at least one occasion (Daniel, 23). Similarly, *The American Hebrew* included writing by W. E. B. Du Bois in 1924, and Cecilia Razovsky's papers demonstrated that she and Charles Johnson both lectured about immigration/migration at a conference on social work.[19] Although vast distances, differences, and disagreements existed among these communities, they clearly knew of one another, at times published together, and were mutually influential.

These historical connections found in literary and journalistic sources suggest the complex discursive web of influence that affected women's writing during this period. Journalists and fiction writers from various communities shaped and revised the meanings of words only after they were "in other people's mouths, in other people's contexts, serving other people's intentions" (Bakhtin, 293–294). In Bakhtin's terms, juxtaposing the writing of these communities dis-

closes the "hybrid construction" of journalistic discourses as well as the
novel. Women writers continually revised discourses of reform and
their fiction in the light of cross-cultural encounters, sharing and refor-
mulating the language of "democracy," "foreignness," and "domesticity," for example. Borrowing not just substance but also rhetorical
strategies from each other, women's fiction and journalism engaged in
dynamic dialogue within and among communities, debating the major
issues of the early twentieth century.

Reform and the Politics of Domestic Fiction

My study recovers the range and complexity of reform politics in
women's fiction. As "Red Progressives," "Race Women," and "New
(Jewish) Women," the authors I consider here worked in reform institutions centrally concerned with domesticity, which explains why so
many authors turned to domestic fiction during the Progressive Era.
Building on earlier studies of sentimentality, I demonstrate how the
domestic ideology of off-reservation boarding schools, organizations
concerned with social welfare and racial uplift, or immigrant aid and
settlement houses served explicit political goals during this period.[20]
These institutions trained women for domestic service, ensuring their
economic marginalization, even as they positioned women in the
home as agents of acculturation and as advocates for social conformity.

Women writers revised these politics in their journalism and in
their fiction. For example, Native women writers exposed the colonialist agenda of domestic training and "model cottages" in boarding
schools; African American women rewrote racist social welfare conceptions of family and domestic labor; and Jewish immigrants challenged the elitism and domestic education of settlement houses.
They also strategically claimed domestic roles to argue for integration
and cultural retention. The marriage plots of women's fiction that
both entertain and reject intermarriage, passing, and cross-class
liaisons are carefully structured by the politics and rhetoric of reform.
By combining institutional critiques with marriage plots, women
writers revised domestic politics and commented on their own
activism in the process. Although a focus on domesticity has been read

as compromising women's politics, I argue that women's domestic fiction was a publicly engaged narrative strategy that positioned gender at the heart of national politics.

As a recovery project, *Reforming Fictions* works toward a deeper, more historically specific understanding of the representation of reform in women's writing. It explores a diverse range of assimilationist and class politics, which are often oversimplified or treated together in an undifferentiated way. Although clearly related in the writing of Native, African, and Jewish American women, the politics of assimilation and class are not identical. Literary critics often elide assimilationism and middle-class politics in their readings because they assume a cause and effect relationship among acculturation, middle-class status, and integration.

However, during the 1910s and 1920s acculturation among racialized groups more frequently did not guarantee civil rights or necessitate material prosperity, as Fauset's representation of the hostile response to African American soldiers during World War I painfully demonstrated. In addition, Mourning Dove's novel argues that Eurocentric practices embraced by her protagonist, Cogewea, do not guarantee social equality and are more likely to result in dispossession than material gain. Even Yezierska's characters who do attain social mobility through acculturation reject it because of the pervasive anti-Semitism that precludes social integration. Of course signs of acculturation, such as boarding school education in Mourning Dove's novel, patriarchal nuclear family structure in Fauset's novels, or Americanized clothing in Jewish women's fiction, do sometimes signal middle-class economic status in literary texts. However, acculturation and middle-class status were not always mutually reinforcing and existed in complex relation to the politics of incorporation.

Moreover, critical accounts of assimilation as simply accommodationist or resulting in cultural loss run the risk of obscuring women's sophisticated political negotiations.[21] Both sociologists and historians have called for more nuanced readings of assimilation. Sociologists generally agree that a monolithic model of assimilation based on an immigrant paradigm has dismissed and ignored the experiences of communities of color.[22] Even an immigrant paradigm of assimilation has suffered oversimplification and has obscured differences within

Jewish communities. According to Hyman, "the term 'assimilation' often does not convey the multiple influences that together forge individual as well as collective identity, the different social contexts in which various aspects of identity are expressed, or the coexistence of the desire for full civic integration with the retention of what we might today call ethnic particularism" (11). Responding to the need for more complex accounts of assimilation, the following chapters explore the dynamic relation between integration and various formulations of group rights among Native, African, and Jewish American women writers within the context of their historical differences. For example, the severe political marginalization of Native and African Americans differed substantially from Jewish Americans for whom there were no significant legal barriers to integration but who struggled against immigration restriction, anti-Semitism, social exclusion, and deportation during this period. African Americans experienced disenfranchisement and legal and de facto segregation while Native Americans met with increasing congressional and Bureau of Indian Affairs (BIA) control over reservation life and resources.

Positioned as racially inferior (in different degrees) and aware of the difficulty of achieving equality in the United States, Native, African, and Jewish American women did not simply sacrifice ethnic particularity or group membership for the promise of inclusion. Often their struggles for human rights and economic prosperity depended on cultural and political cohesion and an articulation of group rights. At times, reform values came at the expense of working-class or less-assimilated constituencies within these communities and compromised demands for equality, collective rights, or ethnic particularism. However, these women also affirmed group racial, ethnic, and religious identities often across class lines and in the face of severe discrimination. Within Native, African, and Jewish American communities there were clear historical divisions between those writers and political figures advocating integration and those advocating separatist politics—tribal sovereignty, black nationalism, and Zionism, for instance. However, these categories were not simply at odds as Jessie Fauset's involvement in Pan-Africanism and Zitkala-Sa's Pan-Indianism demonstrate. A discussion of assimilationist politics that examines cultural retentions, demands for political rights, and individual and group identifications allows for a range of political positionings and better explains both demands for and thwarted integration and equal rights.

My study also attends to the complexities of class differentiation among reform writers, since economic conditions and their significance varied widely among Native, African, and Jewish Americans. As Kevin Gaines argues, the occupations considered middle class among African Americans, like teacher, minister, or barber, could not "be regarded as equivalent with the business, managerial, and craft labor occupations among whites from which blacks were largely excluded" (14). Similarly, economic conditions as well as definitions of status varied among Native Americans, according to reservation and tribal affiliation and legal negotiations with the federal government.[23] Moreover, articulations of middle-class or bourgeois politics cannot be explained simply or strictly in material terms. Following Gaines' examination of African American uplift, this study takes up "the cultural or ideological dimensions of status that figured in representations of class, which . . . derived as much meaning from racial and gender categories as from economic or material realities" (14).

Native, African, and Jewish American women's texts defined class status not only in material terms but also through education, social attitudes toward hygiene, sexual expression, mixed ancestry, manual labor, and cultural markers like specific foods, language, or styles of dress. In Ferber's fiction, proprietorship and the ability to employ a maid are less significant as class markers than a shared family economy, which recalled an Eastern European rather than an European American family structure (Bergoffen, 36–38). In very complicated ways, traditional "yichus," or status, accruing to religious scholarship vies with economic prosperity in Yezierska's fiction. Similarly, the importance of family lineage, though partly constructed through economics, contends with material prosperity as a sign of privilege in Fauset's fiction.

Since reform organizations often provided the means for women's publication, it is not surprising that assimilation and middle-class values figure largely in the politics of women's literary and journalistic writing. Social mobility and the racial and economic barriers to it constitute a central theme in these women's writing. Involved in off-reservation boarding schools, racial uplift, and immigrant aid, all of these women negotiated a precarious balance between outsider and insider status in the United States and within and among their cultural groups. Further, it was against the exclusionary 1920s trends of failed Dawes era policies, segregation, and immigration restriction that these writers argued for civil rights and access to "American" institutions. In their periodical journalism and fiction, they worked in imaginative and complex ways to refute colonialist, racist, and anti-immigrationist rhetoric.

Multiculturalism and Literary Politics

Multiculturalism, in my study, is neither the sum total of works by ethnic writers nor a fluid exchange of common experiences and ideas. For one can read Native, African, and Jewish American women's writing together without erasing cultural differences or suggesting a political coalition where historically one did not exist.[24] Rather, I chronicle networks of influence, jagged and often uneasy, that show how the shared use of rhetorical tropes did not always reflect shared experience. The figure of the *Mayflower*, for example, which suffers a colonialist critique in Mourning Dove's *Cogewea* (1927), returns under the pen of Jewish journalists, bearing immigrants who seek religious freedom. Often even the common political goal of integration led writers to work against each other rather than in concert. While, for instance, African American writers emphasized the opposition between "American" and "foreigner" to reinforce their own positioning in the United States, Jewish American writers tried desperately to dismantle that opposition. In their turn, Jewish writers (Fannie Hurst and Edna Ferber in particular) employed racist representations of African Americans to situate themselves as white and assimilable.

Reforming Fictions insists on a multiculturalism that moves beyond binary models of inclusion, demonstrating how a varied and strategic politics of incorporation developed within a cross-cultural network of writers. In the following pages, I argue that Native, African, and Jewish American women scripted their positions within U.S. society in relation to one another, at times sharing publishing venues, issues, and rhetorical strategies. While I document negotiations with and varying figurations of U.S. politics and culture, I also suggest that exchange occurred not simply in opposition to the dominant culture but among Native, African, and Jewish American communities as well.[25] This study, then, works in at least two directions: it foregrounds women's literary politics by reading fiction in relation to their journalism, and it argues for a historical approach to multicultural reading, one built on the actual associations and networks of exchange among communities of women.

Native and African Americans share a long history of interaction in the United States, as do African and Jewish Americans. Moreover, all three of these groups spoke to one another, as I will demonstrate, through institutional affiliations during the Progressive Era. For example, vocational schools like Hampton Institute, off-reservation boarding schools, and settlement houses or immigrant schools exchanged a varied assimilationist and domestic politics which influenced writers in all of these communities. I also chose to examine the writing of these women together because of the abundance of Native, African, and Jewish American journalism and fiction written in English. Historically, journals in English were more likely to include writing from members of several cultural groups. Not surprisingly, membership in the organizations that produced English-language journals, such as Du Bois associate membership in the SAI or Jewish American participation in the NAACP, also provided evidence of cultural exchange (Hertzberg, 83). A common language and related institutional affiliations enabled women writers in these communities to share rhetorical and narrative strategies across cultures.[26]

In order to reconstruct the historical connections among women writers most effectively, I have organized my book by community. Moving from Native to African to Jewish American writers, I include for each a first chapter on journalism and a second on fiction. This approach avoids homogenizing the politics of each community. I use the contradictory polemics of journalism to uncover the diversity within each community and to read literature as negotiating in-group as well as cross-cultural dynamics. Each chapter on women's journalism gives voice to a number of writers whose varying positions and rhetorical strategies create a rich and contested political field mined by women's fiction. Only through a careful elaboration of the sophisticated dialogue between journalism and fiction in each community can we hear the larger conversation that occurred among communities of women writers.

Each journalistic chapter reconstructs the overlooked history of women's publication through political affiliations and recovers a body of writing previously ignored. Generally, I chose journals from prominent political organizations that employed women in editorial positions. *The American Indian Magazine*, *The Crisis*, *The Jewish Woman*, and *The Immigrant* combined women's editorial writing and influence with political articles and literary pieces by women. Differences in approach to women's journalism in these chapters reflect the needs of various fields of scholarship.

My work on Native American women's journalism, for example, focuses on the interrelated and accessible journals of the SAI and boarding schools but only begins to redress the absence of work on Native women journalists during this period. Women's writing for Native language presses as well as the many articles authored by women in Littlefield and Parins' bibliographies are important and little-read sources. Although a survey of women's journalism in *The Crisis* and other important periodicals needs to be undertaken, I focus on Jessie Fauset because of her prominent position as a journalist and literary figure during the Harlem Renaissance and because the politics of her journalism and fiction have been controversial but not fully historicized. Although critics have examined Josephine St. Pierre Ruffin's *Woman's Era* (1890–1897), the newsletters of African American women's church auxiliaries and clubs, such as the National Association of Colored Women's *National News*, are largely unexamined sources during this period and need investigation as do the newsletters and papers of Native women's organizations (Cott, 92; Streitmatter, 62, 69). I chose to look at the journals of the NCJW because women's writing in the Jewish English-language press has received little attention. These periodicals also provided the opportunity to examine women's journalism edited and written by and for Jewish women.

In chapters addressing periodical journalism I have focused primarily on one or two issues contemporary to the period and the specific community: citizenship, boarding school education, and reservation politics in American Indian periodicals; patriotism, civil rights, and participation in World War I in African American women's journalism; and immigrant aid, religious freedom, and secularization in Jewish women's writing. These choices were influenced by the distinct positionality and history of each of these groups, by the journals I selected, and by women's concerns within those forums, as well as by literary preoccupations during the period.

Each literary chapter begins by taking up current controversies over women's politics. I use journalistic forums to answer questions about the appropriation of Mourning Dove's text by her non-Native editor Lucullus V. McWhorter. Similarly, I read Jessie Fauset's fiction in relation to her larger political role as a journalist to answer charges that Fauset's literature is limited by a politics of respectability and accommodation. Finally, debates over immigrant aid provide a rationale for reading Anzia Yezierska's, Edna Ferber's, and Fannie Hurst's fiction in dialogue. The relationships among Eastern European immigrants and more acculturated Jewish women in the United States help explain Yezierska's contradictory attitudes toward the ghetto and clarify Ferber and Hurst's attitudes toward Jewish immigrants.

By juxtaposing literature with a multivalent history as expressed in political journalism, I argue that text and context can only be discovered simultaneously. Many of the reform politics examined here, as expressed in both literature and journalism, are partial, contingent, and at times compromised. The partial success of these politics, their very contingency, represents the everyday quality of women's commitment to and struggle for political justice, civil rights, and equality. Taken together, including across ethnic boundaries, women's political contributions through literary and journalistic forums are significant and compelling. They suggest the contours of a broad continuum of political writing by women and provide specific evidence of the difficult, day-to-day political choices women made in early twentieth-century America.

I

"Her Rightful Place in the New Scheme of Things"

Native American Women's Journalism in the Dawes Era

> The Indian girl of today lives in a very different environment from that of her great-grandmother. Since the allotment of land in severalty the chances are that the girl lives with her parents on their allotment away from any other people. The rest of the tribe are also scattered, each family on its own allotment, missing the old environment and companionship of the community life and lacking the education and training for appreciating and using the new to advantage. . . .the girl of today is baffled and confused, and is struggling, consciously or unconsciously, to find her rightful place in the new scheme of things.
>
> —Ella Cara Deloria

Native American women journalists argued for incorporation through a wide range of rhetorical strategies during the Dawes Era, attempting to keep in play a dialectic between integration and separatism, cultural adaptation and preservation. In writing that represents the contradictions of its time, Native women advocated both Pan-Indianism and many assimilationist policies, including citizenship, mainstream education, or allotment. Yet while many of their articles reproduced dominant discourses of assimilation and reform, when taken together they also significantly altered those discourses. Rejecting claims about their racial and cultural inferiority, they articulated both the promise and difficulty of attaining equality in U.S. society. At the same time, Native women journalists affirmed a dynamic Pan-Indian politics.

Not surprisingly, this complexity of purpose is grounded in a set of complex institutional affiliations. Many of the women writing journalism in English attended, were affiliated with, and wrote for the journals of off-reservation boarding schools, which flourished from General Richard Henry Pratt's founding of Carlisle in 1879 to the Meriam

Report's influential critique published in 1928.[1] Through boarding schools, Native women writers were influenced by discourses of domesticity and assimilation. Yet, most of these women also belonged to the Society of American Indians (Hertzberg, 36, 197).[2] I focus primarily on material from this society's journal, the *American Indian Magazine* (1916–1920), whose audience and contributors came from various tribes and white reform organizations. Thus, as it skillfully and subtly negotiates the tensions inherent in their situations, the journalism of these women offers a remarkable and heretofore largely unexamined analysis and appropriation of reform politics in the Dawes Era.[3]

The Dawes Era is generally represented as the period (1887–1934) from the passage to the reversal of the General Allotment or Dawes Act (named for its sponsor, Henry Dawes, who was an advocate of Indian assimilation and chair of the Senate Indian Affairs Committee).[4] Assimilationist policy during these decades changed substantially from the 1880s to the 1920s. While early assimilationist policies advocated "total assimilation"—or what might be called an integrationist program, privatizing land ownership and granting citizenship at the expense of tribal organization—by 1920, the policy had become more explicitly colonialist. Its advocates used ideologies of racial difference to marginalize Native communities and to appropriate Native resources (Hoxie, 147–238). These two approaches worked to alienate Native landholdings and to dismantle tribal cultures. Both total assimilationists and colonialists saw Native Americans as doomed, as "vanishing Indians," whose inability to survive contact justified U.S. ethnocentrism and colonialism. Integrationists used private land ownership as the basis for complete accommodation to U.S. society. Colonialists saw Native resources as "part of the public domain" and embraced "partial assimilation—bringing Native Americans into limited contact with the majority society while dropping the goal of equality" (Hoxie, 161, 152). While the former invited the collapse of differences through the erasure of separate tribal status, practices, beliefs, and organizations, the latter reified differences, insisting on Native inferiority and political marginalization to gain access to resources.

Off-reservation boarding school education reinforced shifting Dawes Era policies. Pratt, an advocate of "total assimilation," described his educational philosophy at Carlisle:

I suppose the end to be gained, however far away it may be, is the complete civilization of the Indian and his absorption into our national life, with all the rights and privileges guaranteed to every other individual, the Indian to lose his identity as such, to give up his tribal relations and to be made to feel that he is an American citizen. If I am correct in this supposition, then the sooner all tribal relations are broken up; the sooner the Indian loses all his Indian ways, even his language, the better it will be for him and for the government and the greater will be the economy to both. (qtd. in Lomawaima, 5)

This integrationist politics was based on ethnocentric and self-serving social evolution theory, which argued that Native Americans were culturally inferior and needed to abandon "primitive" tribal communities for U.S. "civilization" in order to survive. Ironically, the education provided in off-reservation boarding schools was outdated even for vocational schools, focusing on "rural, agricultural education" (Lomawaima, 78). The vocational thrust of boarding school education, according to K. Tsianina Lomawaima, worked against integration and equal rights:

Federal boarding schools did not train Indian youth for assimilation into the American melting pot, but trained them in the work discipline of the protestant ethic, to accept their proper place in society as a marginal class. Indians were not being welcomed into American society. They were being systematically divested of their lands and other bases of an independent life. (99)

These contradictions in Dawes Era ideology give rise to many of the rhetorical strategies and political negotiations in Native women's writing. Native women's early journalism refuses a simple rhetoric of domination, attempting, instead, to argue for inclusion without giving up a tribal or Pan-Indian affiliation.[5] Most journalism advocating integration used a rhetoric that masked the tremendous diversity among Native Americans, however. Often Native women journalists wrote about "the Indian" and addressed problems with the BIA, or reservation politics without reference to particular tribal contexts.[6]

Written from a Pan-Indian perspective, tribally specific politicking may have been viewed as divisive.

Within a Pan-Indian framework, Native women's political rhetoric tended to pursue three strategies, which ranged from an embrace of "total assimilation," to a focus on the preservation of tribal life, to a strategy that mediated between these two positions. The first of Native journalists' rhetorical strategies examined in this chapter accepted integrationist policy but in doing so established Native Americans as a constituency deserving equal rights. Native women, including Lucy Hunter (Winnebago), Evelyn Pierce (Seneca), and Elvira Pike (Uintah Ute), argued for integrationist policy and at the same time implicitly developed a rhetoric of Native rights which assumed a separate Pan-Indian identity. They supported mainstream education, citizenship, and the dismantling of the reservation system in order to refute arguments about racial inferiority and to gain equal access to economic and government structures in the United States. The second approach to discourses of reform tried to preserve Native cultural practices. Women, such as Angel DeCora (Winnebago), refuted the ethnocentrism of assimilationist discourse by arguing that Native cultures were distinct from and relevant to U.S. society. She claimed, for example, that Native arts were not relics of the past but could make vocational training more marketable in the United States. Women who argued against citizenship and integration and for separate nation status were rare in boarding school and Pan-Indian discourse. However, a third strategy employed by Zitkala-Sa and Laura Cornelius Kellogg (Oneida) attempted to combine advocacy for treaty rights and self-determination with an integrationist program. These three strategies also structured a gendered debate over the off-reservation boarding school program of domestic training, which I turn to in the second half of this chapter. This debate was specific to women's writing and, as we will see in chapter 2, powerfully affected women's fiction in form and substance.

Evelyn Pierce, Lucy Hunter, and Elvira Pike attended Hampton Institute, Haskell Institute, and the Phoenix Indian School, respectively, and published in the journal of the Society of American Indians. They drew on boarding school discourse in order to argue for civil rights. When advocating higher education, Pierce, Hunter, and Pike used theories of social evolution to claim an equal position for

Native Americans in U.S. society.[7] They maintained that Native Americans could successfully assimilate if they had access to higher education, challenging existing racist ideology on two grounds: they claimed that Native Americans were not by nature limited to vocational education and manual labor, as colonial educational policy asserted, and they argued that Native Americans could compete *on an equal basis* with whites and integrate fully into society, rather than occupy a marginalized position as inferiors. Paradoxically, by accepting the racist, social evolution premise that Native cultures were evolving from a "primitive" to a "civilized" state, these women tried to avoid racial determinism, which fixed Native Americans as "inferiors." They constructed a political Pan-Indian identity for themselves by arguing for civil rights, but they also reproduced reform discourse that relegated tribal cultures to the "primitive" past.

In an article published in 1915 for instance, Evelyn Pierce advocated higher education for Indian students and at the same time used a rhetoric of colonialism and social evolution. She stated, "at the time of the discovery of America by Columbus, our ancestors were at best but a semi-civilized race" (107). However, she used the ideology of social evolution to criticize social inequity and to argue for integration and a greater investment in higher education for Native Americans:

> Everywhere, we hear the cry for higher efficiency. Can the Indian take his place by the white man, and can he gain efficiency with a common school education that the government gives him? No, he cannot.
>
> The white man today must be highly educated in order to keep his place among the thousands of his race. If he wishes to attain a place higher than that occupied by his fellow men, he must train and educate all parts of his nature to their highest possibilities.
>
> If all this is necessary for the white man, how much more so is it for the Indian who is already handicapped by his ignorance of the English language and customs. (108)

Unlike proponents of vocational Indian education who argued for lower educational expectations and opportunity, Pierce believed that Native Americans deserved a better education than non-Natives. She relied on ethnocentric social evolution theory to make her point, but she argued against racial inferiority and for equal opportunity: "In almost every instance where the Indian has had higher academic training he has demonstrated his ability to compete with the whites in the activities of life" (109).

Like Pierce, Lucy E. Hunter employed social evolution theory to argue against vocational education and the racial inferiority it implied. Hunter prefaces an article entitled "The Value and Necessity of Higher Academic Training for the Indian Student" with a history of "progress" from "ancient history['s] . . . people who had no permanent dwelling places but roamed the country and lived on nature's raw products" to "nations, kingdoms, and empires; and even wonderful cities" (11). She claimed "And so, mankind has been on an onward, upward march since the world began; and every time such an awakening has been felt by a people it has been a sure sign of progress" (11). Hunter used discourses of "primitivism" and "civilization" to argue for integration and against economic marginalization. To get a good job and the best wages, she argued, one needs education "of the mind as well as the hands" (13).

Elvira Pike promoted the integration of Indian children into the public school system as an alternative to vocational education. Pike repeated ethnocentric boarding school discourse at the same time that she argued for equal rights. She claimed that "the success of the Indian race depends upon making their interests one with those of the white race" ("Public Schools" 59–60). However, Pike's acceptance and imitation of "white" society did not replace her critique of boarding school education as limiting and ethnocentric. She stated that "Indians as a race and as students, have not been fairly treated" (59). She argued for self-determination in and against vocational and agricultural education:

> The question has often been asked, "What shall be done with the Indian student, or what shall be made of him?" and it has been said "make farmers out of the boys, and farmers" wives of the girls'—as though they were a lifeless piece of clay to be moulded into shape, as suited the whim of an experimenter.

> The Indian student has a will and impulses of his own which must be reckoned with.   ("The Right Spirit" 401)

Using early assimilationist ideology politically to demand equal rights proved a difficult task, often resulting in a rejection of or a conflicted stance toward tribal culture. While Pierce, Hunter, and Pike rejected ideologies of racial determinism and inferiority, they undermined their own arguments by depicting tribal cultures as "primitive" and U.S. society as "civilized." To a very real degree, however, they were able to construct a Pan-Indian identity through a rhetoric of Native rights, arguing against vocational education and for equal opportunity. Their Pan-Indianism is evidenced, in part, by the fact that other writers (such as those I turn to next) addressed, extended, and disagreed with these positions.

Rather than demanding equal rights in U.S. society, Roberta Campbell Lawson (Delaware) and Angel DeCora focused on preserving Native cultural practices. Like Hunter, Pierce, and Pike, they struggled with social evolution theory, but their emphasis on tribal cultures tended to work against the goal of integration. Lawson collected Native American music and artifacts, wrote a book entitled, *Indian Music Programs*, served on the Women's Committee of the National Council of Defense during World War I, held membership in a number of clubs including Hyechka Music, Indian Women's Hobbies, and La-Kee-Kon, attended a 1934 Pan-Pacific conference in Hawaii, and assumed presidency of the Oklahoma Federation of Women's Clubs from 1917 to 1919 and the General Federation of Women's Clubs from 1935 to 1938. DeCora attended Hampton Institute, was a member of the Society of American Indians, and taught at Carlisle. She illustrated the work of several prominent Native American writers including Zitkala-Sa, Francis LaFlesche (Omaha), and Charles Eastman, as well as at least two of her own stories published in *Harper's New Monthly Magazine*.[8]

These women wrote about tribal culture within the context of anthropological discourses on preservation and the popular fascination with Native American cultures, both of which reinforced social evolution theory. Native arts had already found a place in U.S. society as curios and artifacts, evidence of dying cultures (Hoxie, 122). Photographer Edward S. Curtis, for example, titled a famous photo, "The Vanishing Race," and explained, "the thought which this picture is meant to convey is that the Indians as a race, already shorn of their tribal strength and stripped of their primitive dress, are passing into the darkness of an unknown future" (qtd. in Dippie, 209). The marginalization of Native Americans was supported by an ideology that constructed tribal identity as static and nearing extinction. Scientific interest in tribalism worked politically to create an image of Indians as "primitive," as part of America's past, as antithetical to contemporary society. This version of the "vanishing race" helped write the narrative of national progress through conquest (Dippie, 207).

Lawson argued for the collection and preservation of Indian music, but her writing reproduced the discourses of ethnologists with whom she worked, relegating tribal music to the past. She claimed that tribal songs "carry much of the manner and customs, religion and history of a fast disappearing race" (447).[9] Lawson's political work did help to preserve tribal culture. Ideologically, however, her belief in social evolution left those cultures without a future. Displaced by "civilization," she argued that "these songs, like their singers, come from we know not where or whence and while many of them are crude and often far from tuneful, they are the outward expression of the inward soul and feeling of a primitive people" (447). Here, Lawson's discussion of tribal music and cultures valued them only as antecedents to U.S. society.

As the art instructor at Carlisle, Angel DeCora embraced tribal culture without relegating it to the past but was conflicted in her attitudes toward integration. She argued against the ethnocentrism and conformity of boarding school education, for example, but drew on a problematic rhetoric of racial difference: "Heretofore, the Indian pupil has been put through the same public school course as the white child, with no regard for his hereditary differences of mind and habits of life" (527). Similarly, while DeCora rejected social evolution theory, she questioned Native Americans' ability to assimilate:

> The method of educating the Indian in the past was an attempt to transform him into a brown Caucasian within the space of five years or a little more. . . . The Indian, bound up as he is in tribal

laws and customs, knew not where to make a distinction, nor which of his natural instincts to discard, and the consequence was that he either became superficial and arrogant and denied his race, or he grew dispirited and silent.   ("Native Indian Art" 527)

DeCora suggested that the effect of ethnocentric schooling on Native Americans was either the denial of cultural affiliation or marginalization and silence. As we will see in the next chapter, Mourning Dove shares discursive ground with DeCora as she refuses ethnocentrism but more successfully advocates for integration through a representation of Cogewea's mixed ancestry.

Significantly, DeCora's journalism critiqued boarding school education without maintaining, as the government did, that Native American cultures were inferior. Her articles departed from colonial rhetoric because she represented Native art as relevant to U.S. society rather than as evidence of a distant past or of Native "savagery and degradation." DeCora did not argue for the demise or inferior status of tribal culture. Instead, she argued for the preservation and usefulness of tribal cultures in contemporary U.S. society:

We can perpetuate the use of Indian designs by applying them to modern articles of use and ornament that the Indian is taught to make. . . . I believe that we shall be ready to adapt our Indian talents to the daily needs and uses of modern life. We want to find a place for our art even as the Japanese have found a place for theirs throughout the civilized world. The young Indian is now mastering all the industrial trades, and there is no reason why the Indian workman should not leave his own artistic mark on what he produces.   (528)

DeCora created a use for Native arts within a non–Native cultural context. However, the decorative aspect of her economic plan is telling in its inability to challenge vocational education and the political marginalization of Native Americans in the United States. By arguing that industrial arts inscribed with tribal designs could signify Native identity and culture, DeCora did depart significantly from an anthropological discourse of past achievement. Although unable seriously to critique vocational education, she believed that Native arts could make Native Americans more competitive economically in U.S. society.

Jane Zane Gordon (Wyandotte) opposed integration and citizenship altogether but represented a minority voice in boarding school and Pan-Indian journals. In a 1924 article for *Indian Tepee*, she argued that Native Americans would have more autonomy and control over their resources as separate nations than as citizens: "the United States Government has always dealt with the Indian in his tribal and national capacities, and never as individuals in propria persona" (2). She questioned the government's authority over Native Americans as either "subjects" or "wards" and she argued for self-determination: "the Indian has, by his seclusion exercised some slight authority inside of his municipal domain. The Federal Government assumes to control all that its citizens may eat, drink, or wear, where he shall go, and what he shall do. The Indian does not want the shell of a nut" (3).

Zitkala-Sa and Laura Cornelius Kellogg (Oneida) attempted to mediate between the competing demands of integration and separatism. In their journalism they argued for treaty rights, control over Native resources, and the preservation of tribal cultures without reinforcing the marginalization of Native Americans in U.S. society. In addition to writing for and editing the *American Indian Magazine*, Zitkala-Sa held office in the Society of American Indians. She founded the National Council of American Indians in 1926 which attempted to organize a Native American vote to influence U.S. policy. Her collection of folklore, entitled *Old Indian Legends*, was published in 1901 and her fiction, *American Indian Stories*, in 1921. Kellogg is best known as founder of the Iroquois land claims movement, but she occupies an uneasy position in Oneida history because she was accused of fraudulent dealings by tribal elders (Hauptman, 161).[10]

Paradoxically, Zitkala-Sa argued for Native rights by supporting U.S. citizenship.[11] In an article on the Black Hills Council, Zitkala-Sa advocated the break-up of the reservation to argue for citizenship: "In view of this situation it is quite apparent that the sooner the tribal corrals are thrown open, the sooner the Indian will become Americanized. There need be no fear that he may not measure up to the responsibilities of a citizen. Even after the blighting stagnation of the Indian reservations, the Indian will be equal to his opportunities" ("The Black Hills" 5).

However, Zitkala-Sa advocated dismantling the reservation system, not to break down tribal organization, necessarily, but as a means of protecting political rights and treaties. She argued that civil rights would provide the legal mechanism to protest invasive government policy and to advocate for individual and tribal self-determination. She claimed that the reservation system marginalized Native Americans in U.S. society and that the separatism of reservation life did not guarantee self-determination. Mourning Dove's novel *Cogewea* echoes this critique of the reservation as a space without legal recourse and open to U.S. exploitation. Without citizenship, Zitkala-Sa argued, tribes were unable to sue the government because "three-fourths of the Indian race being non-citizen, have no legal status" and "Indian tribes are by express statute excluded from the general jurisdiction of the Court of Claims; and in order to present their grievances, they must first obtain the consent of Congress, of which they are non-constituents" ("The Black Hills" 5). Zitkala-Sa saw citizenship as a means to support the legal petitioning for tribal rights. She also advocated self-determination, arguing that tribes should retain their own council rather than accept advice and council from the Indian Bureau, which consistently failed to represent tribal concerns.

Elsewhere, Zitkala-Sa protested a Senate resolution to control the use of Ute pasture land as well as the Indian Bureau's leasing policy. According to Zitkala-Sa, "the Senate resolution states that the Ute Indians are not making an economic and adequate use of their grazing land; and will not in the future be able to make economic and adequate use of it" ("The Ute" 8). She pointed out the futility of the government's effort to have Utes farm allotted land with an inadequate water supply, and she argued for Ute control over grazing land "with the hands of the Indian Bureau strictly off" ("The Ute" 9). Zitkala-Sa argued for self-determination, protesting government control over the use of tribal land. However, her argument is somewhat problematic in that she failed to challenge Dawes-Era notions of "progress" and development. In general, biographical accounts of Zitkala-Sa recognize that her life was characterized by a struggle to maintain tribal identity while participating in U.S. society; however, they have often neglected the extent to which her politics embraced assimilationist policy as well as tribal institutions and culture.[12]

Although most of Zitkala-Sa's political discourse struggled with U.S. policy and constructed a Pan-Indian political coalition, she did argue for cultural preservation in a few pieces. In her article, "A Protest Against the Abolition of the Indian Dance," for example, she defended "Indian" dance by questioning notions of "barbarism" and "civilization." She was responding to statements like the Commissioner of Indian Affairs' in 1901, "Indian dances and so-called Indian feasts should be prohibited. In many cases these dances and feasts are simply subterfuges to cover degrading acts and to disguise immoral purposes. You are directed to use your best efforts in the suppression of these evils" (qtd. in O'Brien, 76). She opposed reigning representations of tribal cultures as primitive, static, and thus doomed to extinction.

In her article, Zitkala-Sa represented Native American culture as a partially frozen river waiting only for the spring to "rush forth from its icy bondage." Assimilationists chipped away at the surface of the river muttering "immodest" and "this dance of the Indian is a relic of barbarism." According to Zitkala-Sa, not only were these attempts at destroying ceremonialism in vain, but they were also "unconscious . . . of the river's dream, which he may have disturbed; forgetful, too, of the murmuring water-songs he has not released through his tiny tapping." For Zitkala-Sa this partially frozen river dreams of the spring when "its rippling songs shall yet flood its rugged banks." Criticizing their marginalization, Zitkala-Sa represented Native cultures as vital, about to be rejuvenated and unleashed, and much more powerful than non-Natives tapping at the frozen surface ("A Protest" 1).

Zitkala-Sa's river played on notions of doomed and static tribal cultures, decentering non-Native society at the same time it asserted a strong Native presence. Mourning Dove's use of river imagery in *Cogewea* also plays with narratives of victimization.[13] Here, the metaphor can be read as a critique of assimilationists whose attempts to destroy tribal cultures are wrong-headed and ineffectual; their work will only unleash the river's vibrant forces. However, the figure of the river can also be read as ambivalent. If the partially frozen river represents tribal cultures at which whites are chipping away, then the spring thaw could also be read as the furthering of reformers' ambitions: the thaw implies at least a transmutation of tribal cultures. In the figure of the thawing river, Zitkala-Sa suggests Native cultural rejuvenation rather than extinction; however, she does not necessarily guarantee a vital tribalism.

Later in the article, Zitkala-Sa is more explicitly ambivalent about "the Indian dance," claiming that "the old illiterate Indians, with a past irrevocably dead and no future, have but a few sunny hours between them and the grave. And this last amusement, their dance, surely is not begrudged them. The young Indian who has been taught to read English has his choice of amusements, and need not attend the old-time one" ("A Protest" 1).

Here, Zitkala-Sa draws on the rhetoric of the "vanishing Indian." I examine Zitkala-Sa's defense of "the Indian dance" rather than her better-known essay, "Why I Am a Pagan," as evidence of her legitimation of tribal culture because it is more characteristic of the ambivalence most of her political writing displays. In spite of her ambivalence toward "old-time" practices, Zitkala-Sa did consistently question notions of "civilization," "barbarism," and stasis. In doing so, she legitimated cultural practices while she critiqued the marginalization of tribal cultures just as she did in her arguments against disenfranchisement.

Laura Cornelius Kellogg responded to "A Protest" by arguing that tribal dances were "debased" and could "only undo honorable labor," and consequently slow assimilation ("She likes Indian" 1). Like Zitkala-Sa, Kellogg wrote a conflicted politics, trying to sustain a tribal identity without excluding Native Americans from the mainstream. She condemned the reservation system in order to reject notions of racial inferiority, and she insisted on a position of equality for American Indians in U.S. society. However, in so doing she tended to reinforce ethnocentric notions of "progress" as well. Nevertheless, her emphasis on political equality eventually led her to question social evolution and to argue for a tribal orientation in education.

Initially in her 1913 article entitled, "Some Facts and Figures on Indian Education," Kellogg critiqued Native Americans' status as wards on the reservation:

The Indian child's environment is the reservation, a world of deficits. The group has really custodian care. *There is no real per-*

sonal liberty in wardship; there is no incentive in the community for any
special effort; there is no reward for right doing; the social life is not
organized. A group of Indians may dance a whole week without
impairing their personal estates. There are no markets of their
own making and their own responsibility. There is no money
continually in circulation. . . . There is nothing being learned by
the adult population from necessity.   ("Some Facts" 44)

However, she reinforced popular notions of "progress" by rejecting
reservations as unproductive in her statements about dance. Ultimately, she used her critique of the reservation system to expose the
inequity between Native and non-Natives. She argued that: "We have
allowed the country to discriminate against us in the segregation of the
Indian from the rest of the population. We have allowed ourselves to
be cooped up for thirty-five years away from the same advantages the
rest of the country is getting" ("Some Facts" 39).

Boarding school education failed to measure up to education for
non-Natives. Kellogg argued that Indian school officials were poorly
educated, criticized the inadequacy of health care in boarding schools,
decried the graft in Indian education, and bemoaned the pervasive
ethnocentrism which denied Native children pride in their heritage:

Culture is but the fine flowering of real education, and it is the
training of the feeling, the tastes and the manners that make it
so. When we stop to think a little, old Indian training is not to
be despised. The general tendency in the average Indian schools
is to take away the child's set of Indian notions altogether, and to
supplant them with the paleface's. There is no discrimination in
that. Why should he not justly know his race's own heroes rather
than through false teaching think them wrong? Have they not as
much claim to valor as Hercules or Achilles?   ("Some Facts" 37)

To some extent, Kellogg's critique of education as ethnocentric did
conflict with her representation of the reservation as unproductive.
However, this critique was fundamentally an extension of her earlier
political commitment to social equality and her rejection of wardship
and racial inferiority. For her, both the reservation and boarding school

educational systems were corrupt, inequitable, and unpragmatic in a capitalist marketplace. In Kellogg's work, as in Zitkala-Sa's, a defense of tribal culture combined with a critique of the reservation system to undermine exclusive government policies. In spite of the controversy surrounding Kellogg's activism, her work on land claims and her use of tribal language and folklore in oratory are evidence of her success in supporting a dynamic tribalism (Hauptman, 161, 166, 172, 175).

The combination of a critique of reservation corruption and an embrace of political and cultural tribalism was an integrationist strategy embraced by Louise Johson Bear (Winnebago), as well. A member of the Society of American Indians, Johnson Bear created a complex narrative of political heroism by affirming tribalism while maintaining a political critique of the reservation necessary to avoid marginalization. She juxtaposed two stories, "A Winnebago Question and a Tale of a Winnebago Hero" in order to discuss both the Winnebago removal and the political success of a young Winnebago youth in Washington, D.C. Initially, she exposed U.S. incompetence, hypocrisy, and abuse and described the ingenuity and fortitude of the Winnebagos: government soldiers starved and raped the Winnebagos after removing them from Minnesota, but the tribe outwitted them and escaped.

Then Johnson Bear told of a modern-day "Winnebago Hero" who walked to Washington, D.C., to petition "for allotments, for schools, policemen to keep order, implements to work with, for houses and cattle to start these Indians to be self-supporting" (153). A nephew of the Winnebago chief, this hero came from the reservation and worked politically to find a place for his people in U.S. society. Although his negotiations with the government yielded only the fruits of assimilation policy, Louise Johnson Bear's hero was significant because he actively created a future for the Winnebagos. This is not the proud warrior hero who was doomed to extinction but a modern Indian, successful in politics and dedicated to his people. Louise Johnson Bear described him significantly as "an uneducated Indian" who "was the future of his people and worked faithfully for them, overcoming all obstacles, conquering poverty, distance, the terrors of an unknown East and he finally won an inheritance for the Winnebagos. His success came because he was not selfish but thought most of his people and his duty to them" (153).

Similarly, Zitkala-Sa used the figure of the soldier in World War I to critique reservation corruption and advocate for citizenship while creating a successful Pan-Indian hero. She reversed the ideology positioning Native Americans as part of the national past, extinct and proof of the triumph of "civilization," even though her hero did advocate for assimilation. Supporting early Dawes Era ideology, Zitkala-Sa's soldier rejected the reservation system: "In my travels with the army I have seen a great world. I did not know till then that I had been living in a reservation wilderness," and later, "the irksome vacuity of reservation exile may require as much heroism, if not more, to live than it did to die in actual battle" ("Hope" 61–62). Zitkala-Sa's description of the reservation as "exile" is further reinforced by her statements implying that Native Americans would gain from associating with non-Natives ("Indian Gifts" 116).

However, Zitkala-Sa wrote about Indian soldiers primarily to argue for citizenship: "America! Home of Democracy, when shall the Red Man be emancipated? When shall the Red Man be deemed worthy of full citizenship if not now?" ("America" 166). By demonstrating that Native Americans were successful patriots, able to contribute to U.S. society, she refuted racist ideology which saw Native Americans as marginal or as part of a disappearing past. Zitkala-Sa argued that Native Americans were not only responsible for past contributions to the U.S., such as the corn and potatoes that replaced wheat in a war economy, but also for contemporary contributions, giving money, clothing, and men to the war effort ("Indian Gifts" 115).

At the same time Native Americans embraced patriotism in Zitkala-Sa's writing, they retained a distinct Pan-Indian identity. She described Native soldiers stereotypically as "clothed with that divine courage which some have called 'Indian stoicism'; and in their company we realize that each and every one of us possess the attributes of heroism, as our divine heritage!" Native patriotism "reveals inherent in the Indian race a high and noble quality of mind" ("Hope" 62). Zitkala-Sa used stereotypes of "stoic" and "noble" not to relegate Native Americans to the past but to show how these qualities fit them to serve and participate in U.S. society.

Mourning Dove also used a patriotic Pan-Indian rhetoric of heroism to the same end in an article on the Red Cross. She claimed, "This splendid patriotism of the thousands of our best young men who joined in the world fight for democracy, attests the true steel of the Red race, hampered though it is by undue Governmental restrictions" (*Mourning Dove* 189, 190). World War I was also used discursively by African American writers, as I will demonstrate at length in chapters 3 and 4. While Native American enlistment in the war resulted in the passage of the Indian Citizenship Act of 1924, African Americans were drafted into a segregated army and faced increasing racism and violence after the war (Debo, 335; O'Brien, 80). Both communities, however, used a wartime rhetoric of patriotism and democracy in an attempt to gain political rights in the United States.[14]

Negotiating the tensions between tribal self-determination and full participation in U.S. society was a complex and difficult venture. The ethnic politics and strategies of resistance that I have outlined here are often problematic; no one strategy emerges as ideal, wholly successful, or even ultimately consistent. However, together, Native women's political journalism in English constitutes an important transgression of oppressive assimilationist and colonial policies during this period. Native women refuted notions of racial biologism and inferiority, demanded positions of equality in U.S. society, and constructed a Pan-Indian political identity which could and did advocate for Native rights. Women like Angel DeCora, Louise Johnson Bear, and Zitkala-Sa also attempted to represent tribal cultures as participants in U.S. society rather than static and doomed to extinction. What these strategies have in common is the desire to represent Native and non-Native cultures in complex negotiation with one another. They argue implicitly that integration does not require the abandonment of Native rights or the marginalization of tribal cultures. Instead, they position Native communities as dynamic, adaptive political forces in the United States.

Although they appeared rarely, a few articles from the *American Indian Magazine* and boarding school journals focussed directly on gender and debated the colonial versions of domesticity that were clearly a part of reform and boarding school discourse. Articles ranged from an embrace of domesticity as a tool of integration to more frequent critiques of domestic ideology as politically marginalizing, as disrupting tribal family and kinship networks, and as reinforcing social evolution theory. Native women also used their critique of off-reservation boarding schools' program of domestic training as an occasion to stress the value of tribal gender roles. Together, these women rewrote the politics of incorporation and reform from a gendered position and influenced the form and politics of Native women's domestic fiction.

Off-reservation boarding schools were run on the "half and half" (academic and vocational) system. Girls' vocational training was confined to domestic science, which they learned by performing the labor needed to run the boarding school. They sewed uniforms, mended and washed clothing, cleaned kitchens and dormitories, and canned, prepared, and served food for hundreds of students (Lomawaima, 83–84). Actual job placement in domestic service was minimal, however, and Lomawaima argues, "the only employment available in domestic service for many young Indian women graduating from boarding schools was in the boarding schools themselves" (86; Trennert, 287).

Moreover, domestic training served the political goals of the Dawes Era. Domesticity and a "civilized" home supported the individual landowning/farmer ethic of the General Allotment Act. Boarding school attitudes toward women's bodies also betrayed beliefs in racial inferiority and social evolution theory, as Lomawaima argues: "Indian girls' attire, comportment, posture, and hairstyles betrays a deep-seated, racially defined perception of Indian peoples' corporal physical bodies as 'uncivilized'" (82).[15] In an analysis of two photographs, Laura Wexler also documents the colonial transformation of Native American women into Victorian ladies at Hampton Institute (20–26). Through labor and the regulation of women's bodies, domestic vocational education fostered a politics of subordination meant to serve the larger political goals of the Dawes Era.

However, Native women coming from communities with widely disparate gender and sexual mores often used tribal culture to resist domestic ideology in boarding schools.[16] That Native Americans rejected gender differentiation in federal policy is clear in Angie Debo's description of changes in the General Allotment Act. Land was initially allotted as

> 160 acres (a "quarter" of the mile-square "section") to each head of a family, smaller amounts to unmarried men and children. But the Indians expressed so much opposition to this alien 'head of a

family' concept—in their society married women and children had property rights—that in 1891 the act was amended to provide equal shares to all—80 acres of agricultural, 160 acres of grazing land. (300)

The activism of women like Zitkala-Sa and Laura Cornelius Kellogg is in itself further evidence of Native American women's ability to reject colonial paradigms of domesticity.

That Native American women engaged and adapted gendered discourses of reform is evident in their affiliations with women's organizations. Zitkala-Sa and Elizabeth Bender Roe Cloud were both active in the Society of American Indians and in the Indian Welfare Committee (later the Indian Affairs Committee) of the General Federation of Women's Clubs (GFWC) (Fisher, "Zitkala-Sa" 235; Hertzberg, 48). Roberta Campbell Lawson was president of the GFWC (Gridley, 74). Native American women's association with the General Federation of Women's Clubs was used primarily to gain philanthropic support and as a platform to advocate for Native rights.[17] Mourning Dove was one of the founders of a local Native women's organization, the Eagle Feathers Club, in 1928 (Miller, "Introduction" xxv). Ella Cara Deloria was also involved in women's reform organizations through the Young Women's Christian Association (YWCA), for which she served as health education secretary for Indian schools and reservations in 1919 (Picotte, 230). These affiliations informed the fiction of Zitkala-Sa, Mourning Dove, and Ella Cara Deloria, who wrote short stories or novels in addition to journalism.

Elizabeth G. Bender (Chippewa), an active member of the Society of American Indians and the National Congress of American Indians, held office in the General Federation of Women's Clubs and attended Hampton Institute (Gridley, 34; Hertzberg, 48). Bender combined early assimilationist ideology with a defense of domestic training in order to argue against Dawes Era beliefs in racial inferiority. Her article, "Training Indian Girls for Efficient Home Makers," supported colonial boarding school attitudes toward domesticity. Since "the home is the very core of any civilization," Native Americans' successful integration into U.S. society was in the hands of its women, according to Bender (155). She dismissed the reservation as a place of "unkempt homes which are breeding places for filth and disease" and where land is "lying idle" and argued that "no people advance any faster than their women and the home is conceded to be the core of the Indian problem" (155). Bender praised Carlisle for building a "model home cottage" which taught Native women "how to cook over a common stove, to take care of kerosene lamps, and to prepare three meals a day in the most wholesome and economical way. . . . to learn the art of cooking cereals, vegetables, eggs, fish, bread, cake, and pastry, besides the proper setting of a table and the preparation and serving of family meals" (155).[18] Bender's acceptance of women's domestic roles combined with her critique of reservation life in order to promote integration and, more problematically, allotment.

Emma Johnson Goulette (Potawatomi), a member of the Society of American Indians, also saw the home as central to integration (Hertzberg, 118). However, Goulette did not define women's place in U.S. society through their ability to perform domestic labor. Critical of the limited scope of the program of domestic science at Carlisle, Goulette again makes clear that these journal articles represent an active dialogue among Native women writers and activists:

> Some of our Indian schools have cottages for the purpose of teaching home duties. Is it possible to teach the real, practical home duties by this method? Does the child get the practical knowledge of his duty to his father, mother, relatives and neighbors? Does he have a chance to observe and experience town and city ordinances? Does this method afford him the opportunity of hearing home interests, county, state and national affairs and laws discussed?   ("Common School" 302)

Goulette criticized the political marginalization of Native American women within a vocational education system focussed on women's domestic labor.

In this article by Goulette and in the writing of Ella Cara Deloria (Yankton Sioux), Dawes Era policies that positioned Native women as farmer's wives were rejected. According to Goulette, domestic training disrupted Native American family and kinship networks. Similarly, in the 1924 passage I've used as an epigraph to this chapter, Deloria combined a critique of allotment with a domestic argument about the disruption of family and gender roles. Deloria wrote three books on Sioux language and culture and a novel entitled *Waterlily*, while working with Franz Boas. She also taught at Haskell Indian school (Picotte, 230–231).

Goulette, Deloria, and Marie L. Baldwin (Chippewa) also took on social evolution theory by using the language of domesticity to reverse racist stereotypes of Native women as subjugated laborers. Baldwin was a member of the Society of American Indians, an employee of the Bureau of Indian Affairs, a lawyer who litigated the land claims of the Turtle Mountain band of Chippewa, and a suffragist (Hertzberg, illustration caption; Welch, 121–126). She argued explicitly against racist stereotypes directed at Native women's labor, "one of the most erroneous and misleading beliefs relating to the American Indian woman is that she was both before and after marriage the abject slave and drudge of the men of her tribe" (5). Claiming instead that Native men would learn how to exploit women from white men "who have no respect for self or use for a woman except as a servant, child bearer, home manager and bread winner," Goulette inverted racist stereotypes even as she subtly remarked on the exploitation that occurred under the auspices of domestic training ("The Returned" 135). Even more significantly, Baldwin advocated the powerful positions and "absolute equality" of Native American women in tribal culture:

In a large number of tribes she was on an absolute equality with her sons and brothers in the exercise and enjoyment of the several rights and patrimony of her people; and by exceptional environmental conditions she established matronymical or matriarchal institutions, in which she was supreme in the choice of her rulers who were of course her sons and brothers, and whose titles to office were hereditary in her own right and over which she had the absolute right of recall. She herself in some cases exercised executive functions in the various activities of her people. (1)

This assertion of the powerful roles Native women played in tribal communities is rare in the *American Indian Magazine* and, not surprisingly, the journals of boarding schools, probably because it was seen as conflicting with the goals of integration. Baldwin's article articulates this tension when she admonishes Native women that, "to secure welfare and happiness she must adapt and wisely adjust her inherent and acquired talents to these modern surroundings. Many of the things that were useful and necessary, yea, sacred, to her own mother must now be laid aside" (7). As Pan-Indian activists, Native women writers strategically employed a boarding school focus on the home to critique non-Native domestic roles as limited and politically marginalizing and to argue for integration.

Out of complex institutional affiliations and the access they provided to periodical publishing, Native women produced a rich discourse on reform politics. They critiqued Dawes Era policies, social evolution theory, and off-reservation boarding schools. Their writing also provided a rich source of material for Native women's highly politicized domestic fiction. Featuring a graduate of Carlisle, Mourning Dove's novel, *Cogewea*, took up the question of intermarriage to weigh integration against the legal positioning and separatism of reservation life. Cast in domestic terms and critically aware of boarding school discourses of assimilation, Mourning Dove's novel negotiates reform, like Native journalists, to establish "her rightful place in the new scheme of things."

2

" 'Wantin' to Wear th' Breeches and Boss th' Hull Shebang' "

Reservations and Romance in Mourning Dove's *Cogewea*

As a literary reformer, Mourning Dove reconfigured many of the political debates taken up by Native women journalists in her novel, *Cogewea*. That Mourning Dove was an activist is clear from her role in tribal politics. Among other activities, she worked to increase Native employment in the Biles-Coleman Company on the Colville reservation, lectured the Omak Commercial Club on fishing rights, protested the misuse of tribal funds, served on the Colville Council, and founded a Native American women's organization, the Eagle Feather's Club, organized after the non-Native General Federation of Women's Clubs (Miller, "Mourning Dove" 161–179; "Introduction" xxv–xxvi).[1] Through her controversial editor, Lucullus V. McWhorter, she would have been aware of the political debates of such organizations as the Society of American Indians, as well.

At the same time McWhorter was working with Mourning Dove on her manuscript he was writing to prominent Pan-Indian leaders Carlos Montezuma (Apache), Charles E. Daganett (Peoria), and Arthur Parker, who were all involved in the Society of American Indians. The catalogue of McWhorter's papers details his correspondence with these figures from at least 1909 through the 1920s (Ault, 37, 45, 47, 49, 58). *The American Indian Magazine* itself featured McWhorter in its 1917 edition (MacLean, 154–159). Mourning Dove may even have met such figures as Carlos Montezuma, stationed at the

Colville agency in 1893 or Angel DeCora who lived in Pullman in
1915 and Spokane in 1918.[2] Certainly, Pan-Indian politics reached as
far west as Washington State at the turn of the century whether
Mourning Dove personally knew these figures or not.[3]

Current literary criticism has subordinated the political activism of
Mourning Dove's novel *Cogewea* to questions of editorial appropriation. Edited by a non-Native, male, Indian rights activist, *Cogewea* is
often read as McWhorter's political vehicle.[4] Ironically, this reading
reiterates a central thematic in the novel—the exploitation of Native
women by Euro-American men. The tribal history narrated by the
Stemteema, the abandonment of Cogewea by her own non-Native
father, and the victimizing romance with Easterner Alfred Densmore,
which structures the novel, all narrate Native women's dispossession.
Critics have plotted Native women's dispossession at one more
remove. This chapter suggests an alternative and politically active role
for Native women in the novel and for Mourning Dove as novelist by
reading *Cogewea* in the context of Native women's debates over allotment, reservation, and boarding school politics.

Although Mourning Dove mailed a completed draft of *Cogewea* to
McWhorter, at this point no copy of her original draft has been found
(Fisher, "Introduction" xii). Consequently, McWhorter's influence on
the manuscript has been largely deduced from their correspondence
and matters of style. A well-known activist for the Yakimas,
McWhorter easily may have influenced Mourning Dove's politics and
almost certainly inserted his own into the novel. Textual evidence
supports Fisher's claim that McWhorter included his own work on the
Nez Perce, for example (Fisher, "Introduction," v; Mourning Dove,
Cogewea 141). However, the extent of his political appropriation is
contested.[5] Political statements against the Bureau of Indian Affairs
(BIA), for example, are thought to be McWhorter's contribution
because of his politics and the diction of these passages, while the
Stemteema's stories and the folklore in the novel are attributed to
Mourning Dove.[6] Yet despite differences in diction, the Stemteema's
stories share with the BIA passages a critique of colonialism. More-
over, during the Dawes Era, both non-Native reformers and Native
Americans were critical of the BIA. Mourning Dove's original man-

uscript positioned Densmore as an Indian agent dispossessing a Native woman (Miller, "Introduction" xx; "Mourning Dove" 165).[7] Furthermore, she claims in her autobiography that "everyone was at the mercy and whim of the Bureau of Indian Affairs because the courts had decided we were 'wards' of the government. This injustice has been a great handicap to our advancement and self-respect" (*Mourning Dove* 182). To attribute the "didactic" characteristics of *Cogewea* to McWhorter and Okanogan folklore to Mourning Dove denies Mourning Dove a political voice as an Okanogan woman.

Cogewea, the central character in the novel, is a graduate of Carlisle and lives with her sister Julia on a Montana cattle ranch. Owned by Julia's non-Native husband, John Carter, the ranch is situated on the Flathead reservation and is run by cowboys who are primarily of mixed ancestry. As the plot unfolds, Cogewea must choose between a romance with non-Native "tender-foot" Alfred Densmore or "mixed-blood" ranch foreman, Jim LaGrinder. Cogewea is warned away from Densmore by her sister Mary and her "traditional" grandmother, the Stemteema, who envision the robbery and beating Cogewea receives at Densmore's hands by the end of the novel.

Like Native women's journalism, Mourning Dove's novel is centrally concerned with integration and is critical of the doctrines of racial inferiority and social evolution that read Native cultures as "primitive" and U.S. society as "civilized." Mourning Dove's fiction differs from those political essays that embraced "total assimilation" and claimed that with more "civilization" Native Americans could compete equally in U.S. society. (See my discussion of Pierce, Hunter, and Pike in chapter 1.) Although she favors integration, Cogewea clearly refuses to deny tribal culture as the price for a position of equality. Instead Cogewea embraces tribal culture, not as a precursor to "civilization" but as legitimate in its own right: "If permitted, I would prefer living the white man's way to that of the reservation Indian, but he hampers me. I appreciate my meagre education, but I will *never* disown my mother's blood. Why should I do so? Though my skin is of the tawny hue, I am not ashamed" (41).[8]

Densmore, not Cogewea, spouts early assimilationist rhetoric in the novel. Trying to convince Cogewea of his devotion, Densmore cleverly argues for the integration of Native Americans into U.S. society. He is attractive to Cogewea to the extent that he poses as a reformer, who favors integration even though he also embraces allotment and social evolution theory. A stand-in for figures like General Richard Henry Pratt, Densmore argues that the dismantling of the reservation and individual land ownership is central to Native American "advancement" in U.S. society:

> "It may appear harsh, but the day has come when the Indian must desist from his wild, savage life. The Government is working hard for his betterment, and he should respond with a willingness to advance by adjusting himself to the new order of things. The opening of this reservation to settlement, tends to mingle him with his white brother, leading to an inter marriage of the two races. The tribesman will learn wisdom from his new neighbors, who will teach him how best to wrest his food supplies from the soil. The change was inevitable. . . . You are too broad minded for such antiquated ideas. Educated, you should put improbable concepts aside." (143, 144)

Reform ideologies are contested throughout Mourning Dove's text and can't be dismissed simply as editorial imposition. The speeches of Mourning Dove's characters represent various ideological and rhetorical conflicts, and are "active participant[s] in social dialogue" (Bakhtin, 276). Densmore, for example, is given a double characterization as colonial villain who wants to dispossess Cogewea of her allotment and who uses reform doctrine to win her. Ultimately, he exposes reform discourse as centrally concerned with land-grabbing rather than incorporation and equal rights. As a reformer, however, Densmore cleverly seduces Cogewea with arguments for economic opportunity, integration, and intermarriage: "The Indian is civilized and almost on a social and business level with his Caucasian neighbor. Why should I be ashamed to take a girl of pure American blood, a half-blood girl of refined taste and education?" (231).

Cogewea is attracted to Densmore because in his posture as an early assimilationist who favors intermarriage he refutes conceptions of racial inferiority. Densmore's rhetoric (as opposed to his interior monologues or his actions) represents Native cultures as dynamic, not static. He argues that "people change and advance" (231). Moreover, Cogewea is most interested in Densmore when he tones down his ethnocentrism and argues against racial determinism. The few love scenes in the novel follow these passages.[9] When Cogewea declares that she can only marry someone of mixed-ancestry, Densmore says: "Cogewea! I do not believe you! Is not the pure white race just as good? Why erect an imaginary barrier about your life? A true mate is one who has sympathy for your ideals; who understands and is willing to adapt himself to your ways" (150). Densmore distances himself from ideologies of racial inferiority and suggests his own adaptability even as he convinces Cogewea to embrace intermarriage and Euro-American culture. Mourning Dove's novel casts Cogewea's love affair as a political debate over racial and cultural equality. Cogewea is literally seduced by Densmore's integrationist discourse.[10]

Mourning Dove's critique of the liminal status of the "half-blood" through Cogewea also involves a politics of incorporation. She thematizes mixed descent to critique social inequity and the separate but unequal space of reservation culture.[11] As a "breed" Cogewea is often critical of her marginalization:

> "We breeds are half and half—American and Caucasian—and in a separate corral. We are despised by both of our relatives. The white people call us 'Injuns' and a 'good-for-nothing' oufit; a 'shiftless,' vile class of commonality. Our Red brothers say that we are 'stuck-up'; that we have deserted our own kind and are imitating the ways of the despoilers of our nationality. But you wait and watch!. . . . The day will dawn when the desolate, exiled breed will appreciate our worth. Fate cannot always be against those who strive for self-elevation." (95)

In an echo and revision of DeCora, Cogewea uses mixed-ancestry to reject both the idea that Native Americans can't integrate and are doomed to "shiftless" second-class citizenship and the idea that mixed-ancestry (not to mention boarding school education) results in a denial of tribalism or Pan-Indianism and an embrace of non-Native culture as "superior." By recalling a rhetoric of desertion, Mourning Dove responds to writing like DeCora's, taken up in the last chapter, that was critical of ethnocentrism but also tended to read integration as a form of abandonment.

The novel combines an argument for integration with a critique of the reservation when Cogewea refers to mixed ancestry as a "separate corral." In general the corral functions as a trope for the political marginalization of the reservation in the novel. At times Cogewea (like Zitkala-Sa) argues for integration by rejecting reservation culture as limited, as a "corral." Zitkala-Sa claimed, as we have seen, that "the sooner the tribal corrals are thrown open, the sooner the Indian will become Americanized" ("The Black Hills" 5). Although the novel uses the final villany of Densmore to retreat from an integrationist stance, Cogewea continues to recognize the vulnerability of the reservation and its inhabitants to U.S. exploitation through the trope of the corral: "We despised 'breeds' are in a zone of our own and when we break from the corral erected about us, we meet up with trouble. I only wish that the fence could not be scaled by the soulless creatures who have ever preyed upon us" (283).

Cogewea realizes that her decision to remain on the reservation is to some extent victimizing. The reservation is described as " the corral erected about us," out of which Natives cannot escape but European Americans can enter. Like Zitkala-Sa she represents the reservation as a space without legal recourse.[12] However, to some extent, the larger conceit, whereby the characters use the reservation to corral cattle and wild horses and succeed economically in the United States, functions as a defense of reservation life. Similarly, Jim's ability to thrive in the corral, as he does during the "bucking contest" on the Fourth of July, and Densmore's obvious inability to negotiate the corral as demonstrated in his initial fall at Carter's ranch, ameliorates this view of reservation life as marginalized and at the mercy of white despoilers (53, 72).

Significantly, Mourning Dove's integrationist politics, including her critique of the reservation as marginalized, do not involve an embrace of allotment or the sale and settlement of "surplus" land. She critiques the opening of the Flathead reservation as making assimilation not easier, as reform discourse suggested, but more difficult (141, 148). Government officials proclaimed the advantages of white settlement to Native Americans, arguing that the isolation of the reservation served to delay assimilation. We see this position embraced to a certain extent by journalists such as Zitkala-Sa and Kellogg. Mourning Dove, however, represents non-Native settlement as increasing financial hardships, in this case by diminishing the land needed for raising stock. Choosing to position her characters as ranchers who need large tracts of land rather than as individual farmers subtly works to critique allotment even as it embraces the figure of the western cowboy as an integrationist ploy. Using the highly sophisticated trope of the corral, Mourning Dove carefully critiques the reservation, advocating integration even as she refuses allotment and a doomed or victimized position for her characters.

Similarly, in her autobiography Mourning Dove is critical of the opening of the Colville reservation and its allotment at the turn of the century:

> The reservation was violated again at noon on 10 October 1900 when it was opened for homesteading. The law to enable this was the result of a bill passed and approved by Congress through the efforts of the Indian Department and the secretary of the interior. The Colville tribes had no voice in the matter and only heard about it at the last moment. People were frantic and desperate, being content to always live separately from whites.[13] (180)

Congress opened the northern half of the Colville reservation to Euro-American settlement in 1892, voting to reject payment negotiated with the Colville by the Indian Office. In 1898 the rest of the reservation was opened to mineral exploration (Debo, 295). The Colville valley was opened to settlement in 1906 (Reichwein, 314). Mourning Dove's autobiography details Native protests which delayed surveyors and relates various manipulations of the allotment process. However, overall she argues that allotment resulted in the privatization and loss of land as well as in political marginalization. In her account, like Zitkala-Sa's, a separatist stance does not insure self-determination.

Mourning Dove uses the romance plot of *Cogewea* to maintain a focus on integration even as she mounts a thoroughgoing critique of colonial exploitation and abuse. She discusses broken treaties and stolen lands, particularly those of the Blackfeet. She accuses the Indian Bureau of graft and corruption. She blames whites for the introduction and abuse of alcohol in Native communities. Cogewea challenges Densmore to, "show me a solitary treaty made with us by the Government which has not been wantonly violated; when you cite an Indian war where you have not been the flagrant aggressor; then will I admit the *moral* superiority of the Caucasian, and in beliefs and manner become one of you" (135–36).

Far from reading "civilization" as progress, Cogewea debunks social evolution theory by reading U.S. Indian policy as destructive and unjust. "Civilization" is based on exploitation and corruption and has helped dismantle tribal cultures rather than "uplift" it. This argument contrasts with the stance taken by journalists such as Evelyn Pierce, whose integrationist politics embraced "civilization" through a nationalist rhetoric of Columbus and the "discovery" of America. Unlike the assimilationist discourses of Native journalists who drew on U.S. patriotism to achieve integration, Mourning Dove invokes a national past through a discussion of the *Mayflower* only to indict colonialism: Cogewea says, "Viewed in its proper light the coming of the Mayflower was, to my people, the falling of the star 'Wormwood'; tainting with death the source of our very existence" (133).[14]

This focus on exploitation, however, also reenacts narratives of the "noble" but "dying Indian" unable to survive white contact. Cogewea asks, "where is our once strong and virile race?" (134). Many of Mourning Dove's representations of Native victimization echo the fiction of non-Natives writing at this time which, according to Paula Gunn Allen, "seem to warn Indians against trying to make it in the white man's world. They often reinforce the belief common among both Indians and whites that Indians who attempt to adapt to white ways in any sense are doomed to death" (*The Sacred Hoop* 77). This discourse represented Native Americans as inassimilable. Cogewea exposes white exploitation and attacks racial hierarchies and theories of social evolution, but she also suggests that tribal cultures are weak, that Native Americans are victims, and that tribal cultures are degraded and dying out. Mourning Dove's critique of allotment often combines with a rhetoric of the "vanishing Indian": "When I remain here till nightfall, I can hear the death chant and wailing of the spirit-Indians whose bones are being disturbed by the homesteader's plow. I can see the tepeed villages melting before the blaze of conquest and the shattered nations sweeping desolately towards the ocean-laved portals of the sunset" (147).[15]

Narratives of victimization, the Stemteema's stories reproduce dominant ideologies of the noble but "vanishing Indian," as well. In the Stemteema's first story, the Dead man tells his tribe "your people will be long gone. The land will be no more as it was" (126). This narrative of exploitation and tribal helplessness is reproduced upon women in the Stemteema's telling of "The Story of Green-Blanket Feet" and "The Second Coming of the Shoyahpee" as well as in her final vision of Cogewea. The women in her stories are innocents, falling helplessly in love with their betrayers in spite of their better judgment. They are represented as having to choose between cultures which cannot intermingle. The children of intermarriage always die in the Stemteema's stories, and her invectives against intermarriage suggest that Natives and non-Natives cannot coexist. The Stemteema constructs a static, if gendered, Okanogan history, one which cannot adapt, which is doomed to extinction.

Similarly, the removal and death of the buffalo acts as a powerful metaphor for the plight of Native Americans throughout the novel. Cogewea is critical of the corralling and sale of buffalo to the Canadian government for the danger they posed to "white settlers" (148). While Densmore describes the corralling as "exciting," Cogewea claims that "it was pitiful to see the animals fight so desperately for freedom" (148). This event (witnessed by Mourning Dove) as well as the creation of the National Bison Range in 1908 on the Flathead Reservation represent an historical rationale for Mourning Dove's focus on the buffalo (Brown, "Legacy Profile" 51–56; Dippie 225). However, Mourning Dove clearly draws on the rhetoric of the "vanishing Indian" in her use of the buffalo as well. In a highly conventional passage, Cogewea compares the fate of Native Americans with the buffalo: "With her people had vanished this monarch of the plains. The war-whoop and the thunder of the herd were alike hushed in the silence of the last sleep—and only the wind sighing a parting requiem" (31). Cogewea's fictional reverie over the stuffed buffalo head in Julia's house is quite similar to historical discourses such as early conservationist George Bird Grinnell's reminiscence:

> On the floor, on either side of my fireplace, lie two buffalo skulls. They are white and weathered, the horns cracked and bleached by the snows and frosts, and the rains and heats of many winters and summers. Often, late at night, when the house is quiet, I sit before the fire, and muse and dream of the old days; and as I gaze at these relics of the past, they take life before my eyes.   (qtd. in Dippie, 226)

The use of the buffalo in conjunction with "vanishing Indians" to symbolize a national past was a popular motif during this period. As Dippie claims, "American stamps, paper currency, and coinage all honored the buffalo between 1901 and 1923—and each had its plains Indian counterpart. . . . After 1913, the buffalo and the Indian were in fact what they had long been in popular fancy, two sides of the same coin" (225). Despite her position as an Okanogan (for whom salmon, not the buffalo, was the central economic and cultural mainstay), Cogewea terms the buffalo, "Colleague of my race, with him went our hopes, our ambition, and our life" (143).

On the one hand, Mourning Dove's reliance on popular discourses of the "dying Indian" is anti-integrationist, reinforcing the inability of Native Americans to survive in U.S. society. Used in popular discourse to establish a national past, the "vanishing Indian" reinforced colonial ideologies of racial and cultural "superiority" through a history of conquest. On the other hand, the integrationist thrust of Mourning Dove's novel is evidenced through her manipulation of a discourse that positions Native Americans as central, if only in the distant past, to U.S. history. She couches her critique of policies like allotment in popular discourse. Cogewea's use of the death of the buffalo to critique white settlement, for example, would have been far more acceptable to her reading public than a direct critique of the loss of the northern part of the Colville reservation.

By the end of the novel, Mourning Dove attempts a revision of narratives of cultural loss through her use of the buffalo and Cogewea's escape from Densmore. Both Cogewea and the Stemteema are represented as fundamentally concerned with the interrelations between

Native and non-Native cultures. Cogewea, for example, retains aspects of an Okanogan belief system. She hears her Okanogan "spirit voice" when she looks at the buffalo skull, for example (Fisher, "Introduction" xxiv). She also lives in a ranch house, was educated at Carlisle, and states her desire to position herself as an equal in U.S. society. The Stemteema, who is positioned as a tribal historian, also evidences changing cultural practices. Although the Stemteema "had adhered to some of the old-time customs—tepee and ground-couch—moccasins and ankle-wraps," her tepee is situated on the reservation cattle ranch of her granddaughter's white husband (41). She is Catholic, understands and speaks English—although she prefers Salish, and dresses in "semi-civilized garb." She tells tribal lore to Densmore even though she says her ancestors would protest. The Stemteema rides on the railroad and contentedly attends powwow versions of sacred medicine and war dances even though the narrator sees the commercialization of these dances as the degradation of tribal culture. She also uses a sweatlodge to interpret Cogewea's current romance with Densmore and ultimately to revise the narrative of the "dying Indian." In the end, the Stemteema's vision rescues Cogewea who, significantly, recovers from Densmore's robbery and beating.

The tension between a critique and embrace of integrationist discourse is most apparent in Mourning Dove's representation of the Stemteema. Although the Stemteema warns Cogewea away from intermarriage by providing her with a social history of colonial abuse and exploitation, she is evidence of the adaptability and relevance of Okanogan practices and beliefs to ranch and reservation life. Densmore, Julia, and Cogewea at one time or another all describe the Stemteema as unable to reconcile herself to "modernity." Unwilling or unable to believe that narratives of Euro-American sexism and colonialism are still pertinent, they dismiss her stories as biased and irrelevant. The Stemteema's critique, however, proves to be an accurate assessment of Densmore's character and motives. Densmore, she tells Cogewea, "is here to cheat you; all that any white man wants of the Indian girl. It is only to put her to shame, then cast her aside for his own kind—the pale faced squaw. . . . All that the pale faces desire of Indian women, is pleasure and riches" (103). The Stemteema's categorical statements that non-Native men will abandon Native women for "the pale faced squaw" as well as her insistence that Cogewea marry her own "class" would seem to support Densmore's assessment of the Stemteema as adopting a form of racial biologism. However, the text suggests that the Stemteema's evaluation of colonial exploitation is not a form of racial determinism but, rather, an historical critique. The Stemteema relates tribal history to provide the proper context in which to interpret Densmore and Cogewea's romance. Moreover, the Stemteema's narratives are critical of non-Native exploitation but include factionalism and injustices among various tribes, as well. The Blackfeet raid the Okanogans for the horses of two white men as well as enslave and half-starve Green-Blanket Feet. Similarly, the text implies that the Stemteema approves not only of Julia's marriage with Carter, who is not Native, but also Mary's liaison with a French aristocrat.

In a subtle echo of the tensions surrounding the Stemteema, Mourning Dove plays with Frenchy's "foreign" and non-Native positioning. Frenchy is initially positioned in opposition to the Native and non-Native ranch hands, as a "foreigner," to suggest their Americanism. As I will demonstrate in the next two chapters, Jessie Fauset uses "foreigners" in a similar way to reinforce the "American" positioning of her African American characters. The integrationist intent of this positioning is reinforced when Mary, the most "traditional" sister, decides to intermarry with Frenchy. However, the French background of Mourning Dove's character, his "foreignness," also enables his sympathetic rendering. France's pivotal role in World War I and the frequent association of the war with issues of self-determination make him a suitable match for Mary, who resists assimilation in the text.

As is evident in the Stemteema's use of tribal history and culture, debates over integration and separatism in the novel are gendered. The Stemteema's narrative focus on rape and dispossession functions not just as a historical warning against the dangers of intermarriage and by extension integration, it also helps dismantle social evolution theory. Mourning Dove also inverts stereotypes of sexual "barbarism" at the races, exposing

> the incessant insults offered the Indian women by the "gentlemen" whites. She regretted with a pang, the passing of an epoch, when there were no "superiors" to "guide" her simple race to a civilization so manifestly dearth of the primitive law of respect

for womanhood; substituting in its stead a social standard per-
mitting the grossest insult and indignity to the weaker, with the
most brazen impunity. (65)

Cogewea critiques sexual exploitation and social evolution theory
together. At the same time, her argument relies on a sexual morality
whereby "gentlemen" protect rather than exploit the "weaker" sex.

Like Native journalists, Mourning Dove's novel embraces domestic ideology in order to refute stereotypes of Native Americans as
"primitive" even while she acknowledges domesticity as implicated in
a colonial project. That Mourning Dove was aware of off-reservation
boarding school discourses on gender is clear in her positioning of
Cogewea as a Carlisle graduate. In keeping with her boarding school
education, Cogewea initially differentiates herself from reservation life
through her domestic etiquette, " 'her a usin' them there han' rags at
th' table' " (35). Moreover, her desire for Densmore is represented as a
desire for "a home—a husband who loved books and who would
appreciate her efforts at making their domicile a place of endearment
and happiness. Refined, he was so particular about his dress and he
never ate with his knife, where in the free, wild range, table manners
were given but slight consideration" (137).[16]

References to "table manners" (recalling Bender's rhetoric in the
last chapter) and the demand for more "gentlemanly" behavior at the
races both suggest that Mourning Dove embraces boarding school
domestic ideology to refute charges of racial inferiority and to challenge stereotypes of Native women as "squaws." The popular stereo-
type of the "squaw" used women to argue for Native "barbarism" and
inferiority, reading Native women's labor as degraded because it didn't
fit definitions of True Womanhood.[17] The statement Secretary of the
Interior Carl Schurtz made in 1881 was typical: "the Indian woman
has so far been only a beast of burden. The girl, when arrived at matu-
rity, was disposed of like an article of trade. The Indian wife was
treated by her husband alternately with animal fondness, and with the
cruel brutality of the slave driver" (qtd. in Trennert, 273).

Boarding schools disseminated a domestic ideology that distorted
Native women's labor, reading it as a sign of "primitivism." Ironically,
boarding schools were notorious for exploiting Native women's labor,

as slogans like "learn the dignity of serving, rather than being served" demonstrated (qtd. in Trennert, 282). They shared with the settlement house movement the goal of creating a cheap labor pool, as Jewish American novelist Anzia Yezierska's critique of a similar rhetoric of domestic exploitation in chapter 6 makes plain.

Although Cogewea embraces domestic "etiquette," she rejects the epithet "squaw" many times in the novel and challenges the opposition between a "lady" and a "squaw" by entering and winning both Native and non-Native women's races on the Fourth of July, as many critics have noted. Moreover, Mourning Dove carefully balances Cogewea's labor against the labor of men on the reservation when she and Julia cook for the ranchers who are rounding up wild horses. One of the few representations of domestic labor in the novel, food preparation during the roundup makes Cogewea and her sister "weary of the endless cooking and constant clatter of dishes, and no wonder! But perhaps their task was hardly less arduous than that of the poor devils who rode in the hot sun from early morning till dark, and sometimes far into the night" (21). Far from endorsing women's domesticity as a "civilizing" force, this representation recalls and acknowledges the strenuousness of boarding school labor.

Like other Native women's fiction during this period, Mourning Dove is critical of the Euro-American home as well, contrasting it to the "superior" space of the tepee. Zitkala-Sa's descriptions of log houses in *American Indian Stories*, for example, are characterized by poverty and "the smell of damp clay. . . the natural breath of such a dwelling" (90, 162). Ella Cara Deloria contrasts the domestic violence of non-Natives, who "actually detest their children! You should see them—slapping their little ones' faces and lashing their poor little buttocks to make them cry!" to the domestic harmony of the Dakota in her novel *Waterlily* (103). In her account, the well-ordered space of the tepee reflects a well-ordered social life. Waterlily, for example, "was an industrious homemaker and her little tipi, which her mothers-in-law had standing ready for her when she arrived, was always as neat as it could be" (171–172).

In *Cogewea*, the Stemteema refuses to live in Julia's ranch house, preferring "The tepee. . . [to] the dwellings of civilization, which had only proven death-traps for her race" (129). Similarly, in her journalistic piece on the Red Cross, Mourning Dove argued, "The casting aside of the tepee and adoption of modern houses has had an evil effect on our race beyond calculation. Fresh air is lacking. Owing to his former mode of life—in the open and well ventilated tepee—the Indian does not understand how the air can become poluted [sic] and deadly" (*Mourning Dove* 192).[18] Although the ranch house in *Cogewea* is not represented in negative terms, the novel sees Julia's domestic ideology as reinforcing a colonial mind set. Julia's domesticity, "her sewing at the table" and encouragement of Densmore's suit, coincides with her mistaken belief at the end of the novel that "civilization was the only hope for the Indian" (32, 274). In contrast, the domestic etiquette in the Stemteema's tepee involves a hospitality that opposes the materialism characterizing Densmore and U.S. colonial policies (97, 98).

Similarly, Cogewea is most often positioned outside the house, on the range, "under the pines," or "on the old buffalo grounds." Cogewea's "forward" range behavior, her facility at "roastin' th' whites!" and her reputation as "a dam' good win' jammer" is represented as opposing the domesticity and assimilationism of her sister Julia (35, 42). In fact, when Cogewea is critical of colonialism, she is seen by others as a New Woman. Silent Bob argues that she should be a suffragette, suggesting that she wants to be " made perlice wimin an jedges an' the main push. Wantin' to wear th' breeches an boss th' hull shebang " (42).[19] This conflation of critiques of colonialism and domesticity in the text ultimately rejects gendered boarding school discourse. Indeed, Mourning Dove's criticism of boarding schools in her autobiography is explicitly opposed to the free movement and political expression she embraces in the novel. Of her experience at the Goodwin Mission school she said, "The school ran strictly. We never talked during meals without permission, given only on Sunday or special holidays. Otherwise there was silence—a terrible silent silence. I was used to the freedom of the forest, and it was hard to learn this strict discipline. I was punished many times before I learned (*Mourning Dove* 28).

Finally, Cogewea's characterization in the novel parallels the role of Native women journalists. As political spokeswoman, she participates in an activist rhetoric. Like women involved in Pan-Indian and Native women's organizations, she argues for Native rights. She rejects domesticity and romance with reformer/villain Densmore to critique allotment and social evolution theory, even as she argues for integration and against the political marginalization of the reservation. She refuses to renounce her Native heritage as the price of marriage or participation in U.S. society and ultimately exposes early assimilationist ideology as masking a colonial agenda. The text does not easily resolve issues of exploitation, integration, and separatism, however. Cogewea decides to marry Jim, of her own "class," and remain on the reservation because she is unable to exist in white society without being exploited. However, the end of the novel resists a return to a romanticized and static representation of reservation life, as we have seen. While the novel sets an implicit debate and dialogic discourse in play, it ultimately fashion's Cogewea as a woman activist/spokesperson—vulnerable to seduction by reform rhetoric and caught up in contradictions but nonetheless a female hero-figure with a voice that defines the public discourse—like Mourning Dove herself.

3

"The Democracy for Which We Have Paid"

Jessie Fauset and World War I Controversies in the African American Press

> . . . when, after the shock of terrific warfare, the world has not yet found its balance—when, in the midst of confusion, justice and truth call loudly for the democracy for which we have paid.
>
> —Addie W. Hunton and Kathryn M. Johnson

Jessie Fauset's remarkable career at *The Crisis*, her editorial support for Harlem Renaissance writers, and her wide-ranging knowledge of the press do not reconcile well with critical accounts of her accommodationist fiction.[1] (The controversy over Fauset's fiction is detailed in chapter 4.) Hired by W. E. B. Du Bois, Fauset helped shape the journal of the NAACP, which had the largest readership of any African American periodical in this period (Wall, *Women* 35). As columnist, literary editor, and managing editor (in Du Bois's absence), Fauset's role at *The Crisis* would have put her in touch with the major intellectual trends of her era. Unfortunately, contemporary critics have discussed Fauset's role as a journalist almost exclusively in terms of her literary patronage and have largely ignored the political significance of her work. Like many other African American journalists, Fauset contributed to a range of debates over equal rights and citizenship during and after World War I.[1]

Born in 1882, Fauset grew up in Philadelphia. She graduated from Cornell University, Phi Beta Kappa, in 1905, took courses at the Sorbonne, and finished M.A. coursework in Romance Languages at the University of Pennsylvania. After teaching at the prestigious M Street High School in Washington, D.C., she worked for *The Crisis* as columnist or literary editor from 1918 to 1926 and also edited a children's magazine with Du Bois and Agustus Dill, entitled *The Brown-*

ies' Book. Fauset belonged to the NAACP, women's clubs, and the Delta Sigma Theta Sorority, through which she attended the Second Pan-African Congress (Sylvander, 40, 67; Wall, *Women* 33–45).[2]

Since her career at *The Crisis* began with "The Looking Glass" column during World War I, it is not surprising that Fauset's politics were significantly influenced by the wartime rhetoric of this period. "The Looking Glass" establishes Fauset's thorough familiarity with the press. This column was made up of excerpted material from major newspapers in cities such as Chicago, New York, Philadelphia, and Boston and from periodicals and lesser known publications ranging from "a white radical paper, *The Battle Ax*," to the Little Rock *Star*, the *Christian Advocate*, the *Jewish Exponent*, and the *Southern Workman*.[3] Fauset's unsigned column demonstrates a consistent concern with the war and lynching from July 1918, when she contracted with Du Bois, to October 1919, when she assumed literary editorship (Sylvander, 53).

The war and postwar journalism of African American men, including W. E. B. Du Bois, Robert Abbot, and A. Philip Randolph has already been taken up in detail.[4] However, Fauset and other African American women's responses to the war have been largely overlooked (Breen, 421–422). Alice Dunbar-Nelson summarized women's war work in *Scott's Official History of The American Negro in the World War* (1919) as did Eva Bowles in the *Southern Workman*. Mary Church Terrell, Addie Hunton, and Kathryn Johnson all wrote accounts of their wartime work in memoirs.[5] In general, the writing of these women during and just after the war discussed their own or other women's work for the government or wartime relief organizations. Fauset's journalism draws on African American women's wartime writing but situates itself, primarily, in the thick of debates dominated by the predominantly male African American press.

Debates over World War I in African American communities focused on segregation, citizenship, and equal rights. The war made plain the incongruity of fighting (in wartime rhetoric) for "democracy" denied to African Americans at home. Disenfranchised and segregated in the Jim Crow South and suffering de facto segregation in the North, African Americans had an ambivalent relationship to wartime patriotism, especially since the war itself resulted in severe forms of discrimination and racial violence.[6] The war simultaneously supported segregation and threw it into question. The segregated military reinforced the denial of civil rights and equal opportunity at the same time that the draft confirmed African American citizenship. Ultimately, as Gaines notes, "black soldiers' service in World War I itself did little to improve the political status of African Americans" (234). Consequently, the increasing racism and white violence in the postwar period resulted in a disillusionment with uplift strategies and a new militancy.[7] According to Gaines, "the wartime rhetoric of world democracy and national self-determination sparked the formation of nationalist organizations and pressure groups such as [Hubert] Harrison's short-lived Liberty League, founded in 1917," for example (236). Throughout the war and postwar period, African American journalists generally took full advantage of the war and its rhetoric of patriotism and democracy to demand equal treatment at home. The use of wartime rhetoric was common in articles that embraced or rejected African American participation in the war. Patriotism was used strategically by some writers to argue for citizenship, but African Americans debated the extent to which this strategy compromised or furthered their ability to demand civil rights.

Jessie Fauset was no stranger to questions of accommodation and protest during this period. Her journalism constructed, participated in, and was fully aware of these debates. In fact she couldn't have missed the controversy generated by W. E. B. Du Bois' 1918 editorial in *The Crisis*, "Close Ranks," in which he took an accommodationist stance toward the war, arguing: "Let us, while this war lasts, forget our special grievances and close our ranks shoulder to shoulder with our white fellow citizens and the allied nations that are fighting for democracy" (qtd. in Ellis, "Closing Ranks" 111).[8] The negative response to Du Bois's article suggested that many African Americans saw patriotism as hypocritical and the war as diverting attention from the lack of civil rights at home. According to Hubert Harrison, leader of the Liberty League, for example, Du Bois' article argued that African Americans should "consent to be lynched—'during the war'—and submit tamely and with commendable weakness to being Jim-crowed and disfranchised" (qtd. in Ellis, "Closing Ranks" 115).[9]

As the editor of *The Crisis* and known for his stance on equal rights, Du Bois may have adopted a patriotic point of view because of the threat that antiradical attitudes and legislation posed to the black community generally and *The Crisis* in particular.[10] Opposition to the war was broadly conceived of as protest against the government, and African Americans were seen as "potentially disloyal and especially receptive to the propaganda of enemy agents" (Ellis, "Closing Ranks" 102). In fact, German propaganda was directed at African American soldiers. Hunton and Johnson demonstrated how German propaganda played on U.S. racism in their memoir:

> "Hello, boys, what are you doing over here? Fighting the Germans? Why? . . . Do you enjoy the same rights as the white people do in America, the land of freedom and Democracy, or are you not rather treated over there as second class citizens?
>
> Can you get into a restaurant where white people dine? Can you get a seat in a theatre where white people sit? Can you get a seat or berth in a railroad car, or can you even ride in the South in the same street car with the white people?
>
> And how about the law? Is lynching and the most horrible crimes connected therewith, a lawful proceeding in a Democratic country? Now all this is entirely different in Germany."
>
> (53–54)

American Indians were also targeted by German propaganda. In her article on the Red Cross, for example, Mourning Dove claimed that:

> this Government will never know the full extent of the German propaganda that was spread among the different tribes, . . . how their vast hunting domains would be returned to them if only the arms of the Kaiser prevailed. To this end the Red man should join cause with his overseas friend. Many disputes arose among the tribes. The old and uneducated sympathized with the Hun, while the younger and more enlightened counseled peace and continued allegiance to our own country." (*Mourning Dove* 189)

The Espionage Act of 1917 and the Sedition Act of 1918 were used to censor journals perceived as radical (Ellis, "Closing Ranks" 101–2). In fact, the NAACP agreed to censor *The Crisis* after a warning from the assistant U.S. Attorney in New York (Ellis, "America's Black Press" 26). Du Bois was not alone in his struggle with censorship. Robert Abbot, outspoken editor of the *Chicago Defender,* also published an editorial that privileged the war effort over African American civil rights after receiving a warning from the government (Ellis, "America's Black Press" 26). Articles excerpted in "The Looking Glass" suggested Fauset's awareness of the precarious nature of protest during this period. In articles protesting "unAmerican" barriers to African American wartime industrial work, there was a careful differentiation between African Americans and "enemy aliens" or "Russian" radicals, for instance.[11] Increasingly, charges of Bolshevism were used against African Americans, as well. A. Philip Randolph and Chandler Owen, editors of *The Messenger,* were jailed under suspicion of having been influenced by white socialists in 1918, and black nationalist Marcus Garvey's newspaper, the *Negro World,* was labeled "probable Bolshevik propaganda" by the government in 1919 (Ellis, "America's Black Press" 26; Tolbert, 29).[12]

Du Bois did not simply replace protest with patriotism, however. In rallying support for the war, he argued that African American morale could be improved if the government introduced antilynching legislation, if the Red Cross, civil service, and navy would accept African Americans, and if the government refused to allow segregation on railroads (Ellis, "Joel Spingarn's" 144). Similarly, most of the articles concerning participation in the war excerpted by Fauset in "The Looking Glass" described African American contributions to the war for "freedom" and "democracy" and then used those contributions to demand equal treatment and the rights of citizenship at home.[13] Arguments for equal rights—equal accommodations on public transportation, equal opportunity in public schooling, suffrage, and various critiques of segregation and resistance to Jim Crow—existed side by side with reports of African American sacrifice and patriotism in the war.[14] For example, Ida Wells-Barnett in her autobiography, *Crusade for Justice,* described being threatened by the "secret service bureau" and charged with "treason" for distributing buttons protesting the hanging of African American soldiers after the Houston riot. At the same time that Wells-Barnett resisted harassment and chastised the black community for failing to actively protest Houston, she documented her own participation in war relief: "While the reporters and secret service men were in my office, I took them back and showed them tables filled with candy boxes, cigarettes, pipes, tobacco, and other things which we were preparing to send to Camp Grant for gifts for the Negro soldiers" (qtd. in Klein, 99–102). War relief work, defined by domestic patriotism, was used strategically by Wells-Barnett as protection against arrest.

In Fauset's "The Looking Glass" and elsewhere, patriotic rhetoric was also often employed satirically and did not necessarily support participation in the war. Protesting the East St. Louis Riot in 1917, for example, African Americans carried signs pointing to the hypocrisy of wartime democratic rhetoric, "Mr. President, Why Not Make AMERICA safe for Democracy?" and "Patriotism and Loyalty Presuppose Protection and Liberty" (Kornweibel, 325). Many of the articles Fauset collected for "The Looking Glass" played with the notion that America was un-American, that U.S. democracy was not democratic. They claimed that African Americans had to meet both the violence and the horror of war in the conflict with Germany and experience discrimination from the military for whom they were fighting. Excerpts condemning lynching also frequently pointed to the hypocrisy of fighting "German tyranny" while innocent African Americans suffered violence without due process at home.[15] These pieces critiqued the U.S. government for its unwillingness to oppose lynching and they paralleled German and American "tyranny." In a pointed reversal one article moved the battle to American terrain, suggesting that lynching served German propagandists, who announced that "we are barbarians, that the country is in a state of riot" ("The Looking Glass" August 1918, 182).

Several African American writers extended this strategic use of patriotism and the negative connotations of "foreignness" to oppose the war explicitly. Francis Grimke, who opposed African American participation throughout the war, wrote in his private journal that,

> Dying here in defense of democratic principles is just as honorable as dying on a foreign soil. Every colored soldier who meets his death here before sailing for France because he resents the insults of southern white bullies, or rather, I should say, cowards,

belongs on the honor roll of the noble dead who die in the laudable effort to make the world safe for democracy.

(qtd. in Kornweibel, 328)

Similarly, an excerpt from Ethel Trew Dunlap's poem from the *Negro World* invoked the French revolution with biting irony to highlight the violence African Americans endured at home while fighting for democracy in France:

> He sleeps in France's bosom!
> Perchance he has a dream
> Of sires who writhed beneath the lash
> Or peon's stifled scream.
> He sleeps in France's bosom!
> O wish him not awake,
> While innocence is martyr
> To mob law and the stake.
> He sleeps in France's bosom!
> The colors o'er him fly;
> They were his prison stripes and then
> They sent him off to die. . .

(Martin, 184)

Combining the French revolution with the imagery of slavery and lynching, Dunlap played with a wartime rhetoric of freedom. She preferred France, where peonage was overturned, to the United States, where "mob law" ruled; but at the same time she rejected the war as exile and a death sentence.

Dunlap and others saw participation in the war as further exploitation. Service in the war aided the United States but did nothing to guarantee democracy to Africans or African Americans after the war (Martin, 182–188). A logical extension of this line of thinking was the rejection of European colonialism altogether. Kornweibel documents a clear rejection of imperialist European powers engaged in the war (324, 325). He describes a cartoon in *The Crisis* that "depicted a mutilated Congolese telling the English king that 'we could be of greater

service to you now if your cousin [Leopold] had spared us our hands'"
(325). The postwar Pan-Africanism and anticolonialism of *The Crisis*,
however, balanced an integrationist politics with a more radical separatism. Nationalist writing in *The Crisis*, affirmed both "Africa for
Africans" and America for African Americans (Hutchinson, 146). As
Hutchinson claims, "when *The Crisis* pushed Pan-Africanist ideas in
the years of the New Negro, it did not conceive of this thrust as antithetical to the Americanness of the American Negro, any more than
Horace Kallen, for example, conceived of Zionism as antithetical to
the Americanness of the American Jew" (146). Aware of this emphasis, Fauset focused primarily on conditions in the United States. However, her essay on the Pan-African Congress notably claimed that the
war's "basic motif had been the rape of Africa" ("Impressions" 16).
Moreover, Fauset's novel, *Comedy: American Style*, demonstrated an
awareness and rejection of French colonialism in its representation of
Teresa's French husband, as I will discuss in chapter 4. In her column,
Fauset also excerpted articles that represented World War I as a war for
self-determination, particularly in Africa.[16] Historians note that,
among the African American elite and those writers in the black
press, responses to denied civil rights and violence against African
Americans became more militant in the postwar period.[17] *The Messenger* published an article in 1919 which claimed, "the transition from
shooting a white German is not very far from shooting a white American" (qtd. in Barbeau and Henri, 180). Similarly, after the war, Du
Bois published "Returning Soldiers," which also used African American participation in World War I as the grounds for militant protest:

> We are returning from War!
> We return from fighting.
> We return fighting.
> Make way for Democracy! We saved it in France,
> and by the Great Jehovah, we will save it in the
> United States of America, or know the reason why."
>   (qtd. in Hughes, 1)

Postwar excerpts from "The Looking Glass" demonstrated the use
of the war to support a more militant form of resistance to lynching

and Jim Crow. The April 1919 column quoted S. J. Young as asserting that "a man that has died so often for freedom of others may die for freedom for himself." This was followed by the statement, "It is just as 'sweet and fitting to die' for Democracy at home as abroad" (291). Similarly, the May 1919 column quoted James M. Boyd in a letter to the editor of the New York *Evening Post* as claiming:

> We are not asking favors. We are demanding our rights. If the bigots are counting upon still relegating us to the back door of public hostelries, hat in hand, they are reckoning without their host. If that modern "Ku Klux Klan" thinks that these hard fight-ing, straight-shooting veterans of the World War are the same timid field-hands, crouching in terror, they have another "think" coming.   (29)

The range of editorial/political engagement (expressed through excerpt) that Fauset displayed raises questions about the nature of her accommodation. Fauset clearly represented the patriotic language of freedom and democracy that supported the war but clearly this patri-otic rhetoric did not simply displace protest.

In her own essays, Fauset continued to use the wartime rhetoric of democracy to argue for civil rights at home. She most often used France and the war in her essays to critique racism while claiming the position and rights of an American citizen. She asserted an American identity by representing France as "foreign" in many of her essays. At the same time, she used France to critique an America that didn't live up to its own democratic promise. Like Ethel Trew Dunlap, Fauset invoked wartime France and the French revolution in order to high-light the failings of U.S. democracy. France had a very particular polit-ical and rhetorical valence at the end of World War I. Throughout the war, the U.S. government and military feared the ramifications of African American soldiers participating freely in French culture. They warned the French not to associate with African Americans and dis-seminated racist propaganda. African Americans' experience of equal rights in France directly challenged the segregationists in the U.S. armed forces who were also stationed in France. French society was far more open than U.S. society despite its own colonial racism in relation to Africa. Fauset's embrace of France in this context functioned strategically to critique U.S. discrimination and argue for equal rights by contrast.

Fauset's focus on France, however, was Eurocentric in its privileging of Europe as "high culture." More problematically, Fauset's embrace of France to some extent conflated equal rights with middle- or upper-class values. In her writing, Fauset's persona as a tourist, who could afford civil freedoms through travel, tended to suggest that middle-class positioning was integral to civil rights. Fauset, on the other hand, clearly used France to critique the United States, where neither money nor respectability was sufficient to guarantee civil rights. Strategically employing its "elite" cache, Fauset privileged French over American culture precisely because it offered equality to African Americans and symbolized democracy in complex ways.

Fauset also manipulated notions of "foreignness," relying on the increasingly dichotomized rhetoric around "foreigners" in the United States in order to claim "American" identification for African Americans. Like Grimke, Fauset positioned France as "foreign" and herself as American in an effort to focus attention on democracy at home. At the end of "Yarrow Revisited," Fauset claimed that "In Paris I find myself more American than I ever feel in America" (109). First Fauset explained this contradiction fairly conventionally. She used the "foreign" location of France to define her Americanism and, incidentally, to blur the "color line." Her position as American is defined together with whites in opposition to the French: "I mean that Americans white and black do not act that way" (109). Fauset then shifted her allegiance, suggesting that the real commitment in France to "Liberte, Egalite, Fraternite" expressed in her ability to have tea "at the first tea room which takes my fancy," made France more American than America itself (109). Consequently, Fauset could position herself as "American" opposite "foreigners" at the same time that she implied a critique of America that failed to meet its own promise of democracy.

Fauset's use of travelogue genre often subtly created this political dynamic. Fauset claimed an American identity by positioning herself as a tourist and then used France, with its wartime associations, to critique discrimination in the United States. She ended a discussion of

"The Enigma of the Sorbonne," for example, with a description of Haitian women freely participating in Western academe:

> Two absolutely black girls swing through the rectangle. . . . Their hair stiff, black and fuzzy frames cloudily the soft darkness of their faces; their voices ring clear and staccato; their movements are unrestrained. . . . In this atmosphere so completely are they themselves that tolerance is a quality which they recognize only when they are exercising it toward others.   (219)

Here, Fauset used her tourist persona and the Sorbonne's elite reputation implicitly to critique the limited educational opportunities for African Americans in the United States. Her subtle argument for access to higher education recalls similar demands in Native women's journalism.

Even though "This Way to the Flea Market" doesn't explicitly argue for freedom from discrimination, the essay employed her tourist persona to suggest this political framework. Fauset wandered through a flea market at liberty to go where she pleased. She quietly referenced the war in order to foreground freedom and threats to freedom that resonated beyond France. Reflecting on Paris as a walled city, she wrote, "A fortified city. . . we never have them in America." Her guide replies, "'But you would have them . . . if you had the Germans for neighbors'" (163). Having positioned France as vulnerable and victimized by the war, Fauset ultimately claimed the towers of Sacre Coeur as a "safe" haven: "'Come in', they beckoned, 'you are welcome!' Behind us curved and closed the fortifications; viewed from this side they emanated security, protection. 'Pass in', they murmured, 'You are safe!'" (163). In this essay Fauset rallied support for freedom and democracy in a non-confrontational way by vilifying the Germans. At the same time she invited comparison with the United States. In the context of postwar urban race riots and writings in the United States, her reference to fortified cities, welcome, and safety could be read as ironically extending beyond French boundaries.

Fauset's "Nostalgia" more directly addressed the plight of returned African American soldiers and used a rhetoric of "foreignness," "democracy," and "home" to critique U.S. racism. On routine errands in a U.S. city, Fauset interviewed a number of immigrants, all of whom rejected America for another homeland. The owner of a fruit stand wanted to return to Greece; a "bootblack" dreamt of an Italian homeland; the Jewish father of a girl who frequents a settlement house was a Zionist, while her mother longed for Romania. Both the Italian American, who fought in the war, and the Jewish father, whose Zionism is predicated on an escape from anti-Semitism, prefigured the position of the African American returned soldier at the end of the essay who fought for America and struggled with racism. In a complex identification with "foreign" Americans, who saw their home as elsewhere, Fauset's African American soldier felt at home in a "foreign" land. The soldier claims, "Home?. . . where is it? Do you know, I never knew what home was until I went to France? There in the midst of all those strange people, and the awful food and the foreign jabber, I felt myself less homesick than I have ever felt in my life—yes, than I feel this minute" (156–157).[18]

Unlike immigrants, however, African Americans were positioned as occupying a definitional position in the United States. Fauset argued African Americans live in a "dream-country" constructed in the "Constitution of the United States. . . . the Declaration of Independence, in Fourth of July speeches, in extracts from Daniel Webster, in Mr. Lincoln's Gettysburg address" (157). Unlike recent immigrants whose nationalism was defined by Greek statues, Italian operas, and Jewish religious freedom, African Americans dreamt about a homeland of "Justice. . . Opportunity. . . [and] an escape from Peonage" (157). According to Fauset, they were "like all the other descendants of voluntary and involuntary immigrants of the seventeenth century—Puritan, pioneer, adventurer, indentured servant" (157). With only a passing nod to black nationalism, Fauset dismissed Africa and concentrated on establishing an African American identity, claiming: "the past is too far past for him to have memories" (157).

In "Nostalgia" Fauset used the trope of "foreignness" in at least two ways. She positioned African Americans as foundational to the U.S.—unlike "foreign" immigrants who had various national allegiances, African Americans' homeland was the United States and its democratic tenets. After securing an American identity for African

Americans, she ironically suggested that democracy couldn't be realized in the United States, and African Americans could only find "home" in a "foreign" land. The "foreignness" of France then also functioned to critique the United States. Having fought for a home denied him, the African American soldier, according to Fauset, "is doomed to know homesickness of both body and spirit. In France he will want the comforts of America; in America, he cries out for the rights of man which he knew in France. A nostalgia of body and soul—there is nothing harder to bear" (158).

Fauset's soldier was critical of the "army prejudice" he experienced from "Americans in command" overseas but endured it, hoping for recompense, for an acknowledgement of his patriotism and citizenship on his return to America. Fauset voiced his disillusionment when he was met by a white mob in Arkansas who threatened his life for wearing his uniform. Over his own desire to fight once again for democracy, his uncle prevailed on him to escape. In her essay, the soldier decided to make his home in France, looking for civil rights and economic opportunity, looking for "America" abroad. This journalism imaginatively recast the language of wartime patriotism and antiforeign sentiment into a demand (in domestic terms) for equal rights at home.

Using a rhetoric of patriotism and domesticity to challenge racism and segregation in the United States, much of the wartime journalism written by African American women was born of their war relief work. Alice Dunbar-Nelson founded a Delaware chapter of The Circle for Negro War Relief and worked for the Women's Committee of the Council of National Defense. She wanted to go overseas as a reporter or even "as one of four canteen workers in France" (Hull, *Color* 67). After the war, she became Executive Secretary of the American Friend's Inter-racial Peace Committee (*Give Us Each Day* 467–469). In her diary, Dunbar-Nelson writes that she knew Fauset and admired her journalism (*Give Us Each Day* 21, 45, 367, 428). Eva D. Bowles served on the War Work Council of the YWCA (Emmett J. Scott, 379). She was also a social worker in Columbus, Ohio, and left the YWCA after 27 years of membership (Lerner, *Black Woman* 330). Addie W. Hunton and Kathryn M. Johnson traveled to France with the YMCA as canteen workers. After the war Addie Hunton founded the Circle for Peace and Foreign Relations organization (*Two Colored Women* xix–xxii). Mary Church Terrell was a federal clerk in the War Risk Insurance Bureau, worked in the War Camp Community Service, and was a delegate to the International Peace Congress (*Colored Woman in a White World* 252, 318, 329). Fauset was clearly influenced by the rhetoric of women's wartime volunteerism in her fiction, as I argue in the next chapter.

The writings of Dunbar-Nelson, Bowles, Hunton, Johnson, and Terrell thematized war relief work in ways that combined patriotism with African American women's organizing and protest. Dunbar-Nelson related how war relief work included direct forms of support for the war, such as the preparation of aid kits, canteen work, nursing, hostess houses, and liberty loan drives, but also expanded to include work with southern migrants in the north, social welfare, and labor organizing. Although Dunbar-Nelson at times clearly subordinated protest over racial discrimination in the United States to wartime patriotism, her account of the work performed by women in a network of volunteerism somewhat belied her rhetoric. She argued initially, for example, that, "the women of the race . . . . accepted without a murmur the place assigned them in the ranks. They placed the national need before the local prejudice; they put great-heartedness and pure patriotism above the ancient creed of racial antagonism" (Emmett J. Scott, 376). However, she then recounted the struggle to integrate the Red Cross and overseas nursing. Even more interesting was Dunbar-Nelson's description of organizing done through the Women's Committee of the Council of Defense in 1918. She argued that Mary McLeod Bethune and Eartha White organized throughout Florida

> with a particular concentration on a Mutual Protection League for Working Girls, who had taken up the unfamiliar work of elevator girls, bell girls in hotels, and chauffeurs. From this it was not far to a Union of Girls in Domestic Service, a by product of war conditions that might well be continued in every city and hamlet in the country.   (384)

Although Dunbar-Nelson and other women organizers were limited by their connection to the Women's Committee, which deferred to state committees in the South, they obviously tried to extend the boundaries of patriotism to include challenges to the economic exploitation and marginalization of domestic service (428). Roberta Campbell Lawson (Delaware) was also an organizer for the Women's Committee during World War I.[19]

Dunbar-Nelson was aware both of the racist barriers to African American women's organizing, especially in the South, and of the resistance to patriotism born of racial discrimination as her correspondence during her travel for the Women's Committee demonstrated. While visiting New Orleans, she used her position to critique discrimination in government employment that relegated African American women to domestic service despite educational background. She explained women's disaffection with the war effort, "because government employment bureaus here recognize in every colored girl who applies for work only a potential scrub woman, no matter how educated and refined the girl may be" (qtd. in Breen, 425). Dunbar-Nelson saw her position, promoting patriotism, as even more untenable in Vicksburg, where she had arrived just after the wife of an African American soldier had been tarred and feathered (Breen, 425). The contradictions expressed by African American women active in wartime service were acute, especially when trying to organize in the South.

Like Dunbar-Nelson, Mary Church Terrell also documented a conflicted politics during and after World War I. She, too, discussed the discrimination she experienced as a beneficiary of wartime government employment, describing the humiliations of federal segregation and her own marginalization. Her work became both more protest-driven and more problematic as she traveled throughout the South with the War Camp Community Service (WCCS) in 1918 (*A Colored Woman* 329). Terrell used her position to document and protest the racist conditions under which southern African Americans lived. The WCCS program attempted "to do something for the colored women and girls living in the cities where little or nothing had been done for them," according to Terrell (*A Colored Woman* 318). Describing Southern resistance to African American women organizing, she exposed racist beliefs in African American inferiority and the exploitation of African American women's labor through domestic service, as did Alice Dunbar-Nelson. A Pensacola, Florida, man told

Terrell "the white people here want colored people to do their wash-
ing and ironing, and they get mad as fire when they don't. They don't
care a whoop about trying to 'elevate' them" (*A Colored Woman* 325).
Arguing against the racism that offered African Americans only manual labor, that positioned them as, in another man's terms, "a mule. He
is a good animal, so long as you keep him broken," Terrell adopted a
rhetoric of uplift (325).

By failing to mention the resistance of southern African American
women to the WCCS, she also revealed her own class bias, explicitly
as she attempted to gain "consent to permit competent workers to lift
colored women and girls to a higher plane" (327). Displacing her
expose on Southern racism, Terrell claimed that organizers were
needed to effect social change, to help "undesirable, ignorant and
immoral" women (327). Terrell's writing was engaged in political
struggle. Her direct confrontation with segregation in her travels suggested that she was aware that organizing African American women
in the South posed a challenge to a racist social order. At the same
time, her desire to disprove charges of racial inferiority led her to
pathologize working-class rural women.[20] As we have seen, a similarly
conflicted politics developed among Pan-Indian women journalists
who cast tribal cultures as "primitive" to argue against ideologies of
racial inferiority. Jewish journalists also distanced themselves from
immigrant women by casting them as "immoral" in order to establish
their own "respectability" and capacity for integration, as we will see
in chapter 5.

African American women's wartime organizing built on a network
of women already involved in social reform.[21] Outside the context of
war relief work, for example, Addie Hunton, Mary Church Terrell,
and Eva Bowles were all African American welfare workers (Gordon
580). Social welfare among African American women was primarily
aimed at education, health, and settlement house work and was circumscribed by domestic bourgeois values. However, Gordon acknowledges the complex politics of these women as she states that, "despite
the sense of superiority among some, the black women reformers
could not easily separate their welfare from civil rights agitation" (580).
Similarly, although the "'home sphere'" was central to African American women's uplift work, according to Wolcott, it used the "ideals of

domesticity and self-help to build institutions that would aid African-American women and men" (28). Moreover, the Progressive Era emphasis on home was used by African American women "to bargain for the state services that were beginning to improve whites' lives but were denied to African Americans" (Gilmore, 152).[22]

Addie Hunton and Kathryn Johnson's account of their overseas work with the YMCA during World War I, *Two Colored Women with the American Expeditionary Forces* (1920), clearly combined discourses of war, domesticity, and reform. In addition to methodically documenting racism among combat and noncombat troops, officers, and privates in various divisions, Hunton and Johnson used the war to focus on the denial of equal rights in the United States and to combat pernicious stereotypes of racial inferiority and sexual immorality. They argued that African American participation in the war represented a challenge to the United States and a "plea for democracy" (97, 239). More specifically, they rejected U.S. propaganda in France which reinforced the racist sexual ideologies underpinning lynching. They claimed the French "had been systematically informed that their dark-skinned allies were not only unworthy of any courtesies from their homes, but that they were so brutal and vicious as to be absolutely dangerous" (184).[23] Hunton and Johnson's refutation invoked a rhetoric of bourgeois respectability. They claimed through a French General that African American soldiers, "all showed superior mental capacity, and were much loved by all the French citizens because of their splendid behavior and gentility of manners" (213). Moreover, they characterized their wartime service in domestic terms. Hunton and Johnson claimed that, "over the canteen in France, the woman became a trusted guardian of that home back in America" (178). They articulated their role as "to establish a connecting link between the soldier and the home, that home which ever kept for him a beckoning candle in the window and a fire that was ever aglow" (22). Fauset too played with a domestic rhetoric of home and homesickness, as we have seen, in her essay "Nostalgia." These women demonstrated that domesticity and issues of respectability were an integral part of women's patriotism and protest during World War I.

The discourse on women's war work provides an historical rationale for Fauset's representation of World War I in domestic fiction. In fact, Fauset reviewed Hunton and Johnson's *Two Colored Women with the American Expeditionary Forces* favorably in the 1921–22 issue of *The Crisis* (Sylvander, 106).[24] Although the title of her first novel, *There Is Confusion*, has been read as a comment on Fauset's narrative style, it almost certainly derives from Hunton and Johnson's memoir (quoted in my epigraph), suggesting that political protest and not narrative confusion is at the heart of this novel. It is not surprising that Fauset used wartime rhetoric in her journalism and fiction. She was clearly aware of African American journalists widespread use of patriotic rhetoric to argue for human rights, for democracy at home. It is surprising, however, that the explicit politics of Fauset's domestic fiction and the sophistication of her rhetorical maneuvering has been to a large extent ignored. Fauset's domestic fiction does not retreat from political engagement. Instead, armed with rhetorical strategies from women's political writing and the African American press, it takes up the fight for equal rights and protests democracy too long denied.

4

"An 'Honest-to-God' American"

Patriotism, Foreignness, and Domesticity in Jessie Fauset's Fiction

Jessie Fauset's literary politics draw on journalism during and after World War I to represent a historical crisis over integration among elite African Americans.[1] Specifically, her novels combine discourses of Americanism with a conflicted domesticity to negotiate increasing racism in the United States. Employing a rhetoric of patriotism and "foreignness," Fauset's fiction argues against exclusion from U.S. society and aims to establish her characters as citizens deserving political rights. Fauset engages in a sophisticated conversation, playing with journalistic discourses that are already dialogic. Her embrace of Americanism does not come at the expense of protest, just as her embrace of bourgeois domesticity does not wholly support white middle-class hegemony. Unlike the relatively straightforward wartime literary propaganda written by Alice Dunbar-Nelson, Fauset's integrationist politics combine controversies over patriotism with bourgeois domesticity to weigh individual against group rights and to join debates over the place of African Americans in U.S. society.

Fauset saw herself as a "race woman," involved in the politics of racial uplift which, at its best, argued for a collective response to U.S. racism but which too often adopted white middle-class values and culture to argue for positions of equality in U.S. society (Sylvander, 40, 67; Wall, 43, 50; Gaines, 1–3). When historian Willard Gatewood describes African American elites' embrace of middle-class "respectability," he might as well be summarizing the critique of Fauset's fiction. "Respectability," according to Gatewood, included a patriarchal, nuclear family, male wage-earning and female domesticity, education, family lineage, and a code of social decorum defined by "gentility" (190).[2] As Cheryl Wall and Barbara Christian have recognized, Fauset's writing is clearly circumscribed by these domestic and middle-class themes. Her failure to represent folk culture or draw on working-class African American experience and institutions has sustained charges of elitism.[3]

Shifting historical circumstances following World War I, however, undermined confidence in social mobility as the road to integration. Fauset, like other African American elites, was forced to recognize the ineffectiveness of class status and bourgeois values in gaining civil rights. Ann duCille, Deborah McDowell, and Carol Sylvander all document Fauset's loss of faith in the politics of middle-class "respectability."[4] The violence directed at African American soldiers, who embodied the values of respectability and Americanism embraced by the middle class, demonstrated their failure. Urban riots during the "red summer" of 1919 and disillusionment with African American participation in the war resulted in a more militant demand for equal rights. Historian Kevin Gaines argues that Alice Dunbar-Nelson and other elites experienced

> a shift from racial uplift ideology to a New Negro militant consciousness, . . . [as] a response to the elevation of segregation to the level of national policy in the years preceding the war and later, racial polarization, with an attendant rise in black consciousness in the northern urban black communities created by the mass migration of southern blacks.   (214)

Fauset's fiction represents, in sometimes contradictory terms, the shift from bourgeois values to a more militant stance.

In *There Is Confusion* (1924), Fauset depicts conflicting attitudes toward integration through her characters' participation in World War I. She uses a rhetoric of patriotism to demonstrate her characters' capacity for American citizenship and then foregrounds discrimination in the war, U.S.-sponsored antiblack propaganda in France, and the lack of U.S. democracy at home in the postwar period to argue against the denial of civil rights. In an ambivalent embrace of the war, she represents African American soldiers as heroic but disillusioned, unable to take their rightful place in U.S. society but more able to see and resist racism after serving in the war. Her ambivalent patriotism suggests the difficulty of combining a demand for integration and political rights with an awareness of increasing U.S. racism, segregation, and violence.

The two principle characters in *There Is Confusion*, Peter Bye and Joanna Marshall, exemplify struggles over Americanism. The novel argues ironically that Peter's slave past constitutes him as an American citizen. When given the opportunity to travel to France as a musician to free himself from discrimination, Peter refuses and claims America as his homeland: "I don't want to leave America. It's mine, my people helped make it" (*There Is Confusion* 182). He echoes these sentiments when deciding to participate in the war, "America makes me sick, you know. . . but darn it all, she is my country, my folks helped make her what she is even if they were slaves" (*There Is Confusion* 207). His Aunt also assures him that his great grandfather, who participated in the Revolutionary War, and his two uncles, who fought in the Civil War, present him not only with military models but an American lineage. In these passages, Peter's Americanism and capacity for citizenship is ironically defined by a national history of participation through soldiering and exclusion and exploited labor through slavery.

Joanna also becomes a public symbol of ambivalent Americanism, after having achieved notoriety as a dancer despite racial discrimination. Specifically, she is barred from dancing in important venues, on racist grounds, until a patriotic Greenwich Village production, "the Dance of the Nations," hires her. Joanna is initially hired to dance the African American role, which is one of three roles ("American," "black," and "red") representing America in her entirety. Fauset's decision to include American Indians rather than immigrants in her patriotic representation of America probably indicates her awareness that American Indians used participation in World War I to argue for U.S. citizenship, which they received in 1924. Fauset's association with Du Bois and her familiarity with Hampton Institute's journal *The Southern Workman* may have acquainted her with this discourse. She taught at Hampton and cites *The Southern Workman* in her April 1919 "Looking Glass" column (Sylvander, 66, 67).

A white dancer is hired for the role and is competent at performing "America" and the "red" role but can only adopt a minstrel portrayal of African Americans. In an ironic reversal, Joanna wins not only her place performing African American culture and the American Indian role but also plays white America, behind a mask, which she removes. Like Peter, the unmasked "Miss America" claims, "I hardly need to tell you that there is no one in the audience more American than I am. My great-grandfather fought in the revolution, my uncle fought in the civil war and my brother is 'over there' now" (*There Is Confusion* 269, 232). Critics have read this scene as evidence of Joanna's accommodationism, missing the larger context for and critique of patriotism in the novel as well as the scene's dual acknowledgment of national participation and exclusion.[5]

Following the historical movement in the press toward greater militancy, the prewar patriotism and optimism of the novel is gradually replaced with a clearer critique of racism suffered by African American soldiers during and after the war. Peter's vexed integrationist politics are subtly represented through his decision to attend the African American officer's training camp at Des Moines. Historically, W.E.B. Du Bois' support of this camp was extremely controversial because the camp, a segregated facility, was seen as endorsing a segregated military at the same time that it tried to move African Americans into positions of authority in the army.[6] Similarly, Fauset combines a patriotic embrace of African American participation in the war with a critique of segregation and increasing disillusionment. On the one hand, African Americans in the war, unlike their hypocritical white compatriots, exemplify the meaning of the democracy for which they fight. In *There Is Confusion*, the real heroes of the war are those African American soldiers whose bravery is measured by a "persistent . . . cheerful(ness) in the face of the hateful prejudice that followed and flayed them in the very act of laying down their lives for their country" (*There Is Confusion* 259). The novel's patriotism here reads as accommodationist—African Americans, excluded from the political rights of the nation, are nevertheless "cheerful" as they die for the nation's political ends. On the other hand, Fauset's fiction does not shy away from documenting the extreme alienation and oppression of African Americans in the war effort. Peter's arrival in France is full of conflict and racial violence, prompted by a segregated U.S. military:

> First white Americans and Frenchmen clashed; separate restaurants and accommodations had to be arranged. Then came the inevitable clash between white and colored Americans; petty jealousies and meanness arose over the courtesies of French-women and the lack of discrimination in the French cafes. The Americans found a new and inexplicable irritation in the French colored colonials. . . . Stevedores and even soldiers became cattle and beasts of burden. Many black men were slaves.
>
> (*There Is Confusion* 247–248)

Instead of subordinating African American interests to those of the nation, Fauset's descriptions of racism among U.S. armed forces attempt to reorient the focus of the war away from international conflict toward racial conflict in the states. She also uses the war to highlight the racist ideology behind lynching. She describes white mob violence over the associations between African American soldiers and French women (*There Is Confusion* 250).[7] In Fauset's novel, however, African American soldiers are able to protect themselves from mob violence: "the colored soldiers even taken by surprise gave as good as they took. Between these two groups from the same soil there was grimmer, more determined fighting than was seen at Verdun" (*There Is Confusion* 250). Furthermore, Fauset uses the experience of the war not simply to document service to country but also to argue for increasing militancy. She subtly invokes militant claims in the African American press, like Du Bois's: "We are returning from War! We return from fighting. We return fighting," by suggesting that armed African American soldiers would use their training against the denial of democracy at home (qtd. in Hughes, 1). Ultimately Fauset claims that the overseas experience of an American soldier enables resistance to racial discrimination and strengthens the demand for a life lived "to the full" (*There Is Confusion* 259–260).

Peter meets his white relative, Meriwether Bye, on his way to fight in World War I. The racial politics of this relationship are also used to argue against a segregated army and accommodationism. Fauset uses Peter and Meriwether's kinship to demonstrate that the white and black Byes are essentially the same—Peter and the white Meriwether Bye spring from the same family; they are equally founders of American prosperity; they are both willing to give up their lives for their country; but through the legacy of slavery, they have shared disparately in the monetary and civil rewards of that country. This comparison uses Peter's identification with Meriwether, his ability to imitate white middle-class and patriotic values, as a rationale for equal rights. At the same time, however, Fauset critiques Meriwether as exploitative, accommodationist, and unable to fight discrimination effectively despite his good intentions. Although they are assigned to different regiments in a segregated U.S. army, Peter ends up caring for his mortally wounded white relation in the heat of battle, their bloods mingling in a symbolically integrationist tableau. Fauset uses the trope of family here not just to focus on the history and abuses of slavery or to argue for Peter's ability to imitate Meriwether, but also for the more explicit political goal of arguing for an integrated army.

Moreover, although Meriwether Bye is valued in the text for his ability to recognize racism and for his ability to empathize, he is also represented as accommodationist, as unable to challenge racism seriously. Even though he acknowledges that the Bye wealth is due to African American labor under slavery, he does nothing in the United States to rectify the unequal distribution of wealth. Similarly, Meriwether tells Peter, "I see this war as the greatest gesture the world has ever made for Freedom. If I can give up my life in this cause I shall feel that I have paid my debt" (*There Is Confusion* 245, 246). He undermines this idealism by going abroad with a death wish. His fight for freedom is represented as choosing to escape rather than to grapple with discrimination. Through Meriwether, Fauset indicts patriotic participation in the war as an accommodationist and ineffective challenge to racial discrimination. She also shows important differences between, or gradations of, what too many critics lump together as middle-class and accommodationist stances.

African American soldiers in Fauset's novel suffer severe racial hostility and discrimination on their return home. Peter tells Vera Manning, "The colored soldiers were all sold. Fighting for freedom was a farce so far as they [African Americans] were concerned. But France is all right if the white Americans don't get in too much propaganda" (*There Is Confusion* 273). Vera describes how white southerners "mobbed some colored soldiers in Arkansas because they'd worn their uniforms in the street" and is inspired by the event to dedicate her life to documenting racial violence and lynching in the South (*There Is Confusion* 270). The Vera/Harley subplot in this novel is taken from Fauset's essay, "Nostalgia," discussed at length in chapter 3. Vera is also probably modeled on Walter White, who investigated lynchings for the NAACP by passing (Park, 317, 318). *There Is Confusion* demonstrates a shifting integrationist politics that uses an ambivalent patriotism to focus attention on African Americans' capacity for citizenship, to reject segregation, and to move toward a more militant stance.

In *Comedy: American Style* (1933), Fauset continues to draw on discourses of Americanism as she struggles to position her characters in U.S. society. Instead of using the war as a catalyst for debates over integration, Fauset's last novel follows Olivia Blanchard's attempts to gain political rights by becoming white, through passing and becoming an expatriate. In *Comedy: American Style* Fauset uses a rhetoric of "foreignness" to argue for African American citizenship. In several instances Fauset aligns "foreigners" with African Americans, both of whom suffer discrimination and exclusion in the U.S. When Teresa attends Christie's, a "thoroughly American" elite New England prep school, for example, she knows that, "while the school had no objection to foreigners, Negroes nor Jews, it happened that none had ever registered within their portals" (*Comedy* 70). In addition, Phoebe and Oliver see the plight of Jewish and African Americans as parallel. Phoebe argues that "Jews and colored people—they're the people we're always hearing about being persecuted" and Oliver finds the "unwashed Negroes and Jews" of "South Street" an inspiration for his music (*Comedy* 52, 192).

However, Fauset also draws distinctions among immigrant and African American experiences of discrimination. In two ironic passages at the start of the novel, Fauset parallels the exclusion of immigrants and blacks from the category of "American" even as she differentiates immigrants, whose whiteness enables their participation in American culture. Olivia gains acceptance in public school by passing as an Italian immigrant. Her teacher asks,

> "You didn't mind my speaking of your being an Italian, did you? You know," said Miss Baer, whose grandfather under a difficult name ending in ewski was at that moment painfully tilling a field in a far-off town in Poland, "you know I think that you Italian children are quite as good as us Americans." (*Comedy* 6)

In this satiric passage, Fauset both identifies Olivia with the excluded Italian Americans and distances her from white immigrants, implying their racism and ignorance through Olivia's need to pass. Fauset implicitly compares anti-immigration sentiment to U.S. racism, positioning African Americans as more severely affected by discrimination. Recognizing Italians as American in ironic contrast to African Americans, Fauset exposes the racism of immigrant claims to whiteness. Read in juxtaposition to Fannie Hurst's and Edna Ferber's fiction, this subtle and pointed passage offers a rejoinder to immigrant writers' racist characterizations of African Americans detailed in chapter 6.

In an even more complicated gesture early on, Fauset uses Olivia's mother, Janet, to identify African Americans with "foreigners" even as she carefully situates Janet as more American than immigrants. Passing as white to work in a factory, Janet is promoted by her employer for her ability to "manage" immigrants,

> Finally a harassed foreman, noting that she had a way with her with the foreigners by whom the place was overrun and commenting to himself that here was an "honest-to-God" American who might be able to get some sense into the heads of these "wops," made her an assistant forewoman. (*Comedy* 11)

Through Janet's and her daughter Olivia's passing, Fauset critiques Americanism as exclusive and discriminatory in relation to both immigrants and African Americans. By using the trope of "foreignness," she then manages to position African Americans ironically as more discriminated against and as more American than white immigrants.

Finally Fauset capitalizes on antiforeign sentiment to offer a critique of passing. Although Janet gives up passing, moves to Boston, and marries an African American man, Olivia and her own daughter, Teresa, continue to embrace foreignness to pass as white and are consequently represented as un-American. Ostensibly Olivia passes in order to avoid discrimination, win acceptance as an American, and be accorded the rights of a citizen. However, to succeed she must either take on a "foreign" identity (Italian American), figure her son, whose skin color betrays her African American heritage, as a "foreigner" (a Filipino butler), or become an expatriate in France. "Completely hipped on foreign life," Olivia identifies with foreigners to become white (*Comedy* 315). Fauset suggests the futility of Olivia's passing by documenting the exclusion of foreigners earlier in the novel as I've suggested. That Fauset was familiar with this discourse is also demonstrated by her use of the term "100 per cent. Americanism" (sic) in *Plum Bun* (352). By the end of *Comedy: American Style*, Olivia's desire for integration, her belief that whiteness is equated with freedom and superiority results in her son's suicide and her own and her daughter's impoverished and lonely exile in France. In the end, Fauset equates whiteness with "foreignness" and plots Olivia's decision to remove herself from black community as a rejection of Americanism.[8]

Conversely, the characters who claim an American identity in Fauset's novel embrace black community. Dark-skinned Henry, for example, is positioned as essentially American, "In point of fact with the exception of his skin, he would, with his clear, hard mind, his straight, supple body, his sense of humor, his beauty, have been labelled a typical American" (*Comedy* 123). Moreover, when Teresa asks him to pass for Mexican to avoid discrimination, he ends their relationship, replying, "I'm perfectly satisfied to be an American Negro, tough as it all is" (*Comedy* 143). Although critics have read Fauset's characters' embrace of patriotism as accommodationist, Fauset's texts are critical of those who would avoid rather than fight discrimination. Fauset's "American" characters reject the rhetoric of victimization used to justify passing at the same time they protest inequality.[9] Teresa's inability to face and reject discrimination, her decisions to pass for convenience eventually lead not to incorporation but to alienation and poverty.[10] Fauset's patriotic embrace of America doesn't altogether replace, then, a rhetoric of protest. Her American-ism doesn't guarantee integration but it does demand the rights of cit-izens for African Americans, eschewing, "This senseless prejudice, this silly scorn, this unwelcome patronage, this tardiness on the part of her country to acknowledge the rights of its citizens" (*Comedy* 124).

A brief look at the writings of Alice Dunbar-Nelson throws into relief Fauset's departure from wartime propaganda. At the same time, it establishes that Fauset's rhetorical strategies circulated among other African American women journalists and fiction writers. Dunbar-Nelson enters the same debates over World War I patriotism, Ameri-canism, and foreignness in her one-act play, published in a 1918 issue of *The Crisis*. A journalist herself, Dunbar-Nelson, like Fauset, was aware of the ways in which World War I and, especially, the draft could be used to focus attention on discrimination in the United States. "Mine Eyes Have Seen" is the story of two brothers, Dan and Chris (who has been drafted), and a sister, Lucy, arguing over African American participation in World War I. The play begins by recogniz-ing de facto segregation in housing in the North. Lucy, who currently lives with her brothers in a tenement, reminisces with nostalgia over having once lived a bourgeois domestic ideal, "in the little house with the garden, and you and father coming home nights and mother get-ting supper, and Chris and I studying lessons in the dining-room at the table—we didn't have to eat and live in the kitchen then. . ." (Dun-bar-Nelson, "Mine Eyes" 271). Her disabled older brother, Dan, quickly intrudes on her memory, adding to the scenario the racist burning of their home and unprosecuted murder of their father, his own disfigurement through factory work, and the death from subse-quent poverty and disease of their mother.

Dunbar-Nelson tries to use Dan to argue for equal rights. How-ever, his protest over segregation and racist violence is quickly subor-dinated to a patriotic discourse of Americanism. Establishing their capacity for citizenship, Dan argues that African Americans have a foundational relationship to the United States, having fought "in 1776. . . . Ours was the first blood shed on the altar of National lib-erty. We went in 1812, on land and sea. Our men went through the struggles of 1861" (Dunbar-Nelson, "Mine Eyes" 273). Jewish Jake and

Irish Mrs. O'Neil listen to this speech as Dunbar-Nelson subtly contrasts immigrants, who have foreign national allegiances, with African
Americans' experiences in the United States. Dunbar-Nelson parallels
racism in the United States to the forms of discrimination Jewish and
Irish immigrants faced in Europe, anti-Semitism in Russia and an Ire-
land "bled" (273). She is careful not to inflame antiforeign sentiment
even as she distinguishes between African Americans' central positioning in the United States and the peripheral positioning of immigrants. Although she draws on antiradical and anti-Bolshevik propaganda, for example, she makes both the Irish and Jewish characters
patriotic. The Jewish character, Jake, reveals that Chris has been
attending socialist meetings. However, Jake later claims that despite
severe anti-Semitism the Jewish people are, "loyal always to the country where we live and serve" (Dunbar-Nelson, "Mine Eyes" 274).

Dunbar-Nelson plays carefully with the popular claim that African
Americans were disloyal and influenced by "Bolsheviks" to argue for
Chris's alienation in the United States.[11] Chris decides that he has no
reason to fight for a nation that refuses to claim him. He wants to gain
a draft exemption due to his status as sole bread-winner. Replacing
national allegiance with his own domestic one, he asks: "Shall I desert
the cause that needs me—you—Sister—home? For a fancied glory?"
("Mine Eyes" 272). Dunbar-Nelson suggests that discrimination and
the denial of civil rights, not to mention poverty, stand in the way of
full African American support for the war. She uses patriotic rhetoric as an ironic contrast to the treatment of African Americans in the
United States, which includes sanctioned white violence and murder.
She also parallels wartime atrocities to lynching and violence in the
United States. She points out how discrimination diminishes African
American support for the war even as she uses patriotic rhetoric and
immigrant figures to position African Americans as citizens with a
long history of soldiering in the United States.

Dunbar-Nelson was later disillusioned about African American
participation in World War I as a strategy to gain political rights and
became an active pacifist.[12] However, she ultimately supports the war
in "Mine Eyes Have Seen" as evidence of African American achievement and citizenship. Julia finally states, "it IS our country—our

race—" ("Mine Eyes" 274). Participation in the war, by the end of the play, assumes primary importance, displacing the rhetoric of protest that opens the play.

This is particularly clear in the representation of domesticity. Domesticity is used initially to represent the denial of integration and civil rights. By the end of the play, Chris's desire to provide for his impoverished family represents disloyalty, and participation in the war without political rights becomes the primary strategy for incorporation. Not surprisingly a settlement worker's arrival coincides with Dan's most patriotic (and accommodationist) speech, a speech which argues for participation in the war "above the small considerations of time or place or race or sect" (Dunbar-Nelson, "Mine Eyes" 274). This speech also subordinates the racism that is figured as disrupting African American family life to the disruption of European families through war. Dan argues for Chris' patriotic (and domestic) duty abroad by claiming, "Can't you be big enough to feel pity for the little crucified French children—for the ravished Polish girls, even as their mothers must have felt sorrow, if they had known, for OUR burned and maimed little ones? Oh, Mothers of Europe, we be of one blood, you and I" ("Mine Eyes" 274). The end of the play replaces African American family and the demands for group rights with a domesticity defined by nationalism and wartime participation.[13]

Patriotism and domesticity work hand-in-hand in Dunbar-Nelson's play, not only to advocate for the draft but also to contest racist stereotypes of urban pathology. Historians argue that middle-class respectability was embraced by African American elites to refute racist sexual and primitivist stereotypes that underpinned lynching and Jim Crow. They used a politics of respectability to reject biological theories of racial inferiority.[14] Of course by differentiating themselves through middle-class values and a politics of self-help, elites also reinforced a view of the working class as pathological (Gaines, 4). As Gatewood claims, early in the century elite African Americans blamed the discrimination they suffered on the "vulgar" and "uncivilized" behavior of working-class migrants rather than on white racism (208).[15] Dunbar-Nelson rejects racist theories that positioned African Americans as biologically inferior and she to some extent avoids the classism of elite African Americans by attributing poverty and the breakdown of African American family to racism. Furthermore, Dunbar-Nelson takes pains to represent working-class African American family as moral, not degraded. However, the family's morality is constituted by an embrace of middle-class status and selfless patriotic involvement in the war. Her play endorses middle-class versions of domesticity by representing the nuclear family as "normal" and a household lead by Lucy as traumatized and by symbolically introducing a settlement house worker into the end of the play.

Historically, settlement house and social workers imposed white middle-class models of domesticity on working-class African American migrants and argued that African American family structures were inferior due to a history of slavery. According to Elizabeth Lasch-Quinn, many white reformers simply failed or refused to address the needs of African American migrants but even those who took an interest in African Americans "described the character of blacks as somehow maladjusted and their culture as lacking" (10). Even though they used social or environmental conditions rather than biology to explain racist accounts of inferiority, they still believed, "the harsh system of slavery . . . had obliterated morality, family integrity, social organization, and even culture and civilization itself" (Lasch-Quinn, 10). Gaines argues that among elite African Americans, as well, "formulaic representations of urban pathology were crucial to their self-image of racial respectability" (158). Although it attempts to read working-class African-Americans as moral, Dunbar-Nelson's play finally reinforces a version of settlement house urban pathology by defining morality in middle-class terms and by subordinating the rhetoric of racial protest to patriotic goals. Although her attitudes probably derived from her work in a settlement house in New York City, Dunbar-Nelson's attitudes toward domesticity were far more complex than this play indicates, as her remarkable public political career and lesbian relationships indicate (Hull, *Color, Sex, and Poetry* 54).

Fauset's fiction differs from Dunbar-Nelson's play in its more successful politicizing of domesticity in relation to an ambivalent patriotic rhetoric. Fauset's marriage plots, the domestic framework for many of her novels, are often read as a retreat from political debate (Wall, 78). However, her representations of domesticity draw on and are politicized by the activism of African American women in settlement, social welfare, and war relief organizations. Even critics who read Fauset's representations of domesticity as political argue that she subordinates protest to the goal of attaining a middle-class home. While Fauset's texts substantiate many of these claims, critics have neglected much of the political context for and subtlety of Fauset's representation of domesticity.

Fauset represents settlement and social welfare work to critique white bourgeois versions of domesticity and individualism in *Comedy: American Style*. Olivia Cary is constantly in the company of white club women, who perform welfare work (*Comedy* 158, 206). Fauset's other novels also suggest a knowledge and rejection of social welfare work. She satirized Angela's philanthropic attitude toward her sister when contemplating marriage to the wealthy Roger in *Plum Bun* and is critical of "high brow philanthropists" in *There Is Confusion* (198). Olivia has so imbibed white settlement ideology that she figures her own dark-skinned relatives (her son, Oliver, and daughter-in-law's mother, Mrs. Grant) as domestic workers in her "white" home. Mrs. Grant exposes Olivia's exploitation of her labor and belief in working-class African American inferiority, explaining that Olivia had invited over

> "some of them wite women she's always trailing around after. She brung 'em in en I happened to pass by the parlor door en she sez: 'O there you are, Sarah, just bring us a pot of tea, please, on a tray with four cups. I'll tend to everything else. . .' I said: 'If you want any tea for your poor wite trash you'll have to fix it yo'self!'" (*Comedy* 305)

Fauset also delivers a harsh condemnation of Olivia's choice to gain social rights by becoming white through marriage and motherhood. Olivia marries Christopher Cary for his class status and light skin, to have "white" children (*Comedy* 29). Through domestic discourse, as well as discourses of Americanization, Fauset rejects the idea that African Americans should aspire to white culture. It is precisely this aspiration that tears apart Olivia's home.

Instead, African American family in *Comedy: American Style* represents racial solidarity and an African American collectivity. When both Olivia and Teresa ask Henry to pass for Mexican as a prerequisite to marriage, he refuses to deny black community by posing as a Mexican American in order to be considered "white": "I can help other men to work their way to better conditions. What am I going to do, throw aside all my traditions, all my old friends and be a damned gringo just to satisfy the vanity of two make-believe white women!" (*Comedy* 143). His use of the term "gringo" acknowledges the distance between a Mexican American and white positioning and critiques passing as a "make believe" or failed strategy of incorporation. He embraces African American community as he refuses to imitate white/"foreign" middle-class family in a marriage to Teresa.[16] Teresa, however, takes settlement ideology to its extreme by marrying a racist white Frenchman. Her embrace of white domesticity results in her own alienation from family and involves a racist rejection of black community as her husband talks of Senegalese participation in World War I in colonial terms, "They were all right as cannon fodder," and also spouts racist propaganda about African American soldiers and white French women (*Comedy* 182).

Marriage and domesticity signify racial politics, either alienation from or allegiance to African American heritage and community in *Comedy: American Style*. Fauset critiques social welfare and settlement work and its idealization of white domesticity as racist, responding directly to the racism of Edna Ferber's and Fannie Hurst's fiction, described in chapter 6. In addition, her critique resonates both with Mourning Dove's rejection of Julia's home and belief in "civilization" as colonialist and with Anzia Yezierska's critique of the Hellman Home for Working Girls as exploiting working class women's domestic labor, as we will see. Fauset, like these other authors, uses a domestic plot and representations of the "home" to revise and comment on women's activism during the Progressive Era.

Once again in *There Is Confusion*, the politics of domesticity are dramatically affected by representations of the "home" in the context of World War I discourses and African American women's war relief work. *There Is Confusion* is directly indebted to Addie W. Hunton and Kathryn M. Johnson's historical memoir of African American women's wartime volunteerism. Maggie, like Hunton and Johnson, goes to France with the YMCA to "mother" African American soldiers through canteen work. Maggie represents her role in the war as "race work." She witnesses discrimination and the disillusionment of African American soldiers. Hunton and Johnson also document the abuses of a segregated army and see their own role as breaking through the racist limitations placed on African American women's institutional volunteerism.[17]

It is not surprising that Maggie's service in France during the war also allows for the disentanglement of a secondary marriage plot, as she rejects Peter and offers to marry Joanna's brother Philip. Maggie's role in the war and her marriage to Philip overlap. Philip has been fatally gassed and is disillusioned with the war. He has lost his patriotism as well as his ability to fight racism as he claims that "in the defense of the country which insists on robbing me of my natural joys, I've lost the strength to keep up even the fight for which I let everything else of importance in the world go" (*There Is Confusion* 267). Maggie meanwhile combines "race work" with domesticity as a war relief volunteer and sees marriage to Philip not as a retreat from but as an extension of this role. The domesticity of Fauset's women, then, does not always remove them from a political sphere. Just as Fauset both embraces the war and uses it to critique discrimination, she endorses marriage to Philip, but she refuses "respectability" and a conventional patriarchal family structure. Ironically, Maggie renounces her "selfish" desire to use marriage to procure wealth and "respectability" as she reunites with Philip. Philip's injuries preclude patriarchal wage-earning, and he refuses to marry Maggie. In a revision of bourgeois domesticity, Fauset takes away Philip's wage-earning capacity and Maggie's desire for "respectability" (she offers to be Philip's mistress). Even though Maggie's domesticity is represented in the context of her wartime volunteerism, it isn't necessarily accommodationist, taking an ambivalent stance toward middle-class norms and refusing to serve patriotic goals.

Similarly, Fauset inverts settlement ideology and theories of urban pathology by condemning the white family as victimized by its own racism in *There Is Confusion*.[18] Peter Bye is clearly superior to the white Byes whose social history as slave owners has taken its toll. Meriwether is the last white Bye, despite Aaron Bye's family of ten sons. Moreover, Meriwether's family history eventually results in a death wish, explained by his social positioning: "When I came to realize that all my wealth and all the combination of environment and position which has made life hitherto so beautiful and perfect, were founded quite specifically on the backs of broken, beaten slaves, I got a shock from which I think sometimes I'll never recover. It's robbed me of happiness forever" (245–246).

Fauset claims that the middle-class white family, not the African American family, suffers from a history of slavery. She blames Peter's suffering on white abuse as well when he claims, "my ingratitude, my inability to adopt responsibility, my very irresoluteness come from that strain of white Bye blood" (*There Is Confusion* 297).[19] Fauset critiques white bourgeois domesticity as pathological through the Bye family lineage and its history of exploitation.

The attainment of middle-class status as an integrationist strategy is also critiqued as too individualistic through the representation of Joanna's family. Like her father, Joanna becomes a symbol of America through individual effort, by embodying the American myth of self-help despite discrimination. Yet, she partially rejects this bourgeois mythology by the end of the novel (McCoy, 115).[20] Both Joanna and her father achieve an elite status—he through financial success and she through artistic endeavor. However, even though each one repudiates and breaks through racial barriers, neither is satisfied because each ambition results only in individualistic achievement not in integration and equal rights for African Americans generally.

Dissatisfied with his accomplishments as a caterer, Joel describes his vision of "greatness" not as material success but as "that which gets one before the public eye, which makes one a leader of causes" (*There Is Confusion* 10). Similarly, Joanna is disillusioned with her fame as a dancer that doesn't meet her own desire "to be needed, to be useful, to be devoting her time, her concentration and her remarkable singlemindedness to some worthy visible end" (*There Is Confusion* 236). While valuing her achievement as a dancer, "of course it did mean something to prove to a skeptical world the artistry of a too little understood people," (*There Is Confusion* 274) she is keenly aware of its limitations. "High culture" and Americanism do not guarantee equal rights. Joanna realizes that her impact and ambitions continue to be delimited by racism and segregation. The venues in which she can perform are limited primarily to New York. She states her ambivalence clearly, "this, this was her great success. She loved and hated it" (*There Is Confusion* 275).

By subordinating Joanna's career to marriage, Fauset is also reject-ing the New Woman as self-interested and cut off from black com-munity, a critique she expands in *Plum Bun*.[21] More importantly, Joanna's rejection of her career, her patriotic role in the "Dance of the Nations," suggests Fauset's awareness of a pattern of discourse in the African American press that rejected participation in the war because it did not yield the rights of citizenship. Joanna leaves the "Dance of the Nations," which recalls the rhetoric of nationalism and self-deter-mination coming out of World War I, because she realizes it is fraud-ulent. In a disillusioned echo of Peter's and Philip's attitudes toward patriotism, Joanna recognizes that she is not really represented in the nation. Fauset parallels Peter's, Philip's, and Joanna's ambivalent return "home" to critique the denial of equal rights to African Americans in the United States.[22] Fauset combines domestic and national dis-courses, drawing on journalism that embraced even as it critiqued America as "home." Although Joanna's marriage embraces patriarchal family and self-help through Peter, the complexity of Fauset's ending can only be understood in the context of increasing racism after the war and the recognition that class status and bourgeois values were ineffective strategies for achieving democracy at "home."

The competing domestic ideologies in Fauset's texts do not repre-sent a removal from political discourse. Rather, they engage with and are represented through women's institutional activism, their welfare activity, and related wartime volunteerism. Moreover, Fauset's domes-tic politics attempt to negotiate the historical crisis over integration. At times Fauset's marriage plots argue for integration by embracing patriarchal family and a middle-class rhetoric of self-help at the expense of working-class populations, as critics have argued. When Fauset situates her representations of domesticity in relation to women's institutional activism, however, she is more able to argue for incorporation by protesting discrimination and the denial of equal rights.[23] Read next to political discourses, Fauset's integrationist fic-tion speaks the language of African American women's activism even as Olivia, Joanna, and Maggie represent the failure of democracy and a profound ambivalence toward "home."

Mourning Dove (Okanogan Colville) wrote fiction, collected folklore, was active in tribal politics, and founded a Native women's organization, the Eagle Feather's Club. *(Negative 95-133 from the Lucullus V. McWhorter Collection PC 85, Washington State University Libraries, MASC.)*

Zitkala-Sa (Yankton Sioux) wrote fiction, collected folklore, held office in the Society of American Indians and edited the *American Indian Magazine*, founded the National Council of American Indians, and worked with the General Federation of Women's Clubs' Indian Welfare Committee. *(Tozzer Library, Harvard University)*

Angel DeCora (Dietz) (Winnebago) was a member of the Society of American Indians and wrote for the *American Indian Magazine*, taught at Carlisle, and illustrated the work of prominent Native writers such as Zitkala-Sa, Charles Eastman (Santee Sioux), and Francis LaFlesche (Omaha). *(Tozzer Library, Harvard University)*

Emma Johnson Goulette (Potawatomi) taught at Haskell Insitute, was a member of the Society of American Indians, and wrote for the *American Indian Magazine*. *(Tozzer Library, Harvard University)*

Marie L. Baldwin (Chippewa) was a member of the Society of American Indians, wrote for the *American Indian Magazine*, worked for the Bureau of Indian Affairs, litigated the land claims of the Turtle Mountain band of Chippewa, and was a suffragist. *(Tozzer Library, Harvard University)*

Roberta Campbell Lawson (Delaware) collected Native music and artifacts, wrote *Indian Music Programs*, served on the Women's Committee of the National Council of Defense during World War I, and assumed presidency of the General Federation of Women's Clubs from 1935 to 1938. *(Western History Collections, University of Oklahoma Libraries)*

Jessie Fauset wrote fiction, worked as a columnist and literary editor for *The Crisis*, edited *The Brownies' Book*, attended the Second Pan-African Congress, belonged to the NAACP, and taught briefly at Hampton Institute. *(Prints and Photographs Department, Moorland-Spingarn Research Center, Howard University)*

Alice Dunbar-Nelson wrote literature and journalism, headed the Anti-Lynching Crusaders in Delaware, was active in the National Federation of Colored Women's Clubs, organized for the Women's Committee of the National Council of Defense, and campaigned for women's suffrage. *(Prints and Photographs Department, Moorland-Spingarn Research Center, Howard University)*

Ida B. Wells-Barnett wrote journalism, edited the Memphis newpaper *Free Speech*, founded the Anti-Lynching movement, helped organize the NAACP, legally challenged discrimination by the railroads, established the Negro Fellowship League, and organized and participated in many women's clubs, such as the National Equal Rights League and the National Association of Colored Women. *(Photographed by R.D. Jones, Mary O. Williamson Collection, Prints and Photographs Department, Moorland-Spingarn Research Center, Howard University)*

Addie W. Hunton worked for the YMCA and traveled to France as a canteen worker during World War I. She wrote an account of this work with Kathryn M. Johnson, entitled *Two Colored Women with the American Expeditionary Forces*. After the war she founded the Circle for Peace and Foreign Relations. (*Prints and Photographs Department, Moorland-Spingarn Research Center, Howard University*)

Kathryn M. Johnson worked for the YMCA and traveled to France as a canteen worker during World War I. She was coauthor with Addie Hunton of *Two Colored Women with the American Expeditionary Forces*. (*Prints and Photographs Department, Moorland-Spingarn Research Center, Howard University*)

Mary Church Terrell wrote journalism and an autobiography, *A Colored Woman in a White World*, helped found the NAACP, legally challenged discrimination in restaurants, was the first president of the National Association of Colored Women, and served as a member of the National American Suffrage Association. *(Prints and Photographs Department, Moorland-Spingarn Research Center, Howard University)*

Anzia Yezierska wrote short stories and novels, two of which were made into films. She also worked for Hebrew Charities, lectured to the National Council of Jewish Women, and conducted research for John Dewey among Polish immigrants. *(From the Anzia Yezierska Collection, Department of Special Collections, Boston University)*

Fannie Hurst wrote fiction, sold the movie rights to many of her novels, wrote for radio, and supported the New York Urban League, Hadassah, the United Neighborhood Houses, the Federation of Jewish Philanthropies, and the Campaign for the Relief of Eastern European Jews. She was appointed chair of the Committee on Workman's Compensation for Household Employees, fought for birth contol, and belonged to antiwar organizations. *(Fannie Hurst Collection, Special Collections Department, Brandeis University Libraries)*

Edna Ferber wrote journalism, fiction, and plays, sold the movie rights to many of her novels, covered national party conventions, wrote "war propaganda" for the Red Cross, YMCA, and Salvation Army, and was active in Liberty Loan drives. *(Photographed by Carl Van Vechten, courtesy of the Trust Under the Will of Carl Van Vechten, Special Collections Department, Brandeis University Libraries)*

Cecilia Razovsky (*center*) wrote for and edited *The Immigrant*, was the secretary of the Department of Immigrant Aid for the National Council of Jewish Women, taught classes in English and citizenship for the Jewish Educational Alliance, and worked in Jane Addams' Hull House. *(American Jewish Historical Society, Waltham, Massachusetts, and New York, New York)*

Etta Lasker Rosensohn founded *The Immigrant*, chaired the Department of Service to the Foreign-Born of the National Council of Jewish Women, and worked for Hadassah. With her sisters, Florina and Loula Lasker, she also wrote *Care and Treatment of the Blind in the City of New York*. *(Photograph by Hazel Greenwald, courtesy of Hadassah, the Women's Zionist Organization of America, Inc.)*

Estelle Sternberger was a journalist and radio commentator who wrote for and edited *The Jewish Woman*, was active in the National Council of Jewish Women, the National Conference of Jewish Women's Organizations, the World Conference of Jewish Women, the National Federation of Temple Sisterhoods, and the Jewish War Relief Appeal, among other organizations. *(Photograph found in the American Jewish Archives, Cincinnati, Ohio)*

5

"Why Should You Ask for Ease?"

Jewish Women's Journalism in the English-Language Press

> I quite realize that life would be simpler for you if you were able, as you
> say, to be completely the Jew or completely the non-Jew. Or if you
> could, as a Jew, be completely the nationalist or completely the reli-
> gionist. . . . The position of the intellectual Jew in a modern complex
> society is by no means an easy one to maintain. But why should you ask
> for ease?
>
> —Florence Kiper Frank

Florence Kiper Frank prefers the plight of "the intellectual," who is faced with a range of political allegiances, to any one singular or "complete" position-
ing. As Frank embraces a layered politics, she also suggests the pleasure
and inventiveness of women's political writing. In the period from
1900 to 1930, Native Americans faced BIA corruption, allotment,
and increasing congressional control over Native resources; African
Americans experienced disenfranchisement and legal and de facto
segregation; and Jewish Americans faced limitations on immigration
and a new wave of anti-Semitism, social exclusion, and deportation.
Borrowing from each other, women in these communities developed
a subtle and multivalent politics of incorporation in their intertwining
discourses.

At times Native and Jewish women writers rejected discourses of
Americanism that demanded conformity. At other times they argued
for inclusion and political rights by revising patriotic rhetoric as we've
seen of Native and African Americans during World War I. Jewish
women also claimed a rhetoric of democracy but in the context of
immigration restriction as I suggest below. The integrationist focus of
women's reform work sometimes exacerbated tensions among communities of women. As we've seen, Fauset situated African Americans in opposition to "foreigners" to argue for a central position in the

United States. Similarly, Jewish American fiction writers embraced racist representations of African American domestic servants to argue for their own social mobility through a rhetoric of "whiteness." Class tensions but also ties within various communities were heightened by increasingly exclusionary and disruptive conditions in the United States. Fauset's use of a rhetoric of uplift along with criticisms of elite African Americans and welfare workers plays in the same discursive field as Jewish women's representations of settlement house and immigrant aid workers. The authors considered here simultaneously rewrote discourses of reform, spoke across cultures, and addressed their own communities.

In general, Jewish American women's journalism in English promoted integration during a period in which Jewish national allegiances were called into question. The displacement and refugee status of European Jews in the wake of World War I brought into relief the ugly reality of anti-Semitism and Jewish homelessness in Europe. At the same time, immigration restriction in 1917, 1921, and 1924; deportations, especially during the "red scare" in 1919; Henry Ford's anti-Semitic campaign in the *Dearborn Independent* at its height in 1922 and 1923; and university quotas for Jewish students from 1920 to 1922 signaled a limiting of access to opportunities in the United States.[1]

Jewish American reformers wrote articles on immigrant aid, Americanization work, and Jewish women's club and social work in the two journals of the National Council of Jewish Women, *The Immigrant* and *The Jewish Woman*. A monthly "bulletin" of the National Council of Jewish Women's Department of Immigrant Aid, *The Immigrant* was published from 1921 to 1930 and edited by Etta Lasker Rosensohn and Cecilia Razovsky. *The Jewish Woman*, the official journal of the National Council of Jewish Women, began publication in January 1921 and is still being published as the *NCJW Journal* (Rogow, 171). It was issued quarterly and edited by Estelle Sternberger throughout the twenties. Attending to the plight of Jewish immigrants, *The Immigrant* advocated primarily for the integration and civil rights of Eastern European Jewish populations. Women writing for both journals also used immigrant aid to make their own position as Jews in the United States more tenable. As editors, writers, and activists in immigrant communities, these women positioned themselves between "Americans" and "foreigners."[2] Their journalism refuted criticisms of immigrant aid work as elitist, assimilationist, and as contributing to the loss of Jewish cultural and religious practices.[3] Even as Jewish women's journalism in English provided evidence of these tendencies, it affirmed a strong commitment to a Jewish identity and worked toward alliances with immigrant women.

Journalism in *The Immigrant* and more frequently in *The Jewish Woman* also established the central role gender played in articulations of Jewishness during the 1920s. Written and edited by women, these journals helped to create and sustain an important feminist discourse, including articles on legislation affecting women, such as the Equal Rights Amendment, suffrage, citizenship regulations, and divorce law.[4] In writing that explicitly addressed gender, particularly the role of the "modern" or New Woman, Jewish women journalists wrote self-reflexively, commenting on their relationship to immigrant communities.[5] As New Women, club women, and social workers in immigrant communities, they identified primarily as Jewish women but also as Americans. Jewish women reformers aligned themselves with the figure of the New Woman, embracing "modernity" rather than the "Old World," to claim a place in U.S. society. Simultaneously, they privileged their Jewishness and differentiated their work from the mainstream Americanization movement, resituating the New Woman within a Jewish matrix. These reform strategies and tensions also emerge in and compellingly link the fiction of Anzia Yezierska, Edna Ferber, and Fannie Hurst as we will see in chapter 6.

In spite of the rich complexity of this discourse, little critical attention has been focused on the journals written and edited by Jewish women. Scholarship surveying Jewish journalism generally mentions only Rosa Sonneschein's journal *The American Jewess*, published from 1895 to 1899. Aside from work on Sonneschein, no equivalent to Maxine Seller's excellent article on the women's page of the *Jewish Daily Forward* exists for the "native" Jewish American community.[6] Although the journals of prominent male organizations, such as B'nai B'rith's *Menorah*, have received attention, bibliographies and surveys of Jewish American journalism have tended to ignore the publications of organizations like Hadassah or the National Council of Jewish Women (NCJW).[7] As the primary journal of the Council, *The Jewish*

Woman provides a unique sampling of Jewish women journalists writing in English.[8]

Jewish women's journalism in English focused on integration, foregrounding legal rights and issues of citizenship. Unlike Native and African American women's patriotic contextualization of citizenship and demands for political rights, *The Immigrant* took up citizenship primarily to ameliorate or circumvent immigration restrictions.[9] Cecilia Razovsky, who edited *The Immigrant*, was born to immigrants in St. Louis, taught classes in English and citizenship for the Jewish Educational Alliance, was employed by Jane Addams's Hull House settlement in Chicago, worked as the Secretary of the Department of Immigrant Aid for the NCJW, and had read Anzia Yezierska's work (Antler, 214, 215). Razovsky wrote an influential pamphlet detailing the effects of legislation on citizenship status.[10] "What Every Woman Should Know About Citizenship," explained that under the 1922 Cable Act marriage to a citizen no longer conferred citizenship. Consequently, women who had lost citizenship abroad when they married had no citizenship rights in the United States and none in their country of origin. In the specific context of immigration, Razovsky's pamphlet informed Jewish women of their political rights as citizens or noncitizens. Similarly, articles in *The Immigrant* argued that "aliens whose wives live abroad" acquire and be granted citizenship because, according to U.S. law, "the wife and minor children of an American citizen are entitled to a non-quota immigration status" ("Why the Temporary Committee on Naturalization?" 6). *The Immigrant* also affirmed the teaching of English (Yiddish and Ladino were also taught but only as a last resort) to "illiterate bonded women," who were admitted to the United States on the condition that they acquire literacy, usually in three months time, in order to avoid deportation (Lehman, 6–7).

Arguing for the acquisition of citizenship and English language education at times, however, resulted in ethnocentrism and discrimination—the privileging of English over Yiddish is one clear example. In fact, Julia Richman, district superintendent of the Lower East Side schools, exemplified cultural tensions between German and Eastern European Jews by banning Yiddish in the public schools (Moore, 90–91). Similarly, focusing on the acquisition of citizenship recalled nativist distinctions between citizen and alien. Proposals that discriminated against aliens, limiting naturalization and employment opportunities, for example, abounded. In addition, a bill was introduced to Congress in 1916, requiring aliens to become citizens within three months or face deportation, and in 1918, Congress passed the Revenue Act, which taxed "nonresident" aliens at higher rates than citizens (Higham, 248–250). By and large, however, articles in *The Immigrant* advocating citizenship were strategic and were not aimed at reinforcing the differences between alien and citizen.

Again revealing a political focus on integration, articles in *The Immigrant* often described Jewish women's immigrant aid as Americanization work. However, they carefully differentiated between discourses of conformity that reinforced American hegemonies and their own civil rights advocacy. Razovsky, for example, was critical of "flag-waving, hysterical Americanization" in her article, "The Relation of Nationality to Income," and directed her integrationist politics toward equal opportunity (8). Razovsky argued for wage equity, claiming that, "there is evidence to show that Negro, Italian and Jewish workers suffer from discrimination and denial of opportunity, the Negroes suffering more than others" (8). Although she was centrally concerned with integration, she wasn't suggesting that Jews become like gentiles to gain better treatment. Instead, she examined how America set apart and exploited those marked as different from "Protestant white stock." Razovsky claimed that nationality was linked to better wages, that "clear-cut evidence [exists] of the advantages accruing to Protestant white stock in this land of equal opportunity. From the statistical tables presented, it is apparent that the Protestant workers show a distinctly higher earning power than the Jewish or Roman Catholic workers" (9). Rather than arguing for the abandonment of Jewish "difference" to achieve wage equity, Razovsky argued that America was violating its own principles of equality through wage discrimination. According to Razovsky, American discrimination, not immigration, stood in the way of equal opportunity.

Arguing against anti-Semitism and for integration benefited Jewish reformers as well as immigrant women, however. Florina Lasker, who contributed regularly to *The Immigrant*, worked as National Chairman to the NCJW Department of Immigrant Aid, and wrote *Care and Treatment of the Blind in the City of New York* (1918) with her sisters, Etta

and Loula Lasker, joined debates over Americanization.[11] Like
Razovsky, she defended the immigrant aid and Americanization work
of middle-class women as focusing not on conformity but on access
to U.S. society. In her article, "Native and Newcomer," for example,
Lasker positioned the Jewish "native" between the two poles of American and immigrant. As mediator, it was the Americanization
worker's job to avoid erasing or replacing immigrant culture and to
avoid reifying Jewish difference and marginalizing immigrants as well.
Lasker affirmed her own Jewishness by valuing the cultural specificity
of the immigrant and cautioned against "The American worker [who]
might ignore the cultural heritage of the immigrant, thus seeking to
superimpose on the newcomer his own standards of culture" (6). At
the same time, Lasker affirmed her Americanism, arguing that "the
foreign nationality worker might be prejudiced in favor of Old World
ways and traditions, thus failing to interpret properly American ideals
and institutions" (6).

Lasker inserted herself between the polarities of "American" and
"foreigner" to advocate for immigrant inclusion but also to create a
position for herself, as both Jewish and American. That is, in a subtle
way, Lasker's rhetoric of "American" and "foreigner" distanced the
reformer/mediator from immigrants (even as she identifies with them)
in order to reinforce her own Americanism. Ironically, this strategy
paralleled Fauset's use of "foreignness" to position African Americans
as central to U.S. society. Because any correlation between Jewishness
and "foreignness" ultimately worked against Lasker as well as immigrant populations, she (unlike Fauset) used her "American" position
to push for Jewish integration.

In fact, integration—not acculturation—is the primary focus of
Lasker's work both explicitly, in her advocacy for immigrants, and
implicitly, in her positioning of herself as mediator. Lasker claimed that
the rhetoric of Americanism, which read "Anglo-Saxon" culture as
superior and immigrant culture as a "deAmericanizing" force, was both
racist and exclusionary (7, 8). These anti-immigration sentiments
existed in both the dominant and American-born Jewish communities, according to Lasker. In the role of mediator, Lasker criticized those
who argued for "Anglo" cultural superiority and the erasure of immigrant cultures, those who "insist that the immigrant should at once

throw off all memories of his past existence—that he should immedi-
ately discard all those ideals and values which he has brought with him
replacing them with those generally accepted in this country, to the end
that he soon become a 'full-fledged American'" (7).[12]

Lasker's rejection of conformity paralleled that of Native journalists, Angel DeCora and Laura Cornelius Kellogg, who were critical of
the ethnocentrism of boarding school education and argued for tribal
cultural retentions. Similarly, Lasker's criticism of those who would
restrict full participation in U.S. society resonated with similar critiques in both Native and African American communities. Lasker
claimed that American ideals were relative and constituted by all
Americans with "no distinction between the native and the foreign
born" (8). She argued for a different kind of Americanization, one
that did not replace immigrant traditions but facilitated immigrant
participation in the United States:

> Let us define Americanism to the immigrant not in terms of
> blind or unwilling conformity to existing standards, but, to the
> contrary, in terms of political and intellectual freedom—in terms
> of moral and spiritual integrity. And let us so define American-
> ism to those native born as well who are ignorant or unmindful
> of the finest traditions of their own country.
>
> ("Native and Newcomer" 8)

However, by invoking "morality," Lasker uncomfortably recalled
both the language of immigration restriction and the regulatory discourse of "friendly visitors" and settlement houses.[13] Articles in *The
Immigrant* that depended on an analysis of "morality" tended to reinforce the idea that Eastern European Jewry was culturally inferior.
Similarly, several articles clearly demonstrated that Jewish women
reformers imposed middle-class standards on Jewish immigrants. In an
article entitled "Problems in Adjustment," for example, middle-class
standards of "morality" were clearly endorsed by "the editors" of *The
Immigrant* and dictated to immigrant women. One section of the article told of "Esther" who was "acquiring a wrong perspective of American life from the girls she met on the street. The best things in America were beginning to mean to her tawdry finery, liberal and inartistic

use of lipstick and rouge, and cheap amusements" (7). The article approved the placing of this woman in "the Girls' Home Club of the Council" where she "received valuable lessons in the art of living" (7). In addition, a discussion of the "Americanization of Foreign Born Mothers" addressed the difficulty of recruiting immigrant women to Americanization classes. The solution advocated in the article was to focus on home economics and "American standards of household sanitation and personal hygiene" (12). Ironically, these are precisely the topics omitted from the "Women's Page" in the *Forward*, suggesting a distinct lack of interest in these issues in the immigrant community (Seller, 98). Although Lasker was not immune to elitism, her emphasis on political and intellectual freedom represented a significant revisioning of discourses of Americanization. Her new version of Americanism served both immigrant and acculturated Jews but arguably constructed the most secure position, as a Jewish American, for the reformer.

Estelle Sternberger, the editor of the NCJW's other journal, *The Jewish Woman*, also opposed anti-Semitism and worked to rewrite exclusive definitions of Americanism in her journalism. Born in Cincinnati in 1886, Sternberger had an active career. She belonged to the National Conference of Jewish Women's Organizations, the World Conference of Jewish Women, the National Federation of Temple Sisterhoods, the Cincinnati Jewish Consumptives Relief Society, the Reading Road Temple Sisterhood, the Jewish War Relief Appeal, and the National Conference of Christians and Jews. She also regularly wrote for a number of publications and had a national reputation as a radio commentator (Rogow, 239).[14] In her writing for *The Jewish Woman*, Sternberger revised patriotic discourses to affirm Jewish religious difference as fundamentally American. In the process, she used immigrant issues to establish more firmly her own position in U.S. society. In her 1925 article, "The Birth of Democracy," Sternberger placed "the Bible of Israel" at the center of American democracy and suggested that the Pilgrims were really just like Eastern European immigrants:

the seed of democracy was planted in America by the Pilgrims, who embarked from the Mayflower, holding in one hand their small bundle of personal effects and in the other, the Bible of Israel. As they stood on Plymouth Rock and gazed at the sylvan shore of this new land, America, they must have enheartened themselves by comparing their destinies with those of Israel at the threshold of the Promised Land. America was to be a land where they could set up their own worship of God. America was to be a land where they could follow the dictates of their own conscience and teach them to their children. England had been their Egypt, and the Atlantic Ocean their Red Sea, over which they had passed, through God's providence, unharmed.[15]   (9)

Here Sternberger relied on the colonial subtext of the *Mayflower* (that Mourning Dove rejected) in order to position Jewish immigrants as foundational to the nation. For Sternberger, religious freedom was the basis of democracy and the desire for religious freedom, harkening back to the expulsion from Egypt, was Jewish in origin. Using an immigrant paradigm, Sternberger articulated, at the same time, her Jewishness and her Americanism. Her Americanism, however, rested on colonial discourses of "sylvan shore[s]" and "new [uninhabited] land" ready for the taking. This strategic but troubled invocation of patriotic discourse, as Jonathan Sarna has noted, was a favorite of many prominent Jews (358).

Sternberger's relationship to patriotic discourse became even more difficult as she spoke directly to issues of race. In a long encomium to George Washington, she was forced to confront the racial inequity that gave the lie to her vision of freedom-loving America. She tried to argue that Washington believed in liberty for all "regardless of color," but the inadequacy of her example—that Washington freed his slaves at his death—did more to recall a history of racial inequity than to debunk it. In her "Racial Minorities," Sternberger acknowledged and then ignored racial intolerance and discrimination in her effort to argue that America is fundamentally an open society, a society whose basic principles are Jewish in origin, a society defined by both Jewish particularism and Jewish participation.[16] Sternberger raised the common experience of racial discrimination among "the Negro, the Indian, the Oriental and the Jew" and then abandoned race to the more comfortable terrain of religious intolerance (6). This move suggested that Sternberger, like Fauset, recognized an incipient coalition among racialized groups, but it also demonstrated her willingness to sacrifice common ground for the promise of inclusion.

Sternberger's focus on religion also highlighted her own acculturated Jewish identification. By defining Jewishness as a religion rather than as a lifestyle, people, nation, or race, Sternberger was able to advocate effectively for integration and for acculturated Jews in U.S. society. She argued that religious discrimination, which impugned the American character of Jews, violated fundamental American principles:

> The incompleteness of our Americanism, it may be inferred, is due to our preference for the faith of our fathers and our failure to accept Christianity. This point of view assumes that Americanism and Christianity are inseparable. It is a definition of Americanism that is un-American, for it abandons the cherished American ideal of toleration for people of every creed. (6)

Creating the space for an acculturated version of Jewish religious difference, she claimed that "Christianity and Americanism were not interchangeable terms or doctrines" (7). Sternberger strategically challenged the opposition between American and Jewish "foreigner" by arguing that religious difference both constituted the Jewish contribution to and provided the rationale for participation in American society.

To summarize, journalism in *The Immigrant* and *The Jewish Woman* indicated the extent to which acculturated Jewish women worked for integration and increased opportunity for Jewish Americans in the United States. As reformers, they also used their proximity to Jewish immigrants to affirm their own Jewishness and Americanism. Consequently, their advocacy for Jewish immigrants was both significant and self-serving. Lasker, for instance, refused to subordinate immigrant culture to Anglo cultural superiority. Similarly, Sternberger attempted to redefine Americanism inclusively. In doing so Lasker used the polarities of "American" and "foreigner" to reinforce her own position as a mediator, and Sternberger redefined Americanism to embrace Judaism as religious practice, a view that fit most comfortably with a religious Reform sensibility. Perhaps the most significant effect of this discourse was to establish a rhetoric of group rights, which focussed not on Judaism or Jewishness per se, but on barriers to the affirmation of Jewish community in the United States.

That women like Razovsky, Lasker, and Sternberger were themselves implicated in debates over immigrant positioning in the United States becomes clear in their writing about gender. As club women and social workers active in immigrant communities, these women's writing about gender, specifically women's roles, constituted a self-reflexive discourse. Jewish women journalists writing in English commented on their social work and used it to define their Jewishness in the United States. Implicitly or explicitly they demonstrated again in this forum how intimately their own position as Jewish women depended on their relations with immigrants.

In their immigrant aid and Americanization work, Jewish women reformers were "Progressive New Women," or "social feminists," extending woman's sphere and exemplifying women's independence (Rudnick, 74; Brown, 34). The popular media image of the New Woman, according to Martha Banta, symbolized Americanism and was created in opposition to immigrant populations as well as Native and African Americans (112–113, 123). Immigrants were represented as "Gibson Girls," in shirt waists and on bicycles, only to the extent that they embodied or conformed to the Anglo-ideal of womanhood (108–109). Although the media represented American hegemonies in the figure of the "Gibson Girl" (and later in the figure of the flapper), the meaning and content of New Womanhood was regularly contested during this period.[17]

Middle-class Jewish women journalists' representations of the New Woman suggested the complexity of their American allegiances and the difficulty of maintaining a Jewish identity early in the century. In a number of articles in *The Jewish Woman*, the New or "modern" Woman was constructed as Americanized or assimilated, as her modernity (rather than Old World character) implied. In Jewish women's writing, "Modern" or New Women were most often defined by their labor outside the home, primarily in the field of social work or immigrant aid, and most often for a wage. The "modern" or New Woman was defined by "American" attributes such as bobbed hair, cigarette smoking, or a generational rift. Journalists for *The Jewish Woman* at times positioned the New Woman (and themselves) as Americanized to foreground the need for increased Jewish identification. At other times they used the New Woman's status to secure their own positions in the United States. Although Jewish women reformers worked hard to create a position for themselves as Jewish in the United States, their emphasis on New Womanhood (with a few exceptions) tended to subordinate Jewish immigrant experience and mask or homogenize the diversity in Jewish communities.

This use of the New Woman to suggest American positioning contrasted significantly with Native and African American journalists' emphasis on domesticity in the context of boarding school or World War I discourses to argue for inclusion. Differences in the way Native, African, and Jewish American women discussed their reform work may be partly due to the journals within which these women wrote or their organizational affiliation. As members of a women's organization, the NCJW, rather than the SAI or NAACP, which included both men and women, Jewish journalists may have been more likely to write about their roles as New Women. Considerations of audience might also explain why Native and African American women's domestic fiction more often included representations of New Women in combination with discourses of domesticity. Alternatively, this difference might be explained by the nativist tendency to read Jewish Americans as "alien" or "foreign." This discourse may have rendered tropes of "home" less effective rhetorically than the emphasis on "modernity" or New Womanhood which implied integration in its distance from the "Old World."

A number of articles in *The Jewish Woman* expressed fears over the increased secularization of the New Woman, acknowledging the acculturation of most Council members. They also demonstrated that women active in immigrant aid and Americanization work were worried about their own loss or retention of Jewishness. Ironically, this concern substantiates immigrant claims that middle-class social workers were alienated from and didn't understand immigrant life. It also partly affirms claims like Lasker's that Jewish women reformers worked to preserve Jewishness and did not simply advocate total assimilation.

Nannie A. Reis responded to fears of women's political secularization in her article subtitled "Thou Shalt not Avoid Lectures on Jewish and Religious Subjects Through a Tendency to Arrange for Lectures on Political and General Questions" (6). Reis emigrated from Germany in 1884, actively participated in the Chicago branch of the NCJW and a number of other women's organizations, and wrote for the *Reform Advocate* (Rogow, 236). Reis argued for the centrality of Judaism to community work: "Our Jewish women, be they of the Orthodox or Reform wing, or any of the in-between phases need the unifying influence of a comprehension of Jewish sources and Jewish growth in order to apply the wide vision, the humane implications emanating from these to the solution of general community problems, yes to politics itself" (6). Reis also claimed that Jewish identification should be the principle organizing force in the Council. Jewishness and Judaism, according to Reis, were "the underlying reasons for keeping the group differentiated from the surrounding majority" (6).

In another article advocating women's "full political enfranchisement and actual participation in the government affairs of the world," it was clear that Reis embraced the figure of the New Woman ("In the World" 778). Here, however, her attempt to validate reformers' Jewishness and activism was troubled by her ambivalent representation of immigrant women. She wrote, "that the foes of the women suffrage movement and its program of real progress are those who would have the religious prejudices of the old world become a fixed factor of our American public life. . . . The method of attack is to charge that the women's organizations are 'communistic,' even that they are financed and controlled from Moscow" (779).

Reis saw that the critics of suffrage and Jewish radicalism were the same. Since Jewish immigrant women were very active in the suffrage movement and were also subject to deportation, Reis's statement suggested her knowledge of the response to immigrant women's activism. Later in the article, however, Reis ignored that immigrant women already constituted a strong political force and instead, argued that Jewish Women reformers should take advantage of the opportunity to combine women's and Jewish politics: "If the American woman citizen of Jewish faith, then, could but realize the ideals of her dual opportunity, what a combination for the good of humanity that

would be!" (779). While Reis argued for increased Jewish identification among women, she tended to suppress the immigrant text that
was so obviously a part of Council and social service work.

Women like Reis or Judith Solis-Cohen were part of a rich and
diverse Jewish community. At times, however, their desire to affirm
their own Jewish and American positioning worked to erase Jewish
diversity. This was also true of Pan-Indian journalists who often positioned "Indians" as a political group inside the United States but in
doing so erased tribal affiliation and generally ignored issues of sovereignty. Judith Solis-Cohen's article, "The Jewish Woman of Yesterday and Today," initially described various communities of Jewish
women—Reform, Conservative, Zionist, Eastern European immigrant, Palestinian, and Sephardim—and to some extent disrupted and
revised dichotomized versions of Jewish communities in the United
States, such as German and Eastern European, native and foreign,
New World and Old World, and middle and working class. Furthermore, in the beginning it refused to privilege a "new" generation over
an older one.

However, Solis-Cohen's article was contradictory in its affirmation
of the New Woman, which tended implicitly to affirm Americanization and to erase cultural and political differences within the Jewish
community. She ultimately claimed that all Jewish women were New
Women, that voting and "bobbed hair, prettily turned ankles attrac-
tively displayed, skirts modishly short, the graceful smoking of cigarettes are the attributes of Jewish women regardless of age" (1). She
explained this Americanized version of both the older and newer generation as the result of World War I and women's entrance into the
workforce. After World War I, Solis-Cohen argued, "the conventions
of centuries fell from Jewish women who labored in a variety of occupations and have become successful in business" (2). In order to affirm
Jewish women's Americanism and modernity, Jewishness in all its
diversity, so promising in the heart of the essay, was subordinated and
lost in Solis-Cohen's analysis. Ultimately, Solis-Cohen privileged her
own middle-class positioning. While her New Women worked for
Jewish causes, they were most successfully exemplified by middle-class
women of German descent, as the article states, such as "Fannie
Hurst" and "Edna Ferber."

Even though Jewish women reformers suppressed immigrant women's experience and history, immigrants were central to definitions of themselves as Jewish in the United States. A. Irma Cohon used the paradigm of immigrant aid to represent middle-class women as both Americanized and concerned about Jewish particularism. In "Judaism and the Modern Woman," she collapsed polarities between New Women and "old world" women, between middle-class Americanized women and working-class immigrants in order to underscore "modern" women's Jewishness.[18] Instead of positioning immigrant women as "greenhorns," Cohon argued that immigrant women were already too Americanized! By displacing assimilation onto the immigrant community, she was able to position herself as someone providing immigrant aid, giving advice to Eastern European immigrants, a position acceptable to middle-class Jewish women. Rather than arguing for Americanization in the immigrant context, however, she directed her message toward middle-class women, arguing for their increased Jewish identification.

In this article, Cohon's daughter of immigrants had no understanding of Jewish traditionalism or religion; she was "an 'American.' . . . 'Modernity' was her ideal. She was the 'new woman'" (11). Immigrants were alienated from Jewish traditions, according to Cohon, and "were uprooted beings, trying to send weak tendrils into this new soil. If they had any acquaintance with the old Jewish life, it had been turned toward the unknown New World. They had no understanding of, no appreciation of, no love for the old associations. They had started out empty-handed and empty-hearted" (11).

Cohon later claims that immigrant women's difficult transition into the New World resulted in a "hungry heart" (11). This is probably an allusion to Anzia Yezierska's first short story collection, *Hungry Hearts* (1920), which was made into a movie in 1922. Cohon's positioning of Eastern European immigrants as already assimilated victims of displacement had some historical validity. Hyman and others have documented the influence of the enlightenment on Eastern Europe, how socialists had abandoned religious observation, and how the immigrant community itself was bent on Americanization (Glenn, 33; Hyman, 51–52, 94; Shepherd, 8, 73). However, Cohon's depiction is also a clear distortion, replacing the much more observant Orthodox immigrant community with an immigrant figure who exemplified middle-class Reform religious sensibilities and experience.

Cohon used the New (immigrant) Woman to claim that alienation from Jewish culture made life meaningless and unfit for encounters with anti-Semitism: "Utterly ignorant of the tides and currents of her people's life," the New immigrant daughter is "incapable of sounding the ocean depths of their spirituality. She was unprepared for the adverse winds of open popular antagonism or the lurking shoals and reefs of insidious, pernicious influence" (12). Cohon's solution to the New Woman's modernity and alienation from Jewish culture was a Jewish home.

Significantly, Cohon did not wholly adopt the tenets of True Womanhood, which positioned women as religious authorities in the home. She argued that Americanization had left both men and women ignorant of religion. She also suggested that women's proper role was not to "breathe new life into the Synagogue" where she was "Slow to replace her ignorance by knowledge; overeager to act before prepared [and]. . . . all too often too far removed from her people's tradition to sympathize with it" (12). Her role was in establishing "a religious culture." Here Cohon used the Jewish home not solely or even primarily to assert women's religious authority (which she undermined in the section on synagogue participation). In a domestic role, Cohon argued, woman is most able to reinforce Judaism as lifestyle rather than religion. The New Woman's downfall was not wage labor outside the home, it was secularization and a reductive view of Judaism as confined to the synagogue. According to Cohon, the New Americanized immigrant Woman mistakenly believed

> that custom could not control conscience; ceremony did not spell sanctity; and, above all, food had no relation to faith. Religion should be disembodied spirit! But the humanity of the home-maker has taught her the unity of life. . . . and though she recalls her youthful condemnation of new Yontov clothes as "worldly-minded piety," she knows that waiting until Rosh Hashana to wear the new clothes helps to centre our lives and our children's lives on great days and the significance of those days. And a touch of homely humor begins to tell her that

accommodating the spring house-cleaning to the convenience of the paper-hangar instead of to the date of Pesach, really adds no logic to life, and possibly robs the festival of a bit of its refreshing spirit.   (46)

Cohon's critique of the New Woman in favor of Jewish women's domestic roles went further than simply invoking the tenets of True Womanhood to aid in cultural retention. Cohon reinforced the validity of middle-class women's immigrant aid work as well. The narrator/social worker advocated a Jewish version of domestic hygiene even as the figure of the alienated New Woman was used to argue for increased Jewish identification. Here, Cohon's revisioning of the New Woman in the context of immigrant aid and her emphasis on the home recalls Native and African American women's discussions of domesticity structured through institutional affiliations.

By collapsing the distance between Jewish women reformers and immigrant women, Cohon defied charges of conflict between the two groups and also circumvented nativist rhetoric that argued immigrants were inassimilable. The elitist version of immigrant culture, however—that immigrant women are ignorant of Jewish culture, religion, and lifestyle and require the narrator's guidance—unfortunately functioned to erase immigrant experience and agency. Consequently, Cohon's strategic displacement of assimilation onto the immigrant community, erasing immigrant experience, ultimately undercut her argument for increased Jewish identification. Cohon was most interested in using immigrant culture to situate herself as Jewish and American. In an intricate negotiation with immigrant culture, she defined herself as Jewish against the Americanized New (immigrant) Woman and affirmed her middle-class position as reformer.

In contrast to Cohon, Elizabeth Gertrude Stern used the figure of the New Woman to reinforce Jewish, immigrant values. Stern is best known as a novelist and the author of *I Am a Woman and a Jew* (1926), published under the pseudonym Leah Morton. She was also very active in immigrant aid, wrote a column in the Philadelphia *Record*, and was a contributing editor to *The Ladies Home Journal* ("Women in Social Service—1924" [91]).[19] Stern claimed that embracing wage labor and endorsing women's participation in the labor force even after marriage expressed women's responsibilities toward the family in shared income earning.[20] Stern contrasted the volunteerism of club women, which extended domestic roles into the public sphere, with New Women.[21] The volunteer worked, "cleaning up the homes of the city, feeding and caring for the children of her community, insuring the health of men and women workers, and seeing that there be passed laws to protect every home, every school, every nook and cranny of human life" (6). Differing from the volunteer generation, "modern" women embrace wage earning. Differing from the generation of career women who eschewed marriage, the New Jewish Woman combined career and home. Like Cohon, Stern moved away from the Cult of True Womanhood even though she embraced domesticity. The New Jewish Woman, according to Stern,

> finds herself an admirable executive, or an excellent business woman, a splendid teacher, or a keen scientist, and then she falls in love and marries—and she cannot see why, having done so, she must make for her marriage a sacrifice which her husband is not called upon to make also. She insists on a career, a hus-band—and babies too—all at the same time.   (7)

Stern argued that women's wage labor was a part of Jewish women's responsibility to the home. The New Jewish Woman, according to Stern, can "point . . . to Proverbs" to justify women's wage labor:

> the woman there described "seeketh wool and flax, and worketh willingly with her hands; she bringeth bread from afar." Like the admirable business woman, this woman of the Bible "consid-ereth a field, and buyeth it; she perceiveth that her merchandise is profitable. . . ." and though she is a splendid executive . . . she never neglects her home or her children, for she "sees that all her household are clothed in scarlet, and she looketh well to the ways of her household." And while following her career, and taking charge of her home too, she does not forget her duties to society, for "she reacheth out her hands to the poor."   (7)

Stern argued that wage earning for Jewish women was not simply an extension of domestic values into the public realm, as it was for the volunteer generation or True Women, and it did not represent a break away from the home either, as it did for the gentile New Woman.[22] Instead wage-earning women expressed Jewish values: "It is not that she feels primarily the need of 'expressing herself' that the modern married woman holds her job. She does so because she feels it is part of her duty; because she wishes to feel that she is not being a burden to the man whose wife she is. She shares in the economic planning for the children who are their mutual responsibility" (7).

While Stern's emphasis on "modernity" (her discussion of various generations of True and New Women) suggested a distance from the old world, she clearly developed a New Jewish Woman, who worked not for her own self-fulfillment but to practice shared income-earning, as was common in Eastern Europe and on the Lower East Side. Cohon and Stern's revisioning of domesticity through cultural values recalls Marie L. Baldwin's and Mourning Dove's rewriting of boarding school domestic ideology to include tribal and more politically engaged positions for women.

Reis, Solis-Cohen, Cohon, and Stern suggested the complexity of the figure of the New Woman for Jewish women. Aware of both the immigrant charges of acculturation and of the exclusionary rhetoric of Americanization, Jewish women reformers identified with and strategically deployed the New Woman in their journalism. The majority of articles in *The Jewish Woman* attempted with greater or lesser success to argue both for a position within U.S. society—for "modernity"— and for increased Jewish identification. Similarly, in working for immigrant civil rights and against barriers to Jewish community in the United States, women like Lasker, Razovsky, and Sternberger tried to affirm Jewishness as American and to reject charges of total assimilation. Jewish women's reform discourses suggest both the privileging of middle-class experience and a complicated Jewish identification with immigrants. While middle-class biases found their way into this discourse and Jewish women journalists were not consistently successful in representing or advocating for immigrant women, their revisioning of the New Woman and Americanism, in general, went far toward creating a space both Jewish and American in the United States.

6

"Mingling with Her People in Their Ghetto"

Immigrant Aid and the New Woman in Jewish Women's Fiction

Contemporary literary critics, perhaps unintentionally, have read immigrant and acculturated Jewish women novelists apart from one another. Yezierska is read alongside other immigrant authors such as Mary Antin and Rose Cohen. Edna Ferber and Fannie Hurst are rarely read in the context of their ethnicity, let alone in relation to immigrant fiction.[1] This critical trend suggests that Eastern European immigrant authors have little in common, at best, with middle-class writers of German Jewish descent and, at worst, that Jewishness and Americanism are still being figured as antithetical.[2] In fact, working- and middle-class Jewish women's writing in the 1920s intimately informed one another. A historicized analysis of Yezierska's fiction in relation to the work of her middle-class sisters, Ferber and Hurst, suggests not thematic unity but the rich exchange of rhetorical strategies and sometimes conflicting ideas among Jewish women writers of the 1920s. Yezierska, Ferber, and Hurst's fiction also demonstrates how immigrant and acculturated women writers constructed their ethnicity in relation to one another and in relation to women's writing across cultures, though to a lesser degree.

The biographies of Yezierska, Ferber, and Hurst establish that all three women involved themselves in debates occurring among Eastern European and German Jewish communities, specifically those concerning immigrant aid. Yezierska actually knew Fannie Hurst, who was a member of her New York literary community (Schoen, 61). Yezierska's interactions with middle-class Jewish women ranged from having lived in the Clara De Hirsh Home for Working Girls in 1899 to having worked in a settlement house, to lecturing members of the National Council of Jewish women as an author celebrity.[3] Edna Ferber's father was of Hungarian descent and her mother of German-Jewish ancestry. Her fascination with Jewish immigrant communities is described in her autobiography, *A Peculiar Treasure* (1939). Here Ferber also reveals her awareness of the stratification among Jewish populations and acknowledges her friendship with Lillian Adler, a German-Jewish settlement house worker, who provided the model for a character in Ferber's 1921 novel, *The Girls* (180). Not surprisingly, Fannie Hurst also circulated among Jewish women philanthropists, as is clear in her 1941 tribute to Mary Fels, Rebekah Kohut, and Annie Nathan Meyer (Hurst, "Forward"). Hurst's interest in immigrants was also generally known not only because of her novel *Lummox* (1923) but also because of her writerly reputation for mingling with the working class (for example, she once traveled to Europe in steerage for story material [*Anatomy* 138]). Moreover, despite the objections of her father, Hurst married an Eastern European immigrant, Jacques S. Danielson.

In addition, the Jewish press of the 1920s foregrounded the work of Ferber and Hurst together with Yezierska. Reviews of all three women in *The Jewish Woman* and the *Jewish Tribune* suggest that these women knew of one another and were embraced by the press for their Jewish thematics. Hurst was foregrounded much more frequently than either Ferber or Yezierska in the Jewish English-language press. Articles authored by Hurst on motherhood, marriage, contemporary politics, and writing appeared most often in the *Jewish Tribune* but also in *The Jewish Woman* and *American Hebrew*.[4] Similarly, Ferber was reviewed, interviewed, and singled out in the *Jewish Tribune* more than once as one of America's most important Jews.[5] Like Hurst and Ferber, Yezierska too was embraced by middle-class Jewish women journalists and was reviewed favorably in the early as well as the late 1920s.[6]

Historically, Jewish women's immigrant aid work was a site of ethnic, gender, and class negotiations among Jewish women. Acculturated Jewish women's immigrant aid (also known as Americanization) work included helping Eastern European women come through Ellis Island, locate family and friends, gain employment, learn English, and apply for citizenship. More broadly, it included settlement house activity and homes for working women. Established in working-class immigrant neighborhoods, settlement houses sought to provide social services and respond to the local needs of the communities in which they were situated. Middle-class women, generally, and Jewish women, in particular (like Lillian Wald, who established the Henry Street Settlement in New York City) were active participants in the settlement house movement at its height in the period from 1890 to 1914 (Lasch-Quinn, 13). Historians continue to debate the extent to which settlement houses responded to community needs or consolidated middle-class control in urban ghettos.[7] Furthermore, as we've seen in chapter 4, historians have also recently demonstrated how racist attitudes toward African American migrants exposed the limitations of settlement desires for cross-cultural alliances.[8] At the same time, settlement house workers struggled to cross class boundaries and work across ethnic and racial lines.

As providers and recipients of immigrant aid, Jewish women were strongly influenced by debates over women's domestic and wage-earning labor. Settlement house workers trained immigrants and African American migrants to be domestic servants in ways that were similar to off-reservation boarding schools. They saw instruction in hygiene and homemaking as "civilizing," as central to Americanization and class mobility (Crocker, 78, 91, 160). Reformers argued that immigrants could learn middle-class standards and values from domestic service as they earned a wage. Domestic training could encourage middle-class mores even as it served the middle class by alleviating the shortage of domestics, which occurred between 1900 and 1920, according to Sinkoff (582–583).

By the 1920s, domestic ideals were being challenged by various versions of New Womanhood, which situated women in the work force. The New Woman of the early twentieth century is generally described as concerned with "self-development as contrasted to self-sacrifice or submergence in the family" (Cott, 39). However, the ethnocentrism of the New Woman was contested by fiction writers of the period.[9] As we have seen, Mourning Dove's Cogewea (positioned as a suffragette by ranch hands) never seriously entertains New Womanhood, even though she refuses colonial versions of "home" and domesticity and Fauset critiques the New Woman through Olivia's racist social welfare work. Although Jewish women writers most often embraced the New Woman, they too played with her ethnic and racial positioning. Historically, acculturated Jewish women identified as New Women through their middle-class clubs and social work with Jewish immigrants. Elinor Lerner and Susan Glenn also suggest that Jewish suffragettes and labor activists constituted a radical working-class version of New Womanhood.[10] Yezierska's, Ferber's, and Hurst's texts participate in and suggest the contours of these political positionings and struggles.

Like Jewish women journalists, these novelists thematized immigrant aid in order to enter the urgent community dialogue over Americanization, class positioning, Jewish identification, race, and gender roles and to negotiate shared yet varying experiences of anti-Semitism. Yezierska took up immigrant aid directly, critiquing settlement houses and homes for working women, "the high-hat stuff. . . . the fat mamas giving the glad hand to poor little sister," even as she wrote sympathetic representations of immigrant aid and made a plea for social mobility (*Arrogant Beggar* 24). She used immigrant New Women to oppose the elitism and ethnocentrism of settlement domestic training. "Gratitude you want?" Adele Lindner asks reformers; "For what? . . . Because you crushed the courage out of me when I was out of a job? Forced me to give up my ambition to be a person and learn to be your waitress—?" (*Arrogant Beggar* 87). Yezierska's protagonists ultimately revise reform ideology, rejecting domesticity in favor of other forms of wage labor that allow them the freedom insisted upon by the New Woman.

Ferber created a benevolent relationship between acculturated Jews and immigrants, and she defined middle-class Jewish experience as necessarily embracing immigrant life. Using Jane Addams as a model, Ferber privileges the reformer even as immigrant aid work defines her: "All you see in her face is the reflection of the souls of all the men and women she has worked to save" (*Fanny Herself* 238). Ferber's Jewish New Women exist between "American" and immigrant communities. They reject gentile corporate New Womanhood and struggle to establish their own Jewish identities, influenced by but not quite aligned with the labor and gender radicalism of working-class Jewish women. Hurst's short story, "Roulette," and her novel, *Lummox*, took up immigrant aid as well, using immigrant protagonists to speak the rhetoric of middle-class philanthropy. Although Hurst was advertised in the Jewish press as a New Woman herself, she tended to embrace both middle-class Americanization work and domesticity. She defined these realms as Jewish, but of the three writers, she most clearly embraced settlement house ideology, distancing herself from representations of immigrant life. This isn't surprising since Hurst was the most active in reform organizations.

Ferber and Hurst's gendered discussions of reform also differentially applied settlement house ideologies of domesticity and domestic service to their immigrant and African American characters. Their representations of African Americans expose their own attempts to join the dominant culture by embracing racism. Their inability to argue for social mobility and equality for African American domestics also replays the historical inability of the settlement house movement generally to advocate for African American women. Ironically, even while authors, from especially African and Jewish American communities, were willing to subject each other to the racist discourses they refused for themselves, they found it useful to do so because their struggles were parallel in many ways. Working against social welfare and settlement house versions of domesticity, for example, fiction writers in African and Jewish American communities refused the economic marginalization of domestic service for themselves even as they were willing put other women in that role. As we have seen, Fauset ironically presents African American employment of "Filipino" domestic servants (*Comedy* 208). Edna Ferber and Fannie Hurst both include racist representations of African Americans in domestic service in their fiction as I will discuss in detail below. In addition, Edna Ferber's novel *Cimarron* (1930) relies on racist depictions of both Native and African Americans as domestic servants (192–197, 231).

In the context of the immigrant community, Yezierska avoided replacing Jewish American domestics with Native or African Americans. Known as the "sweatshop Cinderella" and read both as champion of and as alienated from immigrant women, Yezierska's positioning within Jewish communities has been controversial, however. Critical of reformers' work with immigrants, Yezierska was intimately acquainted with Jewish class tensions and participated in debates over immigrant representation in her fiction. However, as a successful author who had achieved middle-class status but who continued to take up ghetto life in her writing, Yezierska negotiated a representational space similar to those working in immigrant aid.[11]

Yezierska writes about immigrant aid explicitly in two novels, *Salome of the Tenements* (1923) and *Arrogant Beggar* (1927). In both pieces of fiction, immigrant women long for social mobility and an escape from the ghetto. Adele Lindner lives in a home for working women (modeled on the Jewish-run Clara de Hirsh Home), and Sonya Vrunsky marries a wealthy gentile philanthropist who runs a settlement house (modeled historically on Rose Pastor Stokes' marriage) (Henriksen, 225–226; Schoen, 39).[12] Both novels expose middle-class desires for social control and the inability of philanthropy to alleviate poverty. Yezierska's characters argue forcefully that self-interest motivates middle-class charity, which aims to make immigrants content with deprivation or, in Yezierska's terms, with "Milkless, butterless, eggless cake" and "cheapness and doing without" (*Salome* 134, 135).

In Yezierska's texts philanthropy is also gendered. It is defined by its domesticity: monied, leisured, female volunteers teach domestic science, domestic economy, and hygiene to working-class, wage-earning women. Attending Columbia on a scholarship in domestic science from 1901 to 1904, Yezierska was well aware of the confluence of philanthropy and domesticity. In *Arrogant Beggar*, Hellman describes domestic service to protagonist Adele Lindner as

> almost a religion with me, this mission of teaching the masses that there is no such thing as drudgery. . . . If only women could bring into their homes this self-sacrificing attitude toward life! Isn't it just as satisfying to the soul to feel you have scrubbed a floor faithfully as to be mistress of the house? In doing your cheerful, conscientious best, in your humble sphere, you are doing your part toward the harmony and perfection of the whole universe. (46)

In dialogic fashion, Yezierska places settlement discourse in the mouth of an assimilated Jewish character, pointing to tensions within and outside Jewish community. Moreover, Adele's refusal to be Hellman's maid (when she discovers that she's being underpaid) and her rejection of the Hellman Home for Working Girls participates in the larger critique of vocational education and domestic training that occurred across cultures. Yezierska's criticism, however, focuses not on colonialism or racism but on the elitism of immigrant aid. Her characters refuse domestic service and the "home" in favor of other forms of wage labor that were historically denied to Native and African American women.

Furthermore, Yezierska's characters' rejection of middle-class domesticity involves a return to a wage-earning Jewish immigrant community and a redefinition of themselves as New Women. Dancing to jazz, dressing in style, and working outside the house, Yezierska's working-class New Women (in *Arrogant Beggar*) are placed in opposition to reformers. They express the historically accurate desire of Jewish immigrant women to perform wage work in factories rather than to work in domestic service because the former paid higher wages and allowed for increased independence (Peiss, 39–40). Adele eventually rejects immigrant aid and flees the Hellman home but not before she exposes reformers' representations of the "poor" as exploitative:

> "Thank God I'm not a lady, so I can tell you to your faces in my own language what I think of you! Hypocrites! Shaming me before strangers—boasting of your kindness—because I had no home—I had no friends—I had no work. Feeding your vanity on my helplessness—my misfortune. Right before the whole world—you had to pull the dirt out of the ash can. You had to advertise to all—'Remember, beggar, where you would have been if it hadn't been for us!'" (*Arrogant Beggar* 86)

Yezierska's rejection of reformers' elitism could hardly be more explicit here. Adele differentiates herself from reformers, accusing them of constructing the working class as "beggar(s)" for middle-class self-aggrandizement.

Adele also rejects marriage within the immigrant community as the alternative to wage labor. For example, given the opportunity to marry Eastern European Shlomoh, who has a Ph.D. and is a teacher,

Adele rejects his mother's "old world" maxim, "God sends always to the spinner his flax, to the drinker his wine, and to the man that is a learner, the wife that will help him go on with his learning" (*Arrogant Beggar* 16). Adele counters, "I knew I could never, never be like that" (*Arrogant Beggar* 16). In gendered terms, Yezierska refuses to subordinate the New Woman's position as wage earner to domestic concerns in an immigrant marriage just as she uses the wage-earning New Woman to resist reformers' domestic ideologies. In ethnic terms, Adele's position as a New Woman is complex. By affirming wage labor outside the realm of the Jewish immigrant home, Adele's position as a New Woman is clearly acculturated. However, having fled the Americanization movement and returned to the ghetto, Adele clearly constructs her identity as Jewish.

As a newspaper columnist and an immigrant woman who dresses in style, Sonya Vrunsky, in *Salome of the Tenements*, is another immigrant New Woman who, like Adele, is seeking upward mobility. Her elaborate scheme to marry "John Manning, millionaire, philanthropist—the man of her dreams" to escape the Jewish ghetto, however, ends in disaster and a similar critique of domesticity and immigrant aid (*Salome* 3). Sonya contrives to marry Manning by enacting his settlement house ideology of domestic economy. Acquiring middle-class clothing and furniture through a Fifth Avenue designer and a loan shark in the furniture business, Sonya creates the romanticized version of poverty that accords with Manning's elitist views. Sonya is more powerful than Adele, initially, because she is able to manipulate middle-class domestic ideology to gain social mobility. However, after her marriage to Manning, Sonya, like Adele, is policed by middle-class and domestic mores both at home and at the settlement house.

Manning's settlement house ideology, like Hellman's, imposes middle-class standards of domesticity and hygiene on immigrants with minimal material aid. Manning tells Sonya,

> "The service I feel myself called upon to render the East Side is to teach the gospel of the Simple Life," he launched forth. "I try to make my settlement house an exhibit of what I mean. I have studied out the furnishings with the most competent artists. Only the inexpensive materials are used. Cheap woods, muslins

and cheesecloth, cotton and scrim, but combined in a way to
bring about beauty."   (*Arrogant Beggar* 75)

Sonya's debt to the loan shark exposes Manning's representation of
immigrants, his romanticized and convenient belief in the "Simple
Life," as false. It is the gap between Manning's desire to mask the problems of the working class and Sonya's desire to improve the conditions
of the working class that ends their marriage. Sonya, like Adele,
rejects immigrant aid and a middle-class home when she leaves Manning in favor of wage labor in the garment industry.

Ironically, in both novels Yezierska's protagonists return to the
ghetto and draw on philanthropy to create alternatives to immigrant
poverty.[13] Although Adele and Sonya initially reject reform for wage
labor in the immigrant community, they ultimately record a carefully
negotiated blend of philanthropy and immigrant culture. In the end,
Yezierska's characters reject middle-class elitism and domesticity.
However, they also become proprietors and conduct benevolent aid
through their establishments. Historically as New Women then, they
are more closely aligned with middle-class social workers than the
labor activists and suffragettes of the working class. In fact, although
Salome of the Tenements is modeled on Rose Pastor Stokes's life, Yezierska suppresses her radicalism, her labor activism, her advocacy for suffrage, and birth control, for example (Antler, 86). The tendency of
Jewish American women writers to replace immigrant experience
with that of reformers is related to African American women's rewriting of working-class migrant characters like Fauset's Maggie.

In *Arrogant Beggar* Adele partially reenacts domestic and reform
ideologies. By remodeling her tenement apartment with the domestic skills she acquires at Hellman's Home for Working Girls, Adele creates a wage-earning enterprise, a cafe. Like the Hellman's home,
Adele's cafe attempts to alleviate poverty by feeding those who can't
afford food—in this case, by serving them on a pay-as-you-can basis.
The cafe reminds its patrons of Parisian rather than shtetl culture and
was probably inspired by Yezierska's trip to Paris where she visited
Gertrude Stein and others after the success of *Hungry Hearts* and
Salome of the Tenements (Henriksen, 195). The cafe also exists, like a
settlement house, within but apart from the ghetto.[14] At the same

time that she provides for the immigrant community, however, Adele creates a reciprocal rather than "benevolent" relationship with the working class. In her revisioning of immigrant aid, Adele depends on immigrant patronage just as they depend on hers.

The end of the novel identifies Adele, the wage-earning New Woman, as Jewish and as and part of the immigrant community. Adele's early rejection of philanthropy and marriage with the wealthy Arthur Hellman in favor of her own wage labor aligns her with shop and factory workers, as does her return to the Eastern European immigrant community. However, her subsequent position in the immigrant community as the proprietor of a cafe is markedly similar to her middle-class sisters. Furthermore, Adele's marriage at the end of the novel reinforces this blend of immigrant and reform experience. On the one hand, she marries a ghetto musician and partly reenacts the Eastern European positioning of a Jewish woman supporting her husband so that he can pursue learning or, here, the secularized arts. On the other hand, Adele's marriage also revises that position. The cafe, as a form of immigrant aid, positions Adele as her husband's and others' benefactor. To some extent, then, he is subsumed under her professional goals rather than the other way around.

In *Salome of the Tenements*, the simplicity and cleanliness of Sonya's rooms, furnished through a loan shark, and her elegantly simple attire, designed by a Fifth Avenue "all rightnik," initially expose the distance between the elitist expectations of reformers and immigrant poverty. After Sonya rejects the settlement house movement and Manning as patronizing and elitist, however, she goes on to find fulfillment as a clothing designer in her own middle-class version of the garment industry. As a new kind of benefactress, she designs simple but elegant clothing for the working class. With Hollins, former immigrant turned Fifth Avenue designer of Paris couture, Sonya plans to open up a dress shop for the working class, "in the midst of the ready-mades of Grand Street, a shop of the beautiful—that's to be my settlement!" (*Salome* 178).

In immigrant communities, clothing was socially significant in a variety of ways. For Jewish immigrants, dressing in style was "an outward sign of cultural adaptation," of Americanization (Schreier, 11). It also offered the possibility of social mobility. The transition to ready-made clothing made upper-class styles available to working-class women and "blurred the distinctions between the 'haves' and the 'have-nots'" (Schreier, 68). Working-class women copying styles of middle- or upper-class women could aspire to positions as sales clerks (Schreier, 66; Glenn, 161). In the garment industry, working-class women used their skills to copy dresses for themselves but were also sometimes employed, like the fictional Sonya, as design copyists, who examined expensive department store dresses and designed economical copies (Schreier, 73). On another level, however, the extravagant working-class styles were also an expression of working class "youth culture" and of independence (Peiss, 56–57). Moving away from imitations of the middle class, "many working-class women rejected the values of understated elegance," according to Barbara A. Schreier (70). Elaborate clothing was also a means by which working-class women parodied or "played with the culture of the elite" (Peiss, 65).

In Yezierska's texts, understated clothing clearly suggests ethnic as well as class positioning. Sonya associates "that beautiful plainness that only the rich wear" with the Anglo-Saxon restraint (as well as wealth) of John Manning (*Salome* 169). At Sonya and John's party, the "Russian Jewess" is represented by Mrs. Peltz's "gaudiest finery of Essex Street" in stark contrast with the Anglo-Saxon elite (*Salome* 123). Moreover, Manning's friends adopt the racialized rhetoric of the 1920s suggesting that Jewish immigrant women are racially "primitive" and oversexed; they see this ideology as reflected in working-class clothing (*Salome* 128).

Sonya initially rejects Manning, his Puritan background, and the anti-Semitism of high society in favor of her own Jewish immigrant community. Contemplating Manning in sleep, "she knew that just as fire and water cannot fuse, neither could her Russian Jewish soul fuse with the stolid, the unimaginative, the invulnerable thickness of this New England Puritan" (*Salome* 147). She also rejects the implicit racialism of her critique of John Manning in the final pages of the novel where she argues that, "at bottom we're all alike, Anglo-Saxons or Jews, gentlemen or plain immigrant" (*Salome* 183). However, Sonya's ethnic politics are complicated by her attitudes toward clothing.

Sonya's passion for simple but elegant clothing is quite startlingly similar to John Manning's settlement ideology, his attempts to create the "Simple Life," to create beauty economically. Moreover, many of Yezierska's characters' attitudes toward clothing emphasize copying rather than parodying the styles of the rich. In *Bread Givers* (1925), Sara is horrified by the excesses of working-class women like Mrs. Feinstein dressing in style. Similarly, in *Salome of the Tenements* Mrs. Peltz's elaborate clothing serves to expose the classism of the wealthy, but her own desire for wealth and her concern with Manning's possessions are made to seem excessive. As a designer, Sonya's decision to make a "simple" dress rather than an elaborately adorned one suggests her investment in middle-class mores.

While Manning's philanthropic ideal of simplicity tries to make immigrants content with poverty, Sonya's agenda is social mobility. This is clear early on when Sonya achieves social mobility through clothing and by manipulating middle-class idealizations of the working class. Unlike Manning, Sonya is fully aware that the distance between the middle and working class is not measured in moral but in material terms. While settlement workers see cleanliness as a "moral" issue, Sonya recognizes middle-class standards of hygiene as elitist; cleanliness can be had but only at a price. Sonya's own story of success and her work as a copyist in the clothing designing trade suggest her investment in social mobility. She also offers a critique of acculturation. She, after all, is not satisfied after achieving a position in the upper class with Manning. Yezierska critiques acculturation while advocating for social mobility, since design work with the wealthy and Jewish Hollins proves tremendously satisfying to Sonya. Hollins, himself, reinforces the critique of acculturation since he is reinvigorated by his proximity to Sonya who brings him "back to his colorful Ghetto days" (*Salome* 174).

Like *Arrogant Beggar, Salome of the Tenements* offers a revised version of immigrant aid, one that advocates for social mobility and embraces Eastern European community. By the end of the novel Sonya is a member of the middle class, working for social mobility by designing affordable middle-class clothing for immigrants. Similarly, by embracing wage labor in the clothing industry and rejecting domesticity in both her marriage to Manning and the critique of his settlement house, Sonya also aligns herself with immigrant New Women. Historically, her position is a combination of middle-class immigrant aid work and working-class labor in the garment industry. Like Adele this dual position is reflected in Sonya's marriage. In gendered terms, Sonya occupies a double position as wage earner and as inspiration to Hollins, both creating the conditions for her husband's artistry to flourish and using him to advance her own professional ambitions. The carefully negotiated positioning of Yezierska's characters recalls Fauset's similar attempt to balance women's war-relief work and domesticity with cross-class alliance in Maggie's marriage to Philip.

Although *Bread Givers* isn't as overtly concerned with Jewish reform as *Arrogant Beggar* and *Salome of the Tenements*, Sara's return to the ghetto as a teacher parallels the roles of philanthropists in her other novels and, historically, the Americanization work of women in the National Council of Jewish Women. Teachers, in *Bread Givers*, function primarily to Americanize their immigrant students through lessons in domestic hygiene and English language pronunciation. Similarly, Sara's prize-winning college essay closely resembles essays written for immigrant aid periodicals. *The Immigrant*, for example, ran an annual essay contest. Immigrant women competed by writing essays on set topics, such as: "Why Everyone in America Should Learn the English Language," "What America Means to Me," "Old World Customs I Should Like My Children to Preserve," and "American Customs and Ways I Have Found Most Useful" ("Our Prize Essay Contest" 1–11; "Our Second Prize Essay Contest" 1–11).

Sara's problematic relationship to her immigrant family at the end of *Bread Givers* can also be read as a negotiation between a reformer and immigrants. When seen in relation to Yezierska's other fiction, *Bread Givers* positions Sara more problematically than either Adele or Sonya as a member of the middle class intent on immigrant aid. The letter from her stepmother accusing Sara of being a fraud—willing to help the "poor" but not her own family—is both dismissed by Hugo and given credence by the larger narrative. Hugo and Sara identify as immigrants and live middle-class lifestyles in the ghetto. However, Sara's attempts to help her working-class family fail, by and large, and register her distance from immigrant life. She can't persuade her mother to have her leg amputated, and her father accepts money from Sara only as filial obligation, continuing to criticize her acculturation and inability to provide a Kosher home.[15]

Yezierska's novels were clearly influenced by an historical involvement with immigrant aid and middle-class Jewish reformers. Her insistence on social mobility was carefully differentiated from the desire of philanthropists to keep Jewish immigrants happy in the ghetto. Yezierska also defines and embraces her characters' Jewishness through their involvement with immigrants. Her version of the New Woman is identified as Jewish by a return to the ghetto. However, Yezierska's novels ultimately record a blend of middle- and working-class Jewish experience. As New Women, Yezierska's characters most closely parallel middle-class Jewish Women social workers. They return to the ghetto to construct their gendered versions of immigrant aid. The complex positionings of Yezierska's heroines (Hurst's and Ferber's too as we will see) reflect the variety of women's political negotiations within complicated social and discursive fields.

In her life and in her fiction, Edna Ferber would seem to suggest that New Jewish Women of the middle class, much like Yezierska's cafe owners, clothing designers, and teachers could be allies of immigrant women. As one of the most successful writers of her time, who prided herself on her focus on the "Little People," Ferber suggests a fluidity of class allegiances. In his excellent chapter on Ferber in *White Collar Fictions*, Christopher P. Wilson problematizes Ferber's ability to speak to and for working-class issues. Drawing on her actual work in the service sector as a sales clerk in her mother's store, on her privileged position as the boss's daughter, and on her role as successful author, Wilson argues that Ferber defended the working girl but that her representations of New Women, like Emma McChesney, worked against real advocacy for women's labor issues (83). Wilson explores a passage in *Emma McChesney and Co.* (1915) in which Ferber rejects reformers' efforts on behalf of working women in favor of the seamless relationship between working girls and the New Woman, who is their model and employer. Wilson argues that in her chapter "Sisters under Their Skin," Ferber ignores contemporary labor disputes and highly publicized strikes and instead represents "a broadly based social solidarity, a 'sisterhood' that transcends the condescension represented by intrusive 'reformers'" (83).

While Ferber certainly ignores labor activism in "Sisters Under Their Skin," the alliance between employer and employee is formulated in terms of clothing and functions primarily to critique upper-class reformers. McChesney admires the ability of her employees who, "copied her clothes" and the clothing of the middle class "with a chic that would make the far-famed Parisian ouvriere look dowdy and down at heel in comparison" (*Emma* 179, 180). The reformers, however, see the clothing of the "Laboring Class" as "extravagant, ridiculous, and oftentimes indecent" (*Emma* 192–193). Their focus on "economy of dress," similar to Yezierska's appraisal of Manning's false economy, is an attempt to differentiate and control working-class women. Far from advocating social equality, Mrs. Orton-Wells sees "the factory girl" as "a distinct and separate class" (*Emma* 195). Moreover, the reformers' dumpy clothing suggests a critique. Unable to understand the class implications of clothing, reformers are also unable to advocate for social mobility. Emma's alliance with her employees, then, to some extent suggests her belief in social mobility and a critique of reformers who, coming from the upper class, are patronizing and elitist. The shop girls' alliance with McChesney erases their actual labor relation but acknowledges the role imitation played in the clothing industry and in immigrant social mobility.

It is true that the class politics of Ferber's most Jewish novel, *Fanny Herself* (1917), fracture as Ferber attempts to represent working-class women from her own affluent positioning. However, representations of class in Ferber's work are constructed by Jewish cultural practice as well as by economic considerations (Bergoffen, 34). Reading Ferber's fiction in a Jewish framework, both in relation to Jewish women's reform work and in relation to other Jewish women writers, resituates her class alliances and alters the politics of her work in important ways. Although Ferber's middle-class allegiances continue to influence her ability to advocate for working-class women, her work is intimately tied to questions of reform in ways similar to her literary Jewish sisters. In *Fanny Herself*, Ferber mounts a significant ethnic critique of the financially successful New Woman that self-consciously acknowledges the "benevolent" relationship and distance between middle- and working-class New Women.

Fanny is associated with immigrants initially because her shared-family economy replicates Eastern European family structures. She and her mother work in Brandeis' Bazaar to support a learned man, in this case Fanny's brother, who is a secularized violin virtuoso and has made his reputation composing Jewish music. This association results in a loss of social status, as Wendy Bergoffen has argued, whereby the Brandeis family is seated behind the affluent German-Jewish population and next to Russian immigrants in their small midwestern synagogue (*Fanny Herself* 38). In *Fanny Herself*, as in "The Girl Who Went Right," wage-earning women are forced to deny their Jewish heritage in order to achieve social mobility. Fanny initially rejects her position in an "old world" shared-family economy in order to achieve class mobility. Ultimately, Ferber is critical of the gentile character of middle-class New Women and is also critical of immigrant New Women whose work is subjugated to a male intellectual.

Like Yezierska, Ferber uses her protagonist's proximity to immigrants to revise the figure of the New Woman and embrace her Jewishness. Fanny is employed in a managerial position in the infants' wear department of a mail order corporation only after having denied her Jewish heritage. However, she is still forced to negotiate her Jewishness as a business woman. The Jewish value of "Tzedakah," or charity, becomes a central concern to Fanny. To what extent is she willing to "give" like her Jewish mother or "take" like the capitalist Fenger who lives to advance himself in big business (*Fanny Herself* 225)? To the extent that Fanny identifies with Jewish workers like Sara Sapinsky, who earns less than a subsistence wage at the mail order company, she works against her own interests in a managerial position, which are to make more money for the company and herself.

By the end of the novel Fanny rejects her corporate money-making role for a more philanthropic one that embraces Jewish immigrants. Fanny agrees to support her brother, who returns from Europe as a refugee fleeing anti-Semitism and who states after returning to the United States, "I feel like an immigrant" (*Fanny Herself* 265). More important, Fanny identifies with a Jewish worker who leads the "Garment Workers' Infants' Wear Section" in a suffrage parade (*Fanny Herself* 250). This suffragette represents the "people" Fanny has been ignoring in her climb for monetary success. The suffragette is "A Russian Jewess, evidently" (*Fanny Herself* 250). Her clothing marks her as a member of the working class as effectively as her sign, being "a sort of parody on the prevailing fashion" (*Fanny Herself* 250). And her face was the history of a people. You saw in it that which told of centuries of oppression in Russia. You saw eager groups of student Intellectuals, gathered in secret places for low-voiced, fiery talk. There was in it the unspeakable misery of Siberia. It spoke eloquently of pogroms, of massacres, of Kiev and its sister-horror, Kishineff. You saw mean and narrow streets, and carefully darkened windows, and on the other side of those windows the warm yellow glow of the seven-branched Shabbos light.

(*Fanny Herself* 250)

Both of these identifications with immigrants carefully avoid labor disputes. Moreover, Fanny doesn't join the suffrage march as does the woman next to her. She simply represents the Jewish worker in a drawing for the newspaper. This drawing elicits sympathy for the working class. Ella Monahan, buyer of women's gloves, after viewing Fanny's picture of garment workers in the suffrage parade announces, "They don't get a square deal, do they?" (*Fanny Herself* 259).

Although the text seems to value the plight of workers and Jewish radicalism and critiques Fanny's capitalist drive, in the end workers and women's rights are subordinated to a more subtle ideal of philanthropy. The working-class New Jewish Woman would go unnoticed without the benevolent aid of Fanny, whose representation—a cartoon for the newspapers—foregrounds the working-class Jewish woman as significant. Similarly, Clarence Heyl, in his critique of Fanny's selfish desire for money, is not only satisfied by her empathy for the people, he holds up Jane Addams (a central figure in the settlement movement who established Hull House in 1889) as his ideal alternative to capitalism (*Fanny Herself* 237, 238). Ferber, like Yezierska, endorses middle-class philanthropy even as she attempts to affirm a Jewish identity by embracing immigrant New Women.

Unfortunately, Ferber's philanthropic bent is accompanied by a subtext of exclusive Americanism. A racist rhetoric and rejection of "foreignness" pervade the text, as Theodore's German wife is rejected, the Japanese servant of Fenger's is termed "sneaking," and Fanny's African American domestic servant's "black" husband is read as lazy (*Fanny Herself* 177, 271, 302). Like Fauset, Ferber's antiforeign subtext participates in the rhetoric of nativist and anti-immigration movements of the

1920s. Unlike Fauset, Ferber employs racist representations of Japanese and African Americans to position her Jewish characters as white. Within this context of exclusive Americanism, Ferber's embrace of a Jewish identity for Fanny is obviously conflicted. The racialized discourses of anti-immigration and Americanism were also directed against Jewish Eastern Europeans. Ferber's alliance with Jewish immigrants breaks down as she tries to position Fanny as an "American" insider by strategically deploying racism, by opposing her to people of color and "foreigners." Her representation of Clarence, a Jewish mountaineer and naturalist with whom Fanny falls in love, also exemplifies her distance from urban Jewish immigrants and her desire to combine Jewish and American identities.[16] Ferber's use of the West as an "American" terrain opposite urban landscapes is a strategy used briefly by Mourning Dove in *Cogewea*, as well. Mourning Dove positions Native and non-Native cowboys as "American" in opposition to Frenchy, the urban and aristocratic "foreigner."

Hurst's representations of the immigrant community were taken up in the mostly laudatory Jewish press. Hurst was praised for her "deep race consciousness," as one who "spends much of her time on the East Side, for she loves nothing better than mingling with her people in their ghetto" ("A True Daughter of Israel" 1). Compared to Yezierska, Hurst was also critiqued as unauthentic, having written about the Lower East Side without ever having "slept in a vermin-disturbed bed with several frowsy sisters or ate the greasy pottage not only described, but consumed by the author of 'Hungry Hearts'" (Levinger, 7). Similarly, Hurst's immigrant novel *Lummox* was praised in a 1924 *Jewish Daily Forward* article as authentic only in its representation of the Oessetrich family, suggesting that the most successful portion of the novel represents Hurst's own middle-class German American background: "The picture of a German home in war time, trying to outdo the American 'patriots' in 'patriotism' by even taking down the picture of Beethoven is excellently done" ("The Gist of the Story").

Hurst's reviewers situated the question of her relationship to immigrants at the center of her fiction. Within the text of *Lummox*, Hurst also comments on the use of immigrant life by middle-class writers (like herself). She makes the immigrant protagonist, Bertha, inarticulate partly to suggest the inadequacy of middle-class representation.

Only a wealthy poet, Rollo, can describe Bertha, and once he's translated her into a work of art that establishes his genius, he discards her. Hurst, like her reviewers, was clearly aware of middle-class appropriations of immigrant subjects.

As we've seen in all of the women journalists and fiction writers studied here, domesticity is a telling entry point into women's reform politics. Bertha (whose descent is indeterminately Swedish, Teutonic, Bulgarian, or Polish) works as a domestic servant in *Lummox*. Most of the middle-class families who employ Bertha are associated with immigrant aid of one kind or another. Their affiliations range from "the Tenement Hygienic Committee of the Human Welfare League" to the "Society for the Prevention of Cruelty to Children" to the "School of Philanthropy" and the "Christie Street Vocational Guidance School for Girls" (*Lummox* 5, 140, 202, 242). Hurst uses Bertha to challenge middle-class domesticity as an ideal and to expose middle-class women's exploitation of immigrant labor. By following Bertha's employment, Hurst represents middle-class domesticity as self-serving and abusive, but its abuse of power frequently turns back upon itself. Mrs. Oessetrich's desire for control drives away her daughters as well as domestic servants. This critique of the middle class functions as a commentary on the New Woman, as well. Mrs. Ossetrich and her daughter Olga are New Women. Olga works in a settlement house, smokes, and bobs her hair. Mrs. Oessetrich is a middle-class suffragette who wants independent daughters and belongs to a number of charities. Hurst reads these two women as overly materialistic, willing to exploit Bertha's labor, and unable to establish domestic harmony. Unlike Yezierska and Ferber, however, Hurst doesn't recognize and value immigrant New Women. Helga, another immigrant domestic, clearly articulates the poor labor relations between women of the middle and working classes and mentions that domestics are unable to organize. Ignoring actual working-class activism, Hurst creates immigrant women who are subjugated—as prostitutes or char women—and unable to challenge effectively the conditions of their exploitation and poverty. Bertha's economic circumstances force her to give up her own child, while she continues scrupulously to mother the middle class for a wage. Her resistance is silent, obedient service that is rewarded at the end of the novel by her adoption into the Meyerbogen's immigrant family.

Ultimately, Hurst subordinates the labor politics of the text, which demonstrate the inequitable treatment of domestic servants, to the larger text of philanthropy. Bertha becomes a proponent for settlement house ideology. She achieves class mobility through her domesticity, by cleaning well and remaining "moral" despite her poverty. Bertha does not acquire her character or "improve" herself by studying middle-class lifestyles, as settlement ideology promised (Crocker, 160). However, domestic work ensures that she has the skills necessary for her position in a nuclear family. By the end of the novel Bertha's domestic labor enables her to achieve a position of "respectability" in the Meyerbogen family, as a surrogate mother.

Bertha's ability to clean also has a racial valence. The text's insistence on Bertha's cleanliness is echoed in the whiteness of her body. After a day's work at the Farley's, Bertha is described as "Smelling strongly clean of laundry soap. Twenty times a day she washed her arms up to the elbows with the great brown cakes" (*Lummox* 14). She is "White Bertha" to Rollo Farley, who seduces her with, "You are so white, Bertha. To think that I never noticed. Deeply white, like the flesh of a magnolia" (*Lummox* 15). Bertha's cleanliness and ability to clean differentiate her from the dirty and less "moral" immigrant women, such as the abusive Annie, who drinks and runs a sailors' lodging house, and Helga, who turns to prostitution and steals from her employers.

Even though Hurst's text combines whiteness, cleanliness, and morality in the racist terms of the 1920s, unexpectedly, these are the defining characteristics of the "old world" rather than the Americanized immigrant. Bertha, as "peasant" and as the representative of the "old world," has "luminous" toes and a face that remains ever white. Americanized immigrants, on the other hand, are described as dark and dirty. Julie at the Musliners is "a dark, nervous girl" with "a scar across her neck to indicate where a jealous husband had attempted to cut her throat" (*Lummox* 64). Julie announces her difference from Bertha, "That's old country dancing. I'm American" (*Lummox* 75). Helga as a prostitute is "dirty with stinkin' perfume" (*Lummox* 182). She "now wore high heels, half-silk stockings, and a small hat so American that it completely obliterated one eye" (*Lummox* 43). This is contrasted with Bertha, whose "look of steerage" ironically constitutes her as "clean" and "moral" (*Lummox* 43).

Hurst also plays with the racialized discourses of the 1920s by making Bertha at once "Western Teutonic," Scandinavian, and Eastern European (*Lummox* 1, 68). Hurst insists on Bertha's "foreignness" but refuses the racial hierarchy that positioned Eastern Europeans as inferior to other European immigrants. More problematically, Hurst's refusal to designate Bertha's ethnicity erases the specific contexts of immigrant culture. When asked to identify her ethnicity in the context of the Jewish ghetto, Bertha replies, "My people? Why those are my people, . . . Those are my people. Out there. All. Everywhere" (*Lummox* 107). Thus, even though Bertha is "old world," she is acceptable in Hurst's terms because she meets Americanization and settlement house criteria—she is "white," "moral," and the universalized, "every immigrant."

Hurst's 1922 story, "Roulette," also clearly embraces settlement ideology in its representation of Jewish immigrants. *The Jewish Tribune* published the portion of "Roulette" that depicts an Eastern European pogrom, a pogrom that in her fiction occurred in the wake of Kishinev ("When the Pogrom" 1, 20). The press uses this story to claim for Hurst an identification with Eastern European Jewry and a "race consciousness" ("A True Daughter of Israel" 1). In fact, the story as a whole is much more focused on Americanization and motherhood. Twins separated during a pogrom in Eastern Europe grow up in the United States, one with the guidance of his Jewish mother and within her middle-class home, the other under the supervision of a working-class midwife. The first becomes a judge and the second is on trial for murder. Both have the same impulses, the same impetuous and tempestuous "nature" but are depicted as products of their (middle- or working-class) environments. Hurst does attempt a critique of social workers in the story. Social workers fail to remove Jason from his abusive immigrant home and fail to educate him. However, the emphasis on cleanliness and domesticity that redeem the middle-class twin mark Hurst's text as a participant in regulatory and elitist settlement discourse, even though Hurst shifts the terrain from settlement houses to middle-class mothering.[17]

Both Hurst's and Ferber's fiction also predicates Americanization on the subordination of African Americans.[18] Historically, some settlement house workers tried to serve African American communities and argued against notions of biological or hereditary racial inferiority in this context. However, their belief that the black family was maladjusted due to the conditions of slavery continued to reinforce racist notions of African American inferiority as we've seen (Lasch-Quinn, 23). Even reformers who worked with African American populations employed environmental or social theories of African American inferiority, such as Frances Kellor who stated in 1901 that, "there is no race outside of barbarism where there is so low a grade of domestic life, and where the child receives so little training, as among the negroes" (Lasch-Quinn, 18, 197). Domestic ideology, as we have seen, combined with environmental racism to situate African Americans as inferior in this discourse.

Ferber's brief description of the African American woman, Princess, who performs domestic work for Fanny reinforces both racial biologism and environmental determinism. "A biscuit-tinted lady," Princess' class status as a domestic worker is the result of her "dysfunctional" family, whose "very black and no-account husband" keeps her from achieving social mobility (*Fanny Herself* 177). Similarly, as in the settlement house movement historically, the possibility of social mobility for African American domestics is always foreclosed in Hurst's fiction as well as Ferber's. In *Imitation of Life* (1933), for example, Hurst initially positions her white protagonist, Bea, in a "benevolent" relationship with Delilah, an African American woman engaged in domestic service, but Delilah fails to achieve social mobility even after she becomes rich. Delilah's labor in *Imitation of Life* goes unrewarded and unacknowledged throughout the text as Langston Hughes and Sterling Brown long ago pointed out.[19] Delilah is perpetually content to remain Bea's domestic servant. In fact, as a domestic Delilah signifies and creates the possibility of Bea's middle-class affluence. Bea makes a fortune by trafficking in the domesticity that Delilah embodies. Furthermore, in "Roulette," Hurst clearly articulates a belief in environmental determinism. Only Hurst's Jewish or immigrant characters are able to escape their environment. As we've seen, Fauset's fiction rejected these pernicious stereotypes.

Together, Yezierska's, Ferber's, and Hurst's writing on immigrant aid outlines and engages in complex debates over elitism, assimilation, race, and women's participation in the labor force early in the century.

In Yezierska's texts, immigrants rescue themselves from Americanization workers in order to critique the domestic ideologies of the settlement house movement and revise immigrant aid. In Ferber's texts, acculturated Jewish women resist the Americanized position of the corporate New Woman even as they affirm Americanization through racist representations of Japanese and African American domestic servants. Immigrants, in Ferber's fiction, offer both an awareness of anti-Semitism and a Jewish identification. Hurst's immigrants are rescued from the "morally" deleterious effects of poverty by middle-class Jewish homemaking. Although Hurst advocated social mobility for immigrant domestic servants, she predicated that mobility on a denial (like Ferber's) of mobility for African American domestics. Hurst most clearly embraced philanthropic ideologies. However, all three authors used philanthropy to respond to anti-assimilationist rhetoric in the early part of the century. Their literary politics pose various possibilities, more or less successfully, for Jewish American women's integration and social mobility in the United States.

Afterword

A long line of Indian rights, social welfare, war relief, suffrage, settlement, and immigrant aid workers made their appearance in women's journalism and domestic fiction during the Progressive Era. Journalists commented on their own positions as reformers even as they addressed specific political issues. Characters in domestic fiction experienced reform through boarding schools, women's organizations, and homes for working girls and, like their authors, took on public roles as critics and proponents of reform. However, despite its substantial investment in public discourse, this dialogue between journalism and fiction has remained a lost chapter of women's literary and intellectual history.

Moreover, the Progressive Era lives up to its name to an extent that has not been fully realized. Native, African, and Jewish women's writing redefined reform in this period. Suffrage, for example, is only one context in which women wrote about citizenship and the vote. Even when women in these communities used the rhetoric of suffrage itself, they often used it to different ends. Zitkala-Sa saw citizenship as integral to negotiations over land tenure and resource management. In a similar vein, Mourning Dove jokingly compared Cogewea to a suffragette not to comment on women's suffrage but to highlight citizenship in the context of American Indian rights. Fauset wrote about segregation and the denial of citizenship to African Americans, generally, during and after the war. By addressing these politics in her fiction after women won the franchise, Fauset suggested the continued denial of equal rights and representation and the failure of democracy. Razovsky took up citizenship in an effort to avoid deportations and evade immigration restriction. In Ferber's novel, Fanny's cartoon of Jewish immigrant suffragettes served this end as well. Fanny refused to join the suffrage parade and instead positioned herself as an American reformer aiding immigrant women.

Any discussion of women's increasing participation in and push for access to higher education is similarly incomplete without a discussion of how various communities of women rewrote the educational policies of reform institutions. Native, African, and Jewish American women rejected the vocational and domestic aims of boarding schools and settlement houses as economically marginalizing. By opposing an agricultural education "of the hands," Native women also used discussions of educational policy to argue against breaking up communal lands for farming and settlement under allotment. Alice Dunbar-Nelson protested the economic exploitation of African American women as domestic workers that occurred despite "how educated and refined the girl may be." She called attention to the racism that prevented educational attainment from resulting in economic opportunity. Yezierska, Hurst, and Ferber, with more or less success, also rejected education that focused on domestic training and the wage inequity it fostered.

All of these women were critical of the ethnocentrism of educational policy. They argued for access to higher education, refusing the rationale that domestic service would bring women into proximity with European American culture and provide an education, a "civilizing" force, in and of itself. *Cogewea* took up these debates through Densmore's insistence that Cogewea, as an educated woman, should adopt European American and abandon Okanogan beliefs. While she refused, Cogewea did embrace the rhetoric of "civilization" and "refinement" to suggest her character's capacity for higher education and integration. Jessie Fauset problematically argued for integration through her characters' Eurocentric participation in and embrace of French "high culture." At the same time, her displacement of educational opportunity to a "foreign" country and in particular her representation of Haitian women at the Sorbonne, critiqued segregation and the denial of access to higher education in the United States. In debates over immigrant education, Jewish women like Florina Lasker alternated between teaching English and literacy to avoid deportation and refusing Americanization that clearly worked against Jewish identification and replaced immigrant culture.

Native, African, and Jewish American women writers were also critical of the key role domesticity played in women's "municipal housekeeping," or reform, during this period. They exposed domestic training as colonialist, reinforcing government policies like allotment; as racist, disseminating ideologies of black urban pathology; as nativist, imposing social conformity on immigrant women; and as exploitative, creating a cheap labor pool of domestic workers. In response to the domestic program of off-reservation boarding schools, for instance, Mourning Dove situated Cogewea as a cattle rancher, rejecting both the farming ethic underlying allotment policy and a domestic positioning for her main character. Jessie Fauset addressed racist representations of domestic workers through Phoebe's mother even as Alice Dunbar-Nelson tried to manipulate the rhetoric of social welfare and settlement discourse to avoid racist depictions of the black family. Jewish women virtually wrote themselves out of the home in their embrace of New Womanhood. They also used this position to avoid being identified as aliens in the United States. These women wrote domestic fiction, not because they lagged behind modernist writers and embraced a Victorian aesthetic, but because they rewrote the home and the nation together in representations of their own Progressive Era activism. In their examinations of citizenship, educational opportunity, and the role domesticity played in various institutions and policies, they shifted the terms of reform, redirecting it through their journalism and their fiction.

The diverse politics of these writers reinvented Progressivism even as they demonstrated the fragility of political alliances among women across racial and class lines. The grossly racialized stereotypes of African Americans in Ferber's and Hurst's fiction (and of American Indians elsewhere in Ferber's texts) can be seen as a strategic embrace of racism. Positioning themselves as white and embracing a social mobility denied to nonwhites, they used settlement rhetoric to argue for Jewish integration and to deflect anti-Semitism. At the same time, African American women capitalized on antiforeign rhetoric to serve their own integrationist goals. Similarly, Mourning Dove and Zitkala-Sa combined discourses of immigration and Americanism to critique U.S. colonialism. Mourning Dove rejected the figure of the Mayflower that Sternberger embraced, and Zitkala-Sa's short story "The Widespread Enigma Concerning Blue-Star Woman" turned the Statue of Liberty's back to American Indians as she welcomed new immigrants to the United States. These tensions and double standards suggest that women's literary politicking was only partially successful in opposing nativist, racist, and "100 percent American" discourses early in the century.

This study looks forward to literary criticism that will recover the rhetorical and political sophistication of Progressive Era literature informed by journalism and indebted to political activism. Debates over specific issues, such as the Dyer Anti-Lynching Bill (1922) in the African American press offered literature not just substance (as criticism such as Kathy A. Perkins' *Strange Fruit: Plays on Lynching by American Women* has begun to recognize) but also a wealth of political and rhetorical strategies. Similarly, arguments over college limitations (1920–1922) taken up by journalists (who contested the supposed failure of Jewish day students to participate in the sports and social life of colleges) show up in wonderfully satiric ways in the fiction of Anzia Yezierska. The discovery of oil beneath the Osage reservation in 1896 and subsequent debates over corruption through oil-leasing and guardianship in the early twentieth century was reported on and also discussed in Osage writer John Joseph Mathews's *Sundown* and problematically in Edna Ferber's *Cimarron*. This study only begins to suggest how a direct focus on issues taken up in the press might result in rich readings of both the rhetoric and substance of fiction during the Progressive Era.

In addition, attention to the journals and publications of political organizations offer new and cross-cultural contexts for literary analysis. A close examination of the dialogue among Native and African American writers in *The Southern Workman* would provide significant material for readings of literary figures in both communities. Similarly, an analysis of the effect of Pan-Indianism on Pan-Africanism through

Du Bois' membership in the SAI and his knowledge of such writers as Charles Alexander Eastman is overdue. Roberta Campbell Lawson's attendance at a Pan-Pacific conference in Hawaii also suggests the dynamic and largely ignored cross-cultural nature of political coalitions that influenced the intellectual climate and literary production of the period. Similarly, women's organizational networks such as war relief work and later pacifism created a cross-cultural history that would aid in reinterpreting the effect of the war on literary production. Mourning Dove and Ferber's work for the Red Cross, Lawson and Dunbar-Nelson's organizing for the Women's Committee of the Council of Defense, and Sternberger's membership in the War Relief Appeal brought women into contact with one another and generated rhetorical and political strategies that affected their fiction as we have seen in the wartime activism and writing of Hunton, Johnson, Terrell, and Fauset.

As Henry Louis Gates's *Black Periodical Literatures Project* has demonstrated, periodicals in the Progressive Era are a wonderful source of literary writing, as well. The fiction and poetry of Native and Jewish American writers available in journalism from this period still needs to be collected. Similarly, women's political writing in journals and also in the newsletters of women's organizations in all three communities is a rich and virtually untapped historical source for literary critics during this period. As a recovery project, this study demonstrates how Native, African, and Jewish American women articulated their politics in relation to one another and in relation to women of cultural backgrounds different from their own. It begins to suggest how cross-cultural readings of fiction in relation to women's activism and journalism reveal the contested relationships and political negotiations of women writers even as they establish shared concerns. The dynamic language and contradictory politics of periodical journalism contributed to the rhetorical sophistication of domestic fiction and gave it the force to disrupt and redirect the debates and narratives of early twentieth-century America.

The legacy of reform is also relevant in today's political context. BIA corruption, neotermination legislation, welfare "reform," challenges to affirmative action in higher education, and immigration restriction all pose a threat to self-determination, equal rights, and access to opportunity in present-day U.S. society. These policies and the rhetoric and coalitions they engender have antecedents in the early twentieth century. As writers and intellectuals redirecting the political discourses of their day, the authors here offer an initial and varied response useful in speaking to the political challenges that remain unanswered today.

Notes

Introduction

1. Emerging from under the shadow of a modernist criticism and canon focussed on such authors as T. S. Eliot, Ernest Hemingway, and William Faulkner, early twentieth-century writing has lately been reframed and reclaimed as a much wider and more complicated field. Critics such as Elizabeth Ammons, Laura Doyle, Ann duCille, Rachel Blau Duplessis, Philip Harper, Michael North, Priscilla Wald, and many, many others have revealed the ways in which fiction of the 1910s, '20s, and '30s took shape not despite or apart from but rather around and through the racial, ethnic, gender, and class conflicts of the era.

2. For overviews of Zitkala-Sa's political activism, see David L. Johnson and Raymond Wilson, Deborah Sue Welch, William Willard, "The First Amendment," and "Zitkala-Sa: A Woman Who Would Be Heard," and Walter L. Williams.

3. For biographical information on Dunbar-Nelson, see Gloria Hull, *Give Us Each Day* and *Color, Sex, and Poetry* 33–103.

4. For biographical information on Fannie Hurst, see Cynthia Brandimarte and Susan Koppleman. On Hurst's relationship with African American communities, see Wilentz, "White Patron."

5. See Bernardin, Brown, Fisher, and Viehmann for readings of McWhorter as an intrusive but politically sympathetic editor (Brown, "Mourning Dove's Voice"; Fisher, "Introduction"). For discussions of editorial appropriation in *Cogewea*, see Mary Dearborn, *Pocahontas's Daughters* 23 and Elizabeth Ammons, *Conflicting Stories* 138. All of these accounts use an

aesthetic or genre-oriented analysis (when editorial correspondence is inconclusive) to differentiate between McWhorter and Mourning Dove's contributions.

6. See for example, Sylvander, 96–121. Sylvander's ground-breaking discussion of Fauset's political journalism is primarily an aesthetic appraisal (102, 103). Cheryl Wall comes closest to examining Fauset's politics through her journalism. Her emphasis on the personal essay and Fauset's views toward art tend to displace her political analysis, however (*Women of the Harlem Renaissance* 51, 57).

7. Critics document the decline in Hurst and Ferber's literary reputations by noting that today they are known primarily through movie versions of their novels (Brandimarte, 277; Caputi, 697; Horowitz and Landsman, 69; and Christopher P. Wilson, 57).

8. As Laura Wexler summarizes: "The chief problem in coming to terms with Yezierska's genius as a writer is that she struggled so with form, and often lost. There has been no friendly critic yet—no patron, no rescuer, no appreciator—from the time of Yezierska's career to the present who has not felt compelled to point this out" ("Looking at Yezierska" 157).

9. See Carby, *Reconstructing Womanhood*; Peterson, *"Doers of the Word"*; Tate, *Domestic Allegories of Political Desire*; Lichtenstein, *Writing Their Nations*; and Ruoff, "Justice for Indians and Women."

10. Alice Dunbar-Nelson wrote for the Pittsburgh *Courier* from February 20 to September 18, 1926 and January through May 1930. She also wrote for the Washington *Eagle* from 1926 to 1930 (Hull, "Introduction" iii). Jessie Fauset contracted with W. E. B. Du Bois for "The Looking Glass" column in the *Crisis* from July 1918 to July 1919 prior to her position as literary editor of the journal. She worked as literary editor from November 1919 through April 1926. She also edited *The Brownie's Book* with Du Bois and Augustus Dill from January 1920 to December 1921 (Sylvander, 53, 95, 115). Edna Ferber wrote for the *Appleton Daily Crescent*, the *Milwaukee Journal*, and George Matthew Adams' Newspaper Syndicate (Ferber, *A Peculiar Treasure* 103, 108). Fannie Hurst edited and wrote for her college paper, *Student Life*, and in the 1930s wrote articles for the Roosevelt campaign (Brandimarte, 283, 292). Zitkala-Sa wrote for the *American Indian Magazine* and edited the journal from 1918 to 1919 (Fisher, "Zitkala-Sa: The Evolution of a Writer" 235). She also edited the National Council of American Indians' *Indian Newsletter* (Peyer 76).

Others writers, like Anzia Yezierska, were interviewed and published in the ethnic press and at times thematized the figure of the woman journalist in their writing. Yezierska was reviewed in *The Jewish Woman* and published in *The Jewish Tribune*, for example (Levinger 7; Yezierska, "The Lost 'Beautifulness'"). In addition, the protagonist of Yezierska's *Salome of the Tenements* is a journalist modeled on Rose Pastor Stokes.

11. For extensive overviews and bibliography of early Native American newspaper and magazine journalism, see Littlefield and Parins. See Hazel W. Hertzberg for discussions of journalism emerging from Pan-Indian organizations that included women. Hertzberg's indexing of "immigrants" and "negroes" in her study also provides valuable evidence of cross-cultural exchange among Pan-Indian writers. See also James E. Murphy and Sharon M. Murphy. On Cherokee editor, Ora Eddleman Reed's journalism, see Alexia Kosmider and Daryl Morrison.

12. For women's writing in the Yiddish press see Maxine Seller, Norma Fain Pratt, Frieda Forman et al., and Isaac Metzker. For examples of organizational studies of the NCJW that rely on its journals, see Faith Rogow and Seth Korelitz.

13. See for example Evelyn Higginbotham's *Righteous Discontent.* Hull has reprinted some of Dunbar-Nelson's newspaper columns in volume 2 of *The Works of Alice Dunbar-Nelson* and claims that Dunbar-Nelson's journalism has not been substantially attended to ("Introduction," *Give Us Each Day* 31). For a brief discussion of Alice Dunbar-Nelson's journalistic career in which she also refers to the journalism of Gwendolyn Bennett, Georgia Douglas Johnson, and Bessye Bearden, see Hull, *Color Sex and Poetry.* See Sylvander and Wall's *Women of the Harlem Renaissance* for descriptions of some of Fauset's essays in *Crisis.*

14. See Hull, "Introduction," *Give Us Each Day* 15; Sylvander, 66, 67; Gridley, 34.

15. See, for example: Arthur C. Parker, "The American Indian in the World War" 61–63; James Weldon Johnson, "The Larger Success" 427–436; "The National Association of Colored Women" 492–493; Caroline W. Andrus, "Conference of the Society of American Indians" 599–603; "Indian Leadership" 131–133; "Angel DeCora Dietz" 104–105; Ella Cara Deloria, "Health Education for Indian Girls" 63–68; and Alice Dunbar-Nelson, "Negro Literature for Negro Pupils" 59–63.

16. Zitkala-Sa and Elizabeth Bender Roe Cloud were both active in the Society of American Indians and in the Indian Welfare Committee (later the Indian Affairs Committee) of the General Federation of Women's Clubs (GFWC) and Roberta Campbell Lawson was president of the GFWC (Fisher, "Zitkala-Sa: The Evolution of a Writer" 235; Hertzberg, 48, 234; and Gridley, 74, 85).

17. Hazel Hertzberg claims that "educated Indians saw the immigrant experience as a model for the Indian in the manner in which the immigrant

became Americanized through public education and the easy acquisition of citizenship" (23). She also states that, "until the twenties few Jews took an interest in Indian movements. Among the new reformers of the twenties led by John Collier, however, there were a number of Jews" (311). Both John Collier and Edna Ferber spent time on the Taos Pueblo visiting their mutual friend, Mabel Dodge Luhan (Szasz, 13; Ferber, *Peculiar Treasure* 381). See also Richard Henry Pratt's comparison of Native with African and Jewish Americans (Hertzberg, 92).

18. See, for example, Diner, Caputi, and Wilentz, "White Patron." Hurst and Hurston also wrote about each other. See for example: Hurst, "Zora Hurston"; Hurston, "Fannie Hurst."

19. See W. E. B. Du Bois, "A Vision of Tomorrow." Cecilia Razovsky represented the National Council of Jewish Women and Charles S. Johnson presented a paper entitled "Our Newest Migrant—The Negro" at a conference on social work (Razovsky, "National Conference").

20. For a range of positions on the political engagement of nineteenth-century sentimental fiction, see Nancy Armstrong, Ann Douglas, and Jane Tompkins. For analyses of sentimental fiction's racial politics, see Laura Doyle, Claudia Tate, and essays in Shirley Samuels' collection.

21. In a different context, Vine Deloria Jr. comments on how sympathetic but overgeneralized readings of Indian/white relations obscure important political negotiations ("Revision and Reversion" 14).

22. See Philip Gleason for a history of the various uses and conceptualizations of the word "assimilation." Sociologists Richard Alba, Michael Omi, and Howard Winant have been critical of the primary articulation of assimilation through immigrant paradigms. Omi and Winant reject models of assimilation that focus on integration or incorporation along individual lines "in favor of a more radical *racial* identity which demanded group rights and recognition" (20).

23. Hertzberg notes differences between Pan-Indian and African American attitudes toward class: "Although class differences were present and played an important role in Pan-Indian affairs, most Indians did not have as strong a sense of class as did Negroes" (303).

24. Building on the pioneering work of black feminist critics such as Audre Lorde, Hazel Carby has warned against developing a political coalition without acknowledging historical differences in her critique of white feminists. She argues that by attempting to "discover a lost sisterhood and to reestablish feminist solidarity," feminist criticism can erase histories of oppression (*Reconstructing Womanhood* 6).

25. Priscilla Wald, Laura Wexler, and Gay Wilentz have all worked across the disparate fields of Native, African, and Jewish American literature and have situated their readings in specific historical contexts. For a survey of critics working to expand conventional notions of cultural exchange among African American and "white" literary traditions, see Shelley Fisher Fishkin.

26. Historians suggest that women's political writing in Chinese, Japanese, and Mexican American communities was primarily in languages other than English. See for example, Judy Yung's excellent article on early twentieth-century Chinese women's activism as presented in *Chung Sai Yat Po*, Mei Nakano's reference to Japanese American women writing for Japanese language newspapers, and Teresa Amott and Julie Matthaei's discussion of Mexican women revolutionaries and radical journalists who were deported to Texas and writing in journals such as *Regeneracion* during this period (Nakano, 54–55; Amott, 74). The political writing of women in these communities provides a vital context in which to read the fiction of women such as Edith and Winnifred Eaton, Etsu Sugimoto, and Maria Cristina Mena. References to Asian and Mexican Americans in Jessie Fauset and Edna Ferber's fiction suggest the relevance of these discourses to the material presented in this book, as well.

1. *"Her Rightful Place in the New Scheme of Things"*

1. For more information on off-reservation boarding schools and vocational education, see Michael C. Coleman, K. Tsianina Lomawaima, Frederick Hoxie, Margaret Szasz, and Robert Utley. Off-reservation boarding schools tried to "civilize" Native American children by separating them from family and kin, regimenting their lives, forbidding them to speak Native languages or practice tribal customs, and teaching them primarily vocational education with a minimal emphasis on academic training. According to Michael C. Coleman, there were "twenty-five off-reservation boarding schools, claiming an average yearly attendance of over 6,000 Indian students" (*American Indian Children* 44). In 1928, these schools were critiqued by a government survey known as the Meriam Report. Its criticism was wide-ranging, including condemnations of nutrition, health care, discipline, and educational standards (Lomawaima, 30–31).

2. For information on the Society of American Indians and the *American Indian Magazine*, see Hazel W. Hertzberg, 31–209; and Robert Allen Warrior.

3. See Daniel F. Littlefield and James W. Parins's ground-breaking bibliographies of early Native American journalism. See also James E. Murphy and Sharon M. Murphy. On Cherokee editor, Ora Eddleman Reed's journalism, see Alexia Kosmider and Daryl Morrison. Native American women

journalists of an earlier generation, such as Susette LaFlesche (Omaha), are also important sources and paved the way for writers during the early twentieth century. Born in 1854, LaFlesche is known for her opposition to and lectures on the Ponca removal. She also wrote articles and stories from 1883 to 1885 while she lived in Washington, D.C., and edited the *Weekly Independent*, a Populist newpaper, in 1894 in Lincoln, Nebraska (Peyer, 1). For bibliographical information on Susette LaFlesche, see Clarke and Green. Native women were also publishing in venues similar to the *American Indian Magazine* on the local level. Edited and owned by Mrs. W. T. (Estelle Chishom) Ward (Chickasaw), *The Super-Civilized Indian*, which appeared in Oklahoma City in 1926, was one such publication and suggests the wealth of writing by Native women available at this time.

4. The General Allotment or Dawes Act "gave the President the authority to negotiate with Indian tribes for the cession of lands the government felt were 'surplus' to the reservations. As a result of this statute, which was actually a detailed policy directive, U.S. Indian Inspectors were sent to the various tribes to negotiate allotments and reduced reservations" (Deloria, "Revision" 86). Although the size of allotments varied, they were typically 160-acre plots of land. Once land was allotted to an individual, the government held the land in trust generally for a period of 25 years, after which the allotee was given a fee simple title and citizenship. "Surplus" land could be sold by the government and opened to white settlement (Prucha, 224–241).

5. That Native Americans educated in mainstream, boarding, or reservation schools were influenced by assimilationist ideology but also strove to maintain a tribal or Pan-Indian identity during this period is discussed generally in Michael C. Coleman, "Motivations" 42–45; Hertzberg, 22, 57–58; and Williams, 3–4. See K. Tsianina Lomawaima and Coleman, *American Indian Children*, for documentation that Native American students resisted exploitation and shaped their boarding school experiences despite unequal power relations.

6. I am indebted to Priscilla Wald's unpublished essay, " 'Changed But Not Yet Fused,' " on Jewish writer Abraham Cahan for insights into the ways writers during this period homogenize historical experience.

7. See, for example, Hunter; Pierce; Pike, "Public Schools" and "The Right Spirit."

8. On Lawson, see "Lawson," *American Women* 388; "Lawson," *Who's Who*; *Tulsa Tribune*; "Roberta Campbell Lawson"; Gridley, 73, 74; and the American Native Press Archive at the University of Arkansas, Little Rock. For biographical information on DeCora, see McAnulty.

9. Lawson's paper, "Indian Music Saved," had been presented at the Seventeenth Biennial Convention of the General Federation of Women's Clubs in Los Angeles on June 11, 1924.

10. For more information on Kellogg, see Hauptman and McLester. For overviews of Zitkala-Sa's political activism, see Johnson and Wilson; Welch; and Willard.

11. Hertzberg and Debo claim that citizenship was not particularly controversial among Native Americans because it did not affect treaty relationships (Debo, 335–336; Hertzberg, 205). Hoxie documents controversies over citizenship in federal and state government that resulted in diminished civil rights and a "partial citizenship" for Native Americans (230–231). Citizenship rights and the ability to manage resources were compromised by trust status or government determinations of Native American "competency" during this period. For a summary of arguments on the controversial issue of allotment which, like Jane Gordon's, weighed separatism against absorption, see Debo, 301–303, 310–14; and Otis, 42–43.

12. See, for example, Fisher and Welch. For information on the effects of Assimilation policy on Native landholdings, see Deloria "Congress in Its Wisdom" 108–109; Hoxie, 44; and Prucha, 305.

13. The Stemteema's river vision, on the one hand, predicts the dispossession of Cogewea and reinforces a larger narrative of Native victimization and doom. On the other hand, it helps enact Cogewea's rescue, which suggests the relevance of the Stemteema's tribal practices. The Stemteema's vision positions Cogewea over the dark swirl of wild rushing waters. "She was struggling in the grasp of a frightful monster—a human serpent whose eyes were the glitter of gold—whose voice was the clinking of silver. His face gleamed with delight at her torture. . . . At last I recognized the Shoyahpee— he of the luring voice—a vulture whose talons were rending my Cogewea, whose beak was buried in her weakening heart" (270–271).

As we will see in the next chapter, Mourning Dove's novel makes significant use of tropes of the "dying Indian" in other contexts as well.

14. In a significant departure from this use of World War I rhetoric, Arthur Parker (Seneca), who edited the *American Indian Magazine* and served as the SAI president for a time, wrote an Onondaga declaration of war against "the Austrian and the German Empires" to assert sovereignty (Hertzberg, 48, 175).

15. For a description of this dynamic in Zitkala-Sa's autobiography, see Meisenheimer, 115–117.

16. See Laura F. Klein and Lillian A. Ackerman's as well as Nancy Shoemaker's recent collections of essays on Native women's various tribal conceptions of gender and gender negotiations in the United States.

17. On the relationship between Native American women and white women's clubs, see Alison Bernstein, 18–19; Welch, 178, 179; and Willard, "Zitkala-Sa" 13. For information on the work of the Indian Welfare Committee, see Stella Atwood's "Indian Welfare" reports from the Biennial Conventions of the General Federation of Women's Clubs after 1921. Although it appears that most Native American women were involved in white women's clubs to further American Indian politics, Native American suffragettes marched in Washington, D.C., in 1913 ("Indian Suffragettes" 11).

18. On model cottages, see Trennert, 27.

2. "'Wantin' to Wear th' Breeches and Boss th' Hull Shebang'"

1. For biographical information on Mourning Dove, see Brown and Miller.

2. See Iverson, 23 and McAnulty, 183.

3. Robert Allen Warrior includes Mourning Dove briefly in his intellectual history, describing *Cogewea* as an "angry indictment of progressive policy" (42). He claims that Mourning Dove belonged to a generation of writers who departed from the integrationist writing of the SAI (22). Although my reading substantiates Warrior's claim about progressive policy, I see Mourning Dove as centrally concerned with integration.

4. For readings of the McWhorter/Mourning Dove relationship, see Allen, *The Sacred Hoop* 83; Ammons, *Conflicting Stories* 138; Bernardin, 491–492; Alanna Kathleen Brown, "Mourning Dove's Voice in *Cogewea*" 2, 4, 10; Dearborn, 23; Fisher, "Introduction" xii–xiv and *The Transportation of Tradition* 109; Larson, 177, 179; Viehmann, 213.

5. Ammons and Dearborn argue for McWhorter's appropriation of Mourning Dove's text whereas Brown, Fisher, and Viehmann suggest that although McWhorter's additions present problems in the text, politically he and Mourning Dove were in accord. Bernardin argues that McWhorter and Mourning Dove had different conceptions of the novel and that McWhorter was intrusive primarily in his authentication of the work, but she does note that Mourning Dove approved many of McWhorter's revisions (Bernardin, 491–492).

Furthermore, Alanna Kathleen Brown argues that McWhorter's epigrams and choice of ending suggested a tragic outcome for the novel and were at variance with Mourning Dove's own ending and sense of possibility for Native Americans ("Mourning Dove's Voice" 12–13). Bernardin corroborates the debate over a tragic ending of the novel with correspondence but argues that Mourning Dove was able to resist McWhorter's editorial advice in this instance (502). In addition, the narrative of tragic Native Americans doomed through white contact to extinction was not simply imposed by McWhorter. Each of the Stemteema's stories suggests this outcome, and these narratives, are universally considered to have been authored by Mourning Dove.

6. See Brown, "Mourning Dove's Voice" 13 and Fisher, "Introduction" xiv. Louis Owens' comments on voice, in his analysis of her position as a "mixed-blood," are most useful to my argument, since they recognize Cogewea's speech as heteroglossia. He argues that "Mourning Dove's novel introduces code switching and a system of complex hybridization" that moves beyond conflict between Mourning Dove and McWhorter (45).

7. Bernardin substantiates McWhorter's desire to critique the " 'Indian department'" with correspondence. However, Mourning Dove's letters also suggest that she was critical of Indian agents (Bernardin 507). For historical information on Colville agents, see Ruby and Brown's chapter, "Civilizing Agent" 223–243 and Reichwein, 301–303, 313.

8. Like Native women journalists, Mourning Dove generally uses "Indian" in place of tribal designations. She also draws on popular plains imagery, buffalo and tepees, despite the Okanogan/Colville affiliation of her main character.

9. See, for example, *Cogewea* 136, 150, 161. These passages are also significant in that Densmore argues for companionate marriage, which the text ultimately rejects. Cogewea's historical contextualization—" 'the wrongs of centuries stand between us'"—proves more relevant to successful romance and marriage (232). This aspect of the novel offers a subtle critique of New Womanhood.

10. E. Pauline Johnson's (Mohawk) short story, "A Red Girl's Reasoning" uses romance and marriage in similar ways (*The Moccasin Maker* 102–126).

11. As Susan Bernardin argues, mixed-ancestry is described in the language "of social and spatial confinement: 'prescribed sphere,' 'zone,' 'diminutive world,' and 'separate corral'" throughout the novel (502–503). Viehmann also reads the representation of mixed ancestry in *Cogewea* as a political matter. She reads Mourning Dove's representation of mixed descent as socially constructed, as changing "the terms of discourse from blood and biology to culture" (209).

12. This is reinforced at the Fourth of July races when justice is abandoned and at the end of the novel when Cogewea is unable to retrieve her money from Densmore. Zitkala-Sa's short story, "The Widespread Enigma Concerning Blue-Star Woman," represents this idea as well when the Statue of Liberty appears in a vision turning her back on Native Americans (*American Indian Stories* 179, 180).

13. Jeffrey Reichwein argues that assimilation was slow on the Colville reservation and "the reservation headmen in 1906 openly condemned the entire United States Native American policy. In fact reservation wide opposition to the United States government continued far beyond the late 1900s" (314, 320).

14. Jewish journalist Estelle Sternberger uses the *Mayflower* in an immigrant context to argue for religious freedom in the United States in chapter 5.

15. The "vanishing Indian" thematic can also be found in the Stemteema's stories: "our villages made desolate with fire and the graves of our fathers profaned. I saw the death-trail worn smooth by the moccasined feet of the dead and the death wail grew loud on the storm-rack of night. It passed! the lament grew fainter and ceased. There were none to morn for the last of the Schuaylp[k]" (224).

Fisher reads "The Dead Man's Vision" and its pessimism as drawing on the Dreamer religion (Fisher, "The Transportation of Tradition" 111).

16. Trennert discusses the uselessness of domestic training aimed at middle-class etiquette to reservation life (282, 286).

17. See Alexis Kosmider's discussion of popular discourses in which "Squaw conjures negative perceptions of Indian women—women shackled to a demanding and indolent husband" (67).

18. Mourning Dove's correspondence with McWhorter is characterized by her struggles with illness.

19. Although Silent Bob compares Cogewea to a suffragette after listening to her political rhetoric, both Cogewea and Silent Bob make fun of suffragettes. Cogewea never fully embraces the figure of the New Woman, although she rejects colonial domestic ideology. As Elizabeth Ammons argues the figure of the New Woman was often invoked but also critiqued as ethnocentric during this period ("The New Woman" 82–97). I discuss Jessie Fauset's critique of New Women engaged in social welfare work in chapter 4. Chapters 5 and 6 demonstrate that Jewish women writers generally embraced but also revised the figure of the New Woman in a Jewish context. Both Edna Ferber and Fannie Hurst also represent suffragettes (Hurst in a critical way). See note 17 in chapter 1 for historical references to Native American suffragettes.

3. *"The Democracy for Which We Have Paid"*

1. African American women's journalism presents many opportunities for scholarly study. See Wall, *Women*, and Sylvander for examinations of Fauset's journalism. Both critics admire Fauset's ability as an essayist and discuss her journalism as more successful writing than her fiction (Sylvander, 99, 103;

Wall, *Women* 51). They do not, however, place Fauset's work within the context of other political journalism written during the period. George Hutchinson provides this kind of context in his examination of major Harlem Renaissance journals, but he does not take up the journalism of African American women in detail. See Wilbert Jenkins for an analysis of Fauset's literary black nationalism which draws on her journalism. Although she doesn't conduct an analysis of Fauset's journalism, Deborah G. Chay rightly concludes that "the terms of literary discourse have blocked investigation of Fauset's active participation in political debates" (89, 168).

On the neglect of African American women's journalism generally, see Rodger Streitmatter (1–2). Streitmatter provides primarily biographical information on a number of African American women journalists, including prominent nineteenth-century journalists such as Gertrude Bustill Mossell, the woman's editor of *The New York Freeman*, and Josephine St. Pierre Ruffin, who edited *Woman's Era* which became the official journal of the National Federation of African American Women, 1890–1897 (39, 64–69). Streitmatter also discusses Fauset's contemporaries: Delilah L. Beasley, known primarily for her journalism in California; Marvel Cooke, who wrote for *The Crisis* and in the 1950s became the first African American woman "to report full-time for a mainstream newspaper"; and Ida B. Wells-Barnett (73–83, 85). Ida B. Wells-Barnett contributed to numerous African American journals and edited her own newspaper, *Free Speech*. Her journalism is best known for having launched the antilynching campaign (Streitmatter, 49–60). On Wells-Barnett's journalism, see also her autobiography, *Crusade for Justice*; her pamphlets, *On Lynchings*; and Shirley Logan and Mildred I. Thompson. See also Mark Matthews and Karen S. Adler on Amy Jacques Garvey's contributions to *The Negro World*.

Among Harlem Renaissance writers Fauset was not alone as a journalist and literary figure. Zora Neale Hurston, Alice Dunbar-Nelson, Georgia Douglas Johnson, and Gwendolyn Bennet all published essays in or edited a wide variety of periodicals. Gloria Hull discusses Dunbar-Nelson's important role as a journalist in *Color, Sex, and Poetry* and has made selections of her columns available in volume two of *The Works of Alice Dunbar-Nelson*. Hull also mentions "Gwendolyn Bennett's race-conscious, but chatty 'Ebony Flute' contributions in *Opportunity* magazine" and Georgia Douglas Johnson's weekly syndicated column "Homely Philosophy," 1926–1932 (*Color* 84–185). Robert E. Hemenway examines Zora Neale Hurston's role in the creation of *Fire!* and her essays for a variety of periodicals in his early biography of her, as does a more recent study of Hurston's politics by Deborah Plant (Hemenway, 35–59, 162, 288). That Hurston was an active journalist as well as folklorist and novelist is demonstrated by her contributions to a wide range of journals, including *Fire!*, *The Messenger*, *The Negro*, *Negro Digest*, *The Negro History Bulletin*, and *The Stylus*. See Walter L. Daniel for journals in which African American women published.

2. For more biographical information, see Sylvander.

3. See Fauset's column in *The Crisis*: "The Looking Glass," August 1918: 180; October 1918: 279; November 1918: 23; January 1919: 127; and April 1919: 289.

4. See, for example, Mark Ellis, "America's Black Press," "Closing Ranks," and "W. E. B. Du Bois"; Theodore Kornweibel Jr.; William Jordan; Emory J. Tolbert

5. See also articles on the war in Gerda Lerner's collection (*Black Woman* 333, 498).

6. The Wilson administration segregated black federal employees prior to the war and endorsed a segregated military. See Terrell's account of segregated government employment in the "War Risk Insurance Bureau" (*Colored Woman* 252). In a segregated military, African Americans served primarily as laborers, as "stevedores, drivers, engineers, cooks, laundrymen, and the like" (Wynn, 178). Only 42,000 of the 200,000 African Americans in France served in combat positions (Wynn, 178). In addition, African Americans could not participate in the Marines, Coast Guard, or in Army Aviation. African Americans were drafted at a higher percentage than whites who registered, were denied commissions as doctors and dentists and equal opportunity as officers, were provided unequal, inferior shelter, food, entertainment, and medical treatment from the United States, and were subject to the racism of white officers and soldiers at home and abroad (Barbeau and Henri, 37, 50–52; Wynn, 177). African American soldiers, for example, experienced and resisted Jim Crow in the communities in which they trained in the South (Barbeau and Henri, 73–77). Furthermore, although government policy stipulated that U.S. divisions would function autonomously from their allies, four African American regiments were assigned to the French army, where they were integrated and fought with white French troops (Barbeau and Henri, 112–114). As soldiers fighting under France, they were often still vulnerable to U.S. racist propaganda, which attempted to bar African Americans from participating fully in French society. In addition, Intelligence tests given to African American soldiers during World War I supported the increasing scientific racism of the 1920s (Hutchinson 69).

7. After the war, African Americans met with an increasingly racist and violent climate at home. With twenty-six race riots and eighty-three lynchings, the "Red Summer" of 1919 demonstrated hostile resistance to African

American migration and demands for equality in the postwar period (Hughes, 2). Although urban riots and certainly lynchings were common prior to World War I, historians describe the ways in which violence against African Americans was linked to the war. For example, thirteen black soldiers were executed after their involvement in the Houston riot in 1917 (Ellis, "Closing Ranks" 100). In 1919 white veterans made up several violent mobs in Washington D.C. riots (Williams, 26). In other cities African American migrants, taking advantage of increased opportunities during the war, were seen as an economic threat to returning white veterans and became victims of white racism. In other cases black veterans asserted their positions as citizens and were the targets of mob violence, at times simply for wearing a uniform (Barbeau and Henri, 177; Harris, 398–399). As soldiers, and especially as officers, African Americans challenged racial hierarchy because they were armed and held positions of authority over white citizens. As Hunton and Johnson claim, in their account of African American participation in the war, "Southern Congressmen were particularly alarmed over any prospects of colored men learning to use guns" (44). The strength of this challenge can be measured by a number of bills introduced prior to the war to ban African Americans from the military, entirely (Patton, 8, 9).

8. Du Bois later renounced his accommodationism in the "Close Ranks" piece, admitting that he had been caught up in wartime propaganda, according to Ellis ("Closing Ranks" 122–123).

9. For more information on Hubert Harrison, See Gaines, 234–260.

10. See Ellis, "Closing Ranks" 105, 107, 114 and "Federal Surveillance" 14. Whether or not Du Bois wrote "Close Ranks" to help gain a commission as a captain in the Military Intelligence Branch of the government has been the subject of much controversy. See for example, Ellis "Closing Ranks"; "W. E. B. Du Bois"; Jordon "The Damnable Dilemma"; Lewis, 555–557)

11. See "The Looking Glass," December 1918: 80 and January 1919: 129.

12. A. Philip Randolph and Chandler Owen were consistently critical of participation in World War I in their journal, *The Messenger* (Wynn, 176; Ellis, "America's Black Press" 26). In 1918, they were arrested and "charged with inciting resistance to the United States and promotion of the cause of its enemies" (Ellis, "America's Black Press" 26).

13. See "The Looking Glass," August 1918: 178–179; September 1918: 230–231

14. See, for example, "The Looking Glass," September 1918: 232; November 1918: 25, 27; February 1919: 187, 190; December 1918: 79, 81.

15. See "The Looking Glass," February 1919:186; November 1918:23; August 1918:182.

16. See, for example, "The Looking Glass," January 1919: 130–131; March 1919: 235–238; February 1919: 188–189, and January 1919: 130. See also Hutchinson's suggestion that *There Is Confusion* is aware of this discourse (146).

Although Fauset's politics often focus on the positioning of African Americans in the United States rather than on Pan-Africanism or anti-imperialism, her perspective is markedly different from the accommodationism of Mary Church Terrell. Terrell claimed that "Nobody who has a drop of African blood in his veins can fail to honor and love France on account of the way she treats her black subjects. . . . I do not claim that France has always treated her black subjects in Africa as she should have done. . . . [However] the French really treat their dark citizens from their African colonies like brothers and men while they are in France" (339, 340).

17. See Barbeau and Henri, 180, 182, 189; Ellis "America's Black Press" 27; Gaines, 236. Major figures in the Harlem Renaissance responded directly to postwar violence against African Americans. Du Bois and Martha Gruening investigated and reported on the East St. Louis Riot of 1917 ("The Massacre" 215–216). Charles Johnson investigated and produced an early official description of the Chicago riot of 1919 (Doreski, 298). Carter G. Woodson was caught in the Washington D.C. riot of 1919 (Williams, 26). James Weldon Johnson gave the "Red Summer" its name (Hughes, 2, 3). Claude McKay wrote "If We Must Die" in response to the "Red Summer" (Williams, 2). Sylvander points out that Fauset's "Looking Glass" column in September 1921 foregrounds the Tulsa riot (97). See also Mary Church Terrell's account of the Washington D.C. riot (341, 342).

18. Wall sees this piece as "a moving and skillfully rendered formulation" of the search for an African American homeland (*Women* 52).

19. For controversies over the form women's war organizing should take, specifically in reference to segregation and state or local control, see Breen, 426–433; Gilmore, 195.

20. On elite African American women's class bias, see Paula Giddings, 95, 97–99; Lerner, "Early Community Work" 857; and Wolcott, 17–21. Like other reformers, Terrell cast working-class African American women as "immoral" because she, like other reformers, "defined their middle-class status in part by their sexual respectability" (Gordon, 579).

21. African American women helped to create educational institutions and organized through club movements and church auxiliaries to work for social welfare (Gilmore, 152–156, Wolcott, 28). See the large body of historical work on African American women's social activism during this period,

including Paula Giddings, Beverly Guy-Sheftall, Evelyn Brooks Higginbotham, Tera Hunter, Beverly Jones, Cynthia Neverdon-Morton, Dorothy Salem, and Anne Firor Scott.

In addition, women's World War I volunteerism served to bolster this network as well as to highlight racial discrimination, such as women's exclusion from organizations like the Red Cross or from overseas service (Emmett J. Scott, 376–377, 384–386).

22. African American women welfare workers were more likely to combine "public-sphere activism and marriage" in their own lives than were white reformers (Gordon 587).

23. Terrell also documents this form of U.S. racist propaganda (338).

24. Of Hunton and Johnson's text Fauset says: "Though clearly not written as propaganda we find in these pages propaganda of the most effective sort. The dispassionate account,—tempered by a sort of marvelling sadness that such things could be—of the needless, foolish humiliations and distinctions which our boys were forced to undergo in France, leaves an indelible impression. If seas of blood cannot wipe out prejudice what can? Yet the tone of the book is never that of despair" ("On the Bookshelf" 61).

4. *"An 'Honest-to-God' American"*

1. Drawing on both sides of the debate over Fauset's accommodationism, I agree with Elizabeth Ammons that Fauset's work is valuable precisely because her novels "exist in tension with themselves. They want to be utterly traditional yet they fight with tradition" (159). My approach is also indebted to Hazel Carby's reading of the Harlem Renaissance not as "a unique, intellectually cohesive and homogeneous historical moment" but as contested terrain (163, 164) and to Kevin Gaines' careful attention to the intricacy and variety of debates over integration during this period.

2. Evelyn Brooks Higginbotham and Victoria Widgeon Wolcott describe working-class versions of African American "respectability." Higginbotham claims that "the church played the single most important role in influencing normative values and distinguishing respectable from non-respectable behavior among working-class blacks during the early twentieth century" (204). Wolcott claims that "a bottom-up, working-class respectability emphasized religious piety, cleanliness, hard work, and thrift; while a top-down bourgeois respectability emphasized public displays of decorum, sexual restraint, and deportment" (8).

3. Jessie Fauset has been accused of promoting middle-class status and values, bourgeois conventions of marriage and domesticity, and a "mulatto

hegemony" in her fiction. See, for example, Judith R. Berzon, Barbara Christian, Vashti Crutcher Lewis, Cheryl Wall. See Wall for a summary of early critics who dismiss Fauset on these grounds (36, note 7). Claudia Tate sees Fauset's work, like late nineteenth-century African American women's fiction, as optimistically arguing for social equality through this type of domestic depiction, even as it reinforced white bourgeois values (92).

4. A summary of articles defending Fauset's work demonstrates that the desire for integration in her fiction is neither straightforward nor clearly accommodationist. Responding to critics like Robert Bone and Barbara Christian, Carol Sylvander argued early on that Fauset's fiction included a critique of "respectability" and did not simply promote the middle class as a rationale for incorporation (157, 168). More recently Beth A. McCoy has claimed that Fauset debunks the American myth of individualism and specifically the ideal that artistic effort can overcome racial discrimination (115). Moreover, Deborah McDowell's influential readings of the sexual politics of Fauset's fiction, while acknowledging sometimes conflicted endings, argue that Fauset articulated unsentimental views of marriage and introduced sexual themes that hardly met the requirements of gentile society, such as "promiscuity, exploitative sexual affairs, miscegenation, even incest" (87, 94, 95). Since then, Ann duCille has extended McDowell's argument to include women's independence and Fauset's idealization of working-class characters (88–93). Finally, McLendon argues that Fauset focuses on mulatto characters and passing not to create an elite that could achieve integration by separating itself from black migrants but to reject notions of white superiority and to deconstruct black/white binaries (10, 33–36).

5. See, for example, Dearborn, 51, 52, and McCoy, 112. McCoy regards Joanna as giving in "to the 'white father's'" mythologies. Joanna does not transcend dominant ideology; she merely proliferates it" (112).

6. For information on Du Bois's controversial support of the Des Moines officer's training camp, see Levering Lewis, 528–532; Patton, 37–38; Rampersad, 161.

7. Historically, both the United States and the Germans disseminated racist propaganda that charged African American soldiers with the rape of white women (Barbeau and Henri, 143–145, 164).

8. The representation of expatriates as un-American in Fauset's fiction demonstrates her investment in integrationist rather than separatist philosophy. Crutcher Lewis claims that Fauset "echo[es] the sentiment of W. E. B. Du Bois . . . whose integrationist philosophy was diametrically opposed to Garvey's nationalism" by having white racist Roger favor Garvey in *Plum Bun* (380). Hutchinson's brief account of Fauset's short story "There Was One

Time" argues for Fauset's interest in "The Americanness of the American Negro," as well (154–156).

9. In *Comedy: American Style*, dark-skinned Nick refuses to marry light-skinned Phoebe because he is tired of the racism directed toward their association. He identifies with American Indians to explain his refusal to resist racism: "I know it's the fashion to admire the Indian, because he put up such a fight against the invading paleface. But where is he now? . . . Mostly dead . . . his relicts herded on reservations, his oil-lands maladministered" (*Comedy* 261). Fauset is critical of Nick's accommodationist stance and implicitly of his reading of American Indians even as she parallels African American and American Indian responses to oppression.

10. One of the few critics to take up representations of Europe in Fauset's writing, Mary Conde recognizes Fauset's use of Europe to critique "the characters' betrayal of their own identities by moving away from America" (104). See also Deborah Chay (136). Instead of reading Fauset's use of foreignness to critique passing, however, Conde argues that Europe presents an escape from racial politics as opposed to passing, which grapples with issues of discrimination in the United States. This reading neglects the intricate relationship between passing and discourses of Americanism and foreignness in Fauset's writing. However, Fauset's embrace of characters who remain within African American community as American is circumscribed by a "mulatto hegemony" as Crutcher Lewis correctly asserts (378, 384–385).

11. See Fauset's February 1919 "Looking Glass" column for an example of claims in the press that discrimination would drive African Americans to Bolshevism (187).

12. Gaines argues that Dunbar-Nelson's pacifism and work "for the American Interracial Peace Committee during the interwar years stemmed partly from the disillusionment that ensued when the sight of black men in uniform provoked not respect and gratitude, but murderous rage from many whites" (223). In a 1928 newspaper column, a disillusioned Dunbar-Nelson wrote, for example, "The Negro is very much a part of this modern trend against war. No one knows better than the Negro that war is not the kind of thing which will bring about understanding among races" (Hull, *The Works* 2:212).

13. Commenting briefly on the accommodationism of this play, Hutchinson argues that Dunbar-Nelson reinforces Du Bois's "Close Ranks" article (158). Hull sees "the Jewish character and interracialism" of the play as aligned with "the current thrust of the National Association for the Advancement of Colored People" but sees the use of socialism in the play as "almost jingoistic" (72).

Fauset's use of the war to advocate integration is more ambivalent than both Dunbar-Nelson's play and the patriotic literary poetry by Georgia Douglas Johnson. The last two stanzas of her "Homing Braves" suggests a patriotic optimism not borne out by history:

> They shall have paid full, utterly
> The price of peace across the sea,
> When, with uplifted glance they come
> To claim a kindly welcome home.
> Nor shall the old-time daedal sting
> Of prejudice, their manhood wing,
> Nor heights, nor depths, nor living streams
> Stand in the pathway of their dreams!
>   (Hunton and Johnson 111)

14. See Gaines; Gatewood; Giddings; Gilmore; Higginbotham; Lash-Quinn; and Wolcott

15. That Fauset also struggled with and drew on these tensions in uplift ideology is demonstrated in *Plum Bun*. Angela Murray claims that

> Harlem intrigued her. . . . Here were people of a very high intellectual type, exponents of the realest and most essential refinement living cheek by jowl with coarse or ill-bred or even criminal, certainly indifferent, members of their race. Of course some of this propinquity was due to outer pressure, but there was present, too, a hidden consciousness of race-duty, a something which if translated said: "Perhaps you do pull me down a little from the height to which I have climbed. But on the other hand, perhaps, I'm helping you to rise."   (*Plum Bun* 326)

In this passage Fauset establishes elite privilege by displacing charges of inferiority onto the working class.

16. Critics have noticed Fauset's affirmation, however tentative, of African American community in other contexts. Wilbert Jenkins argues, for example, that Fauset expresses an African American cultural nationalism through a rejection of white identity (18). See also Elizabeth Ammons, *Conflicting Stories* (148); Angela Hubler (33); Mary Jane Lupton ("Black Women" 38); and McLendon (36).

17. Alice Dunbar-Nelson's poem "I Sit and Sew" can be read as protesting the limitations placed on women's war volunteerism. The final stanza of her poem, for example, reads

> The little useless seam, the idle patch;
> Why dream I here beneath my homely thatch,

When there they lie in sodden mud and rain,
Pitifully calling me, the quick ones and the slain?
You need me, Christ! It is no roseate dream
That beckons me—this pretty futile seam,
It stifles me—God, must I sit and sew?
                              (Hull *The Works* 2:84)

18. Thadious Davis argues that Maggie's family in *There Is Confusion* refutes social environmentalism because it is "neither defeated by urban poverty, dehumanized by unhealthful tenements, nor isolated from supportive networks" (Foreword xi). However, Maggie's "morality" is dependent on her economic success and investment in uplift ideologies of self-help, which historically reinforced social environmentalism.

19. In an analysis of the figure of the mulatto, McLendon argues that "Jessie Fauset tries to revise the mulatto fiction of precursory white writers simply by reversing the implications of the blood theory" (28).

20. Fauset does reinforce elitist ideologies of self-help in *Comedy: American Style*, however. Alexander remains in the United States because it is a land of economic opportunity:

He liked America. A year in Europe had taught him something of the imperfections of most governments. He was not the type of Negro to disassociate the value of a creed of race equality from the worth of economic opportunity. . . . At twenty-three, being an American of some training and thought and of his national quota of materialism, he had no doubts as to the desirability of being a technically free, but starving, Negro in France or England and a practically free Negro living in the northern United States in relative security and comfort. . . . But he did think America might by now try to live up to some of the tall sayings and implications of her founders.   (90–91)

Moreover, all of the figures who live in poverty by the end of the novel are white or passing, exiled, and considered morally corrupt. While Fauset uses white rather than black poverty to invert stereotypes, she replicates settlement house discourse that argued that working-class poverty was not the result of social inequality but of inherent traits.

Similarly, although duCille is right to suggest that Fauset values working-class characters and female wage-earning and is quite critical of women who marry for money, Fauset's fiction does often reinforce middle-class values by embracing characters who attain economic prosperity through a white-collar profession (duCille, 88, 93). Even her impoverished characters, like Maggie, achieve financial security through entrepreneurialism and, often, proprietor-ship. Fauset's inability to represent working-class characters as respectable, apart from their ability to achieve economic success, can be read as respond-ing to stereotypes of African American inferiority but also as replacing protest with a rhetoric of self-help.

21. For an extended analysis of Fauset's critique of the New Woman see Elizabeth Ammons, "The New Woman" 86–88.

22. Representations of the home in *There Is Confusion* have been highly controversial. Of Joanna's final bourgeois marriage to Peter, for instance, Wall has argued that "the privileging of private over the public, the retreat into domesticity, and the denial of difference ultimately cripple her [Fauset's] fic-tion" (84). That Joanna replaces her independence and dancing career (through which she challenges segregation) with patriarchal family and male professionalism (an adoption of white middle-class norms) is certainly the case. Moreover, Wall's claim has some historical validity since some elite African Americans responded to racial discrimination by using their class sta-tus to withdraw from civic life into the home. Elite African Americans, for instance, relied on the home for socializing as a way to avoid de facto segre-gation (but also perhaps the black masses).

McDowell, on the other hand, suggests the complexity of Fauset's repre-sentations of domesticity by arguing that Fauset uses Maggie to satirize the home as a protective space. However, McDowell ultimately agrees with Wall's assessment of the conservativism of Fauset's representation, arguing that both Maggie and Joanna, "to varying degrees, accede to male-determined roles for women" ("Neglected Dimension" 96, 98). Likewise, although McCoy argues that despair rather than optimism characterizes Joanna's final adoption of bourgeois domesticity, her focus on Joanna's retreat also supports Wall's argument.

23. Fauset's representation of women's political affiliations is limited, how-ever. She never represents church-based institutions, for example, and her representation of domestic politics only briefly acknowledges domestic ser-vice itself. Fauset does respond to stereotypes such as those found in Jewish American women's texts. However, her substantial avoidance of African American women's work in domestic service can also be seen as an attempt to differentiate middle- from working-class populations.

5. *"Why Should You Ask for Ease?"*

1. Immigration restriction included passage of a literacy test in 1917 and a quota system in 1921 and 1924 (Higham, 202–204, 311, 324). See Simon and Alexander for an overview of anti-immigration sentiment during the 1920s

in the popular press. The Immigration Act of 1917 also allowed for the deportation of aliens who were identified as radicals (Higham, 221). In 1918 another law was passed "authorizing deportation on grounds of organizational membership" (Higham, 229). The most prominent deportation occurred during the "red scare" of 1919. Attorney General A. Mitchell Palmer raided the Union of Russian Workers and two communist parties and succeeded in deporting approximately 800 "radicals," most of them Eastern Europeans (Higham, 230–231).

The anti-Semitic *Protocols of the Elders of Zion*, which espoused a worldwide Jewish conspiracy, circulated through the U.S. government during the "red scare." *The Protocols* were serialized in Ford's *Dearborn Independent* in 1922–23, constituting the culmination of Ford's ninety-one issue anti-Semitic campaign (Feingold, 8–9). According to Feingold, the "linkage of Judaism to political radicalism became the most persistent element in anti-Semitic propaganda, echoed in the highest echelons of government" (6).

Finally, Harvard was one of many universities that tried to limit Jewish enrollment during this period. Jewish Americans worked against the Harvard limitation from 1922 to 1925 (Feingold, 14). See also Sorin, 239.

2. Jewish women had also used writing to negotiate tensions between Jewish and American identities in the nineteenth century, according to Diane Lichtenstein. However, combining both Jewish and American identities became more difficult in the 1920s, when the rhetoric of nativism and immigration restriction increased the distance between "American" and "foreign" positionings (Lichtenstein, 7, 95; Higham, 270, 300, 307).

3. Tensions over acculturation among Jews of German descent and Eastern European immigrants in the United States are well documented. See, for example, Baum et al., 163–233; Berman; Berrol, "When Uptown Met Downtown"; Mandel; Rischin; and Sorin. As Nancy Cohen has argued, however, acculturated Jews had an impressive history of involvement with and support for Eastern European immigrants, despite their elitism (211–246). Furthermore, historians of the NCJW support, to some extent, acculturated women's own views on this subject. Seth Korelitz argues that the NCJW's Americanization work, for example, was unique in its cultural pluralism, its embrace of Jewish culture, and its advocacy of public roles for women (177–178). Faith Rogow's study documents elitism but also argues that the NCJW was founded to encourage "Judaism and Jewish interests" and unlike other Jewish charities, never opposed Eastern European immigration (Rogow, 15, 159).

4. For examples of articles on legislation affecting women see Loeb; Sternberger, "Has Women's Vote"; and Ranson. See also "Why the Temporary

Committee on Naturalization" and "Legislative Notes." For examples of arti-
cles discussing the "modern" or "New" Jewish woman see Cohon; Franken;
Kleeman; Mueller-Cohen; Reis, "The Modern Esther"; Solis-Cohen; and
Stern, "The Job, the Home and Woman."

     5. Definitions of New Womanhood in Jewish communities varied accord-
ing to class positioning. Linda Kuzmack discusses Jewish women's social welfare and club work under the heading, "The 'New' Jewish Woman." Her
organizational study primarily defines New Womanhood as acculturated
Jewish women's challenge to religious and communal hierarchies (183). Susan
Glenn, however, thematizes the New Jewish Woman in her chapter, " 'As We
Are Not Angels': The New Unionism and the New Womanhood," discussing primarily Eastern European, working-class Jewish women's labor
activism. See note 17.

     6. See Berrol, "Class or Ethnicity," for an excellent analysis of Son-
neschein's *American Jewess*. On women's contributions to the Yiddish press,
Klepfisz has argued that with the exception of *Fraye Arbeter Shtime*, an anar-
chist paper, the Yiddish press was male-dominated and "women's prose was
published only sporadically" (25, 48).

     7. See for example Goren; Reed; Singerman; Whitfield; Whiteman and
Libo; and "Journalism." In addition to mentioning Sonneschein's journal,
Whiteman and Libo discuss a few women contributors such as Judith Solis-
Cohen, Cecilia Reinheimer, Emma Lazarus, and Henrietta Szold (12, 16,
38). They and Goren also refer to *Die Deborah*, which was a "supplement for
the Daughters of Israel," edited by Isaac M. Wise from 1855 to 1900 (Goren,
203–204; Whiteman and Libo, 55). Finally, Goren mentions Hadassah's
newsletter and magazine very briefly and primarily in a contemporary context (220).

     The Hadassah News Letter and women's Zionist writings, including those
of women like Henrietta Szold and Jessie Sampter, are also very relevant to
discussions of Jewish Americans and national identity but are beyond the
scope of my analysis here.

     8. Rosa Sonneschein's journal, *The American Jewess*, performed a similar
service earlier in the century. Women editors and columnists who wrote regularly in the Jewish English-language press, including Judith Solis-Cohen,
Nannie A. Reis, Cecilia Razovsky, and Etta Lasker, can often be found in
the pages of *The Jewish Woman*. Solis-Cohen and Reis wrote women's
columns in the Philadelphia *Exponent* and the *Reform Advocate*, respectively
(Whiteman and Libo, 12; Rogow, 236). Cecilia Razovsky and Etta Lasker
edited *The Immigrant*. In addition, Anita Brenner and Sara Messing Stern
wrote for, appeared in reviews, or were featured in biographical pieces in *The
Jewish Woman*. Brenner wrote for New York's *Jewish Daily Bulletin* out of Mex-

ico City ("Contributors' Column" 36). On the editorial board of *The Jewish Woman*, Sara Messing Stern was president of the Woman's Press Club of Indiana ("Women in the World's News" 47).

Well-known women reviewers and fiction writers, such as Florence Kiper Frank, Elma Ehrlich Levinger, Emanie Sachs, and Elizabeth Gertrude Stern, also published in *The Jewish Woman*. Levinger, for example, published in *The Jewish Woman* and wrote articles, reviews, short stories, and plays primarily for *The American Hebrew* but also for *The Jewish Tribune*. Fiction writers Frank, Sachs, and Elizabeth Gertrude Stern were interviewed in and published poetry, short stories, or articles in these three journals as well. Stern was also a contributing editor to *The Ladies Home Journal*, wrote a column for the Philadelphia *Record* and also wrote under the pseudonym Leah Morton ("Women in Social Service" 91).

For examples of Levinger's writing, see "The Jewish Woman as Author," "The New Jew in Fiction," "Is the Jewish Home a Myth?" and "It's All For a Good Cause." For biographical information on Levinger see "Who's Who of Contributors" and "The Jewish Woman as Author." Frank published poetry and articles primarily in *The Jewish Tribune*. For examples of writing on or by Sachs and Stern, see "Changing Ideals of Modern Women"; Goldman, "Mrs. Emanie N. Sachs—Author of 'Talk'"; "The Small Town in Fiction"; and Wallach, "A Novelist Who Refuses to Preach Sermons" and "The Job, the Home, and Woman"; Morton, "I am a Woman—and a Jew"; Goldstein, "Intermarriage Will Not Solve the Problem of the Jew," and "Women in Social Service—1924."

9. This journalism worked to circumvent immigration restriction, avoid deportation, and inform immigrant women of the status of current U.S. policies and their legal rights. In 1921 for example, a column in *The Immigrant*, "Legislative Notes," stated that immigration quotas would be determined by "nationality," which in this case meant country of birth, alleviating fears that Jews would be classed as a separate nationality, which would result in substantially smaller numbers of Jews being allowed to enter the United States (11).

10. For biographical information on Razovsky, see Rogow (235) and Antler (214–224). Antler also discusses Razovsky's attitudes toward the Cable Act (217). In addition, Ewen cites an example of Razovsky struggling with class and gender conflicts in an English night course she taught for immigrant men (89).

11. For more information on Florina Lasker see the entry on her brother Albert Davis Lasker in the *American Jewish Yearbook* (166).

12. In an article stressing the value of Jewish women's immigration work, Lasker criticized Willa Cather for assuming that the goal of immigrant aid was

acculturation and the erasure of immigrant culture. Lasker quoted Cather's *New York Times* article which asked,

> Contribute? What shall they contribute? They are not peddlers with something to sell; they are not gypsies. They have come here to live in the sense that they lived in the old world, and if they were let alone their lives might turn into the beautiful ways of their homeland. But they are not let alone. Social workers, missionaries—call them what you will—go after them, hound them, pressure them and devote their days and nights toward the great task of turning them into stupid replicas of smug American types. This passion for Americanizing everything and everybody is a deadly disease with us. We do it the way we build houses. Speed, uniformity, nothing else matters.
>
> ("A Reply to Willa Cather" 1)

Cather's argument against conformity and against coercive Americanization work seems to affirm immigrant culture. Yet, Lasker took strong exception to Cather's piece for implicitly denying the Americanization worker's Jewish identity. Cather's paralleling of social workers with missionaries must have irked Lasker, since Jewish women warned immigrants against missionaries who tried to convert them (Rogow 144). Lasker also objected to Cather's representation of immigrant aid as coercive and to her hands-off approach which might work toward the marginalization of "foreign" cultures in the United States.

13. On the use of "morality" and "character" in immigration restriction, see Higham, 199–101, 204. On the regulatory discourse of "friendly visitors" and settlement houses, see Berrol, "When Uptown Met Downtown" 42 and Sinkoff, 572–573, 583–584. Ewen makes a distinction between early philanthropy, which "perceived poverty as a character flaw" and the social work of New Women, who "saw themselves as advocates *for* the poor" (78, 79). However, she also acknowledges the ways in which middle-class social workers replicated elitism (87, 91).

14. For more information on Sternberger, see Marcus, 745–748.

15. For a broader discussion of this typology and its use by various groups in the United States, see Werner Sollors, 42–50. Mary Antin also uses the conceit of the exodus from Egypt explicitly in relation to Russian Jewish immigrants in her autobiography, as Sollors and Joyce Antler note (Sollors, 45; Antler, 19).

16. Sternberger also critiqued race as a rationale for immigration restric-

tion in "Sane Americanism," advocating the "melting-pot" ideology and Jewish Americanization instead (16).

17. See chapter 2, note 19. Historians have most often discussed acculturated Jewish women's activism as conforming to the tenets of the Cult of True Womanhood (Hyman, 25; Rogow, 4, 155–157; Sinkoff, 581–582). Paula Hyman and Faith Rogow have both argued that middle-class Jewish women in the United States embraced the tenets of True Womanhood as a way of assimilating without giving up Jewish identity (Hyman, 25; Rogow, 52). Lichtenstein's literary analysis argues the same point of Jewish women writers in the nineteenth century (16–23, 80). Because domestic roles positioned women as the conservators of religion, a role alien to shtetl culture, Hyman argues that acculturation actually facilitated, "a measure of Jewish ritual observance among women" (25). Rogow agrees but focuses more on the consequences of domestic ideology on women's positions of authority in Judaism. Rogow claims that the revolutionary potential of positioning Jewish women as religious authorities was contained by the True Woman's emphasis on home, which coincided with Jewish women's traditional responsibilities (64–65, 77–78).

To the extent that Hyman and Rogow argue for the complex positioning of middle-class women both as agents of acculturation/Americanization and as cultural conservators, the gender politics of *The Jewish Woman* support their conclusions. However, by the 1920s, middle-class Jewish women were not simply adopting the tenets of True Womanhood. Jewish women's journalism in English at times embraced women's wage labor as Jewish and also at times questioned a domestic ideology that positioned women in the home or as religious authorities. Exploring the convergence of immigrant aid work and representations of the New Woman demonstrates that acculturated Jewish women of the 1920s defined themselves in terms of the Americanized figure of the New Woman whether they embraced or critiqued her. By the 1920s, paradigms of the New or "modern" Woman became at least as important as the True Woman in Jewish women's understandings of themselves and their work. See note 5.

18. Braude reprints this essay and recognizes Cohon's focus on New Womanhood (157–161). For biographical information on Cohon, see "Samuel S. Cohon," Schneiderman, *Who's Who in World Jewry* 141.

19. For current scholarship on Stern and her work, see Umansky and Zierler, 245–293.

20. On Eastern European Jewish women's roles as income earners, see Baum et al., 15; Glenn, 64; and Ewen, 39, 87, 105.

21. See Sochen for a discussion of generational tensions over the professionalization of social work in Jewish communities (50).

22. My reading of this article differs from Rogow's (84). From the final paragraph, Rogow interprets the article as reinscribing women into the home. I argue that the thrust of the article is to revise New Womanhood so that it values both women's public roles and their roles within the home.

6. *"Mingling with Her People in Their Ghetto"*

1. This dichotomy is due in part to Yezierska's consistent treatment of Jewish themes and Ferber's and Hurst's decision to thematize Jewishness far less often in their extensive writings. Joyce Antler and Janet Burstein examine Yezierska together with Ferber's and Hurst's fiction. However, these authors are treated in separate chapters with an emphasis on immigrant life and Americanism, respectively. Antler, Stephen P. Horowitz and Miriam J. Landsman, and Diane Lichtenstein also discuss Ferber's and/or Hurst's Jewishness but examine their work or ethnicity apart from immigrant writers like Yezierska. Priscilla Wald's chapter on Gertrude Stein is one of the few to situate an acculturated Jewish woman writer in an immigrant context (*Constituting Americans* 237–298).

2. Largely middle-class merchants and manufacturers, Jewish Americans of German descent, for example, typically practiced Reform Judaism and embraced a family structure that relied on a single male wage earner. In New York city, Jewish Americans of German descent were active in immigrant aid and philanthropy and generally lived uptown. Working-class Eastern European immigrants, who were primarily Orthodox in their religious practice and embraced a shared family economy, lived downtown in the Jewish ghetto (Baum, 163; Cohen, 301; Ewen, 23; Sochen, 45). These differences did not preclude significant interchange between these communities, however. See note 3, chapter 5.

3. See Henriksen, 17; Wilentz, "Introduction" xi, and "What the Public Wants" 9. For Yezierska's own critique of her position as lecturer, see Fanya's talk in *All I Could Never Be* 115–122.

4. For articles on or by Hurst, see Maurice A. Bergman; "Fannie Hurst's 'Lummox'"; Lillian G. Glenn, " 'My Success Recipe'" and "What's the matter with Marriage?"; Hurst, "How I Write My Stories," "The Jewish Mother," "My Prophetic Soul," and "Women Who Do Things."

5. For articles on Ferber, see Golda M. Goldman; "Who are the Twelve Outstanding Jews?"; and "Who's Who in Literature—1924." This latter article also includes Fannie Hurst.

6. For articles on or by Yezierska, see N. Bryllion Fagin; "Hall of Fame: Anzia Yezierska"; Elma Ehrlich Levinger; and Yezierska, "The Lost 'Beautifulness.'" Thomas Ferraro documents the negative press Yezierska received from male reviewers in the popular press and in the *Menorah Journal* (53). See also Wilentz, "Introduction," for a summary of negative reviews, including one in the *Forward* (xviii, xxv). However, in reviews that treat Yezierska, Hurst, and Ferber together, both Levinger and Fagin favor Yezierska's work over these more popular writers.

7. For information on the Clara de Hirsh Home for Working Girls, which Yezierska attended, see Nancy B. Sinkoff. For information on the immigrant aid work of the National Council of Jewish Women, see Faith Rogow and Seth Korelitz. On Jewish women's reform work more generally, see Baum, Cohen, Ewen, and Sochen. For an introduction to the extensive literature on the settlement house movement, see Mina Carson, Ruth Hutchinson Crocker, Howard Jacob Karger, and Judith Trolander.

8. See, for example, Crocker and Elisabeth Lasch-Quinn.

9. See note 19 in chapter 2 and note 21 in chapter 4. Ammons has clearly demonstrated that writers like Jessie Fauset and Sui Sin Far critiqued the ethnocentrism and provided alternatives to the racial politics of the Americanized, Anglo New Woman (Ammons, "The New Woman" 86, 92). Furthermore, Lois Rudnick, Elizabeth Ammons, Martha Banta, and Dorothy Brown all argue for the conflicted and various representations of New Womanhood in the early twentieth century. Rudnick claims, for example, "the definition of the New Woman of this era runs the political and social gamut from freedoms related to personal self-development to freedoms related to equalizing the class system" (73).

10. Elinor Lerner looks specifically at working-class Jewish women's push for suffrage in New York. Middle-class Jewish women were also active in the suffrage movement but no Jewish women's organization supported suffrage (Kuzmack 148). See also note 5 in chapter 5.

11. Yezierska encouraged the image of herself as a ghetto writer as Henriksen has argued (1, 2, 157). Ferraro reinforces this point by arguing that Yezierska's descriptions of her life left out "a dozen years of middle-class experience: college, teaching in the public schools, marriage, and motherhood. Absent, too, are a half-dozen years of apprenticeship in the business of writing, during which she courageously acquired, late in her life but ahead of her time, rooms of her own" (55).

12. Although my focus on the journalism of the NCJW precludes a focus on Rose Pastor Stokes' journalism, she is represented as a journalist in Yezier-

ska's *Salome of the Tenements* and wrote a column for the *Yiddishes Tageblatt* and at least one article for an English-language Jewish newspaper, the *American Israelite* (Antler, 80–82). She also published a play, *The Woman Who Wouldn't*, in 1916 and wrote her autobiography (Henriksen 245).

13. In her introduction to *Arrogant Beggar*, Katherine Stubbs argues that Adele and Muhmenkeh represent "alternative(s) to official charity" (xxxi–xxxii). However, Yezierska's choice as a writer to both critique and advocate immigrant aid has yet to be taken up in any detail.

14. Katherine Stubbs rightly reads the cafe as a return to Adele's Jewish heritage. Adele, she argues, serves "mohn kuchen and gefulte fish" and turns the cafe into a salon for Jewish immigrants, artists, and musicians (xxxi). However, the space and artistic milieux Adele creates is more reminiscent of Left Bank expatriates than of shtetl culture.

15. See Gay Wilentz and Laura Wexler for standard readings of Sara's ambivalent relationship to patriarchy and ethnicity at the end of the novel (Wilentz, "Cultural Mediation" 38–41; Wexler, 177–178).

16. Although she doesn't explicitly discuss race, in *Writing Their Nations*, Diane Lichtenstein argues that Ferber employed a rhetoric of Americanism, through regionalist writing, that had Jewish integration as its rationale.

17. Hurst's attitudes toward mothering and domesticity are complicated. On the one hand, secretly married and living apart from her husband for a number of years, Hurst was seen in the press as a New Woman. On the other hand, in an brief article entitled, "The Jewish Mother," Hurst argues that "The emancipated Jewish mother who is stalking away from these fine old ideals on the French heels of modern society, and is letting the flame of her torch bend to the winds of the newest generation, is sacrificing the finest quality in the history of her race—the stern, relentless capacity for motherhood" (9). In both *Lummox* and "Roulette" social mobility is achieved through mothering and domestic skills. The status of domesticity is questioned in other of Hurst's texts, however, as I have argued elsewhere (Batker, 120–122).

18. In a sophisticated reading of Gertrude Stein's work, Laura Doyle discusses the critical tendency to ignore racist depictions of African Americans in Jewish women's texts.

19. See Jane Caputi and Gay Wilentz, "White Patron," for critical responses to the book and movie version of *Imitation of Life* from within the African American community.

Bibliography

Adler, Karen S. " 'Always Leading Our Men in Service and Sacrifice': Amy Jacques Garvey, Feminist Black Nationalist." *Gender and Society* 6 (1992): 346–375.

Allen, Paula Gunn. *The Sacred Hoop: Recovering the Feminine in American Indian Traditions.* Boston: Beacon P, 1986.

"Americanization of Foreign Born Mothers." *The Immigrant* 2 (November 1922): 12.

Ammons, Elizabeth. *Conflicting Stories: American Women Writers at the Turn into the Twentieth Century.* New York: Oxford UP, 1991.

———. "The New Woman as Cultural Symbol and Social Reality." *1915, The Cultural Moment.* Eds. Adele Heller and Lois Rudnick. New Brunswick: Rutgers UP, 1991: 82–97.

Amott, Teresa and Julie Matthaei. *Race, Gender, and Work.* Boston: South End P, 1991.

Andrus, Caroline W. "Conference of the Society of American Indians." *The Southern Workman* 41 (November 1912): 599–603.

"Angel DeCora Dietz." *The Southern Workman* (March 1919): 104–105.

Antin, Mary. *The Promised Land.* Boston: Houghton Mifflin, 1912.

Antler, Joyce. *The Journey Home: Jewish Women and the American Century.* New York: Free P, 1997.

Armstrong, Nancy. *Desire and Domestic Fiction: A Political History of the Novel.* New York: Oxford UP, 1987.

Atwood, Stella. "Indian Welfare." General Federation of Women's Clubs Sixteenth Biennial Convention, 1922: 429, 506–509.

————. "Committee on Indian Welfare." General Federation of Women's Clubs Seventeenth Biennial Convention, 1924: 373–376.

————. "Report of Division of Indian Welfare." General Federation of Women's Clubs Twelfth Biennial Council, 1927: 45–47.

Ault, Nelson. *The Papers of Lucullus Virgil McWhorter*. Seattle: State College of Washington, 1959.

Bakhtin, Mikhail. *The Dialogic Imagination*. Translated by Caryl Emerson and Michael Holquist. Austin: U of Texas P, 1981.

Baldwin, Marie L. "Modern Home-Making and the Indian Woman." Paper delivered at the First Annual Conference of The American Indian Association. Columbus: Ohio State UP (October 1911): 1–7.

Banta, Martha. *Imaging American Women: Idea and Ideals in Cultural History*. New York: Columbia UP, 1987.

Barbeau, Arthur E. and Florette Henri. *The Unknown Soldiers: Black American Troops in World War I*. Philadelphia: Temple UP, 1974.

Batker, Carol. "Fannie Hurst." *Jewish American Women Writers: A Bio-Bibliographical and Critical Sourcebook*. Ed. Ann R. Shapiro. Westport: Greenwood P, 1994: 118–125.

Baum, Charlotte, Paula Hyman, and Sonya Michel. *The Jewish Woman in America*. New York: Dial, 1976.

Bear, Louise Johnson. "A Winnebago Question and a Tale of a Winnebago Hero." *American Indian Magazine* 4 (1916): 150–153.

Bender, Elizabeth G. "Training Indian Girls for Efficient Home Makers." *Red Man* 8 (January 1916): 155–156.

Bergman, Maurice A. "An Interview with Fannie Hurst on Contemporary Problems." *The Jewish Tribune* (March 9, 1928): 2, 18.

Bergoffen, Wendy H. " 'I'm No Greenhorn': Ethnic Tensions and Identity Politics in Anzia Yezierska's *Bread Givers* and Edna Ferber's *Fanny Herself*." M.A. thesis, Florida State U, 1995.

Berman, Myron. "The Attitude of American Jewry Towards East European Jewish Immigration, 1881–1914." Ph.D dissertation, Columbia U, 1963.

Bernardin, Susan K. "Mixed Messages: Authority and Authorship in Mourning Dove's *Cogewea, The Half-Blood: A Depiction of the Great Montana Cattle Range*." *American Literature* 67(3) (September 1995): 487–509.

Bernstein, Alison. "A Mixed Record: The Political Enfranchisement of American Indian Women During the Indian New Deal." *Journal of the West* 23 (July 1984): 13–20.

Berrol, Selma. "Class or Ethnicity: The Americanized German Jewish Woman and Her Middle Class Sisters in 1895." *Jewish Social Studies* 47 (1985): 21–32.

———. "When Uptown Met Downtown: Julia Richman's Work in the Jewish Community of New York, 1880–1912." *American Jewish History* 70 (September 1980): 35–51.

Berzon, Judith. *Neither White Nor Black: The Mulatto Character in American Fiction.* New York: New York UP, 1978.

Bone, Robert. *The Negro Novel in America.* New Haven: Yale UP, 1969.

Boone, Joseph Allen. *Libidinal Currents: Sexuality and the Shaping of Modernism.* Chicago: U of Chicago P, 1998.

Bowles, Eva D. "Negro Women and the War." *The Southern Workman* 47 (September 1918): 425–426.

Brandimarte, Cynthia. "Fannie Hurst: A Missouri Girl Makes Good." *Missouri Historical Review* 81 (April 1987): 275–95.

Braude, Ann. "The Jewish Woman's Encounter with American Culture." *Women and Religion in America.* Eds. Rosemary Radford Ruether and Rosemary Skinner Keller. San Francisco: Harper and Row, 1981: 150–192.

Breen, William J. "Black Women and the Great War: Mobilization and Reform in the South." *The Journal of Southern History* 45 (1978): 421–40.

Brown, Alanna Kathleen. "Mourning Dove's Voice in *Cogewea*." *Wicazo-Sa Review* 4(2) (1988): 10.

———. "Mourning Dove's Canadian Recovery Years 1917–1919." *Canadian Literature* (Spring/Summer 1990): 113–23.

———. "Profile: Mourning Dove (Humishima) 1888–1936." *Legacy: A Journal of Nineteenth Century American Women Writers* 6 (Spring 1989): 51–58.

Brown, Dorothy M. *Setting a Course: American Women in the 1920s.* Boston: Twayne, 1987.

Burstein, Janet Handler. *Writing Mothers, Writing Daughters: Tracing the Maternal in Stories by American Jewish Women.* Chicago: U of Illinois P, 1996.

Caputi, Jane. " 'Specifying' Fannie Hurst: Langston Hughes's 'Limitations of Life,' Zora Neale Hurston's *Their Eyes Were Watching God*, and Toni Morrison's *The Bluest Eye* as 'Answers' to Hurst's *Imitation of Life*." *Black American Literature Forum* 24(4) (Winter 1990): 697–716.

Carby, Hazel V. *Reconstructing Womanhood: The Emergence of the Afro-American Woman Novelist.* New York: Oxford UP, 1987.

Carson, Mina. *Settlement Folk: Social Thought and the American Settlement Movement 1885–1930.* Chicago: U of Chicago P, 1990.

"Changing Ideals of Modern Women: An Interview with Emanie N. Sachs." *The Jewish Woman* 4 (December 1924): 10–11.

Chay, Deborah G. "Black Feminist Criticism and the Politics of Reading Jessie Fauset." Ph.D. dissertation, Duke U, 1992.

Christian, Barbara. *Black Women Novelists: The Development of a Tradition, 1892–1976.* Westport, Conn.: Greenwood, 1980.

Clark, Jerry E. and Martha Ellen Webb. "Susette and Susan La Flesche: Reformer and Misssionary." *Being and Becoming Indian: Biographical Studies of North American Frontiers.* Ed. James A. Clifton. Chicago: Dorsey P, 1989: 137–159.

Clifton, James A. "Alternate Identities and Cultural Frontiers." *Being and Becoming Indian: Biographical Studies of North American Frontiers.* Ed. James A. Clifton. Chicago: Dorsey P, 1989: 1–37.

"Close Ranks." *The Crisis* 16 (July 1918): 111.

Cohen, Naomi W. *Encounter with Emancipation: The German Jews in the United States, 1830–1914.* Philadelphia: Jewish Publication Society of America, 1984.

Cohen, Rose. *Out of the Shadow.* New York: George H. Doran, 1918.

Cohon, Irma A. "Judaism and the Modern Woman." *The Jewish Woman* 4 (October 1924): 11–12, 45–46.

Coleman, Michael C. *American Indian Children at School, 1850–1930.* Jackson: UP of Mississippi, 1993.

———. "Motivations of Indian Children at Missionary and U.S. Government Schools." *Montana: The Magazine of Western History* 40 (Winter 1990): 30–45.

Conde, Mary. "Passing in the Fiction of Jessie Redmon Fauset and Nella Larsen." *The Yearbook of English Studies.* Ed. Andrew Gurr. London: W. S. Maney, 1994: 94–104.

"Contributors' Column." *The Jewish Woman* 4 (December 1924): 36.

Cott, Nancy F. *The Grounding of Modern Feminism.* New Haven: Yale UP, 1987.

Crocker, Ruth Hutchinson. *Social Work and Social Order: The Settlement Movement in Two Industrial Cities, 1898–1930.* Chicago: U of Illinois P, 1992.

Daniel, Walter L. *Black Journals of the U.S.* Westport, Conn.: Greenwood, 1982.

Davis, Thadious. "Foreword," *There Is Confusion.* Jessie Redmon Fauset. Boston: Northeastern UP, 1989.

Dearborn, Mary. *Pocahontas' Daughters: Gender and Ethnicity in American Culture.* New York: Oxford UP, 1986.

Debo, Angie. *A History of the Indians of the United States.* Norman: U of Oklahoma P, 1970.

DeCora, Angel. "Native Indian Art." *The Southern Workman* 36 (October 1907): 527–528.

———. "The Sick Child." *Harper's Monthly* (February 1899): 446–448.

Deloria, Ella Cara. "Health Education for Indian Girls." *The Southern Workman* 53 (February 1924): 63–68.

———. *Waterlily*. Lincoln: U of Nebraska P, 1988.

Deloria, Vine, Jr. " 'Congress in its Wisdom': The Course of Indian Legislation." *The Aggressions of Civilization: Federal Indian Policy Since the 1880s*. Eds. Sandra L. Cadwalader and Vine Deloria Jr. Philadelphia: Temple UP, 1984: 105–130.

———. "Revision and Reversion." *The American Indian and the Problem of History*. Ed. Calvin Martin. New York: Oxford UP, 1987: 84–90.

Diner, Hasia. *In the Almost Promised Land: American Jews and Blacks 1915–1935*. Westport, Conn.: Greenwood, 1977.

Dippie, Brian W. *The Vanishing American: White Attitudes and U.S. Indian Policy*. Middletown: Wesleyan UP, 1982.

Doreski, C. K. "Chicago, Race, and the Rhetoric of the 1919 Riot." *Prospects* 18 (1993): 283–309.

Douglas, Ann. *The Feminization of American Culture*. New York: Knopf, 1977.

Doyle, Laura. *Bordering on the Body: The Racial Matrix of Modern Fiction and Culture*. New York: Oxford UP, 1994.

———. "The Folk, the Nobles, and the Novel: The Racial Subtext of Sentimentality." *Narrative* 3(2) (May 1995): 161–186.

———. "Resisting Assimilation: The Three Lives of Gertrude Stein (One of Them Ours)." Narrative: An International Conference, Gainsville, Fla., April 5, 1997.

Du Bois, W. E. B. "A Vision of Tomorrow: In the Year 2000, The New America." *The American Hebrew* (September 26, 1924): 529, 573.

———. *The Souls of Black Folk*. New York: Penguin, 1989.

duCille, Ann. *The Coupling Convention: Sex, Text, and Tradition in Black Women's Fiction*. New York: Oxford UP, 1993.

Dunbar-Nelson, Alice. "Mine Eyes Have Seen." *The Crisis* (Easter 1918): 271–275.

———. "Negro Literature for Negro Pupils." *The Southern Workman* 51 (February 1922): 59–63.

DuPlessis, Rachel Blau. *Writing Beyond the Ending: Narrative Strategies of Twentieth-Century Women Writers*. Bloomington: Indiana UP, 1985

Duster, Alfreda M., ed. "Introduction." *Crusade for Justice: The Autobiography of Ida B. Wells*. Chicago: U of Chicago P, 1970.

Eastman, Charles. *From the Deep Woods to Civilization*. 1916. Boston: Little
    Brown; Lincoln and London: U of Nebraska P, 1977.
Eaton, Edith (Sui Sin Far). *Mrs. Spring Fragrance*. 1912. Chicago: AC
    McClure; Urbana: U of Illinois P, 1995.
Eaton, Winnifred (Watanna, Onoto). *Diary of Delia*. Garden City, N.Y.:
    Doubleday, 1907.
————. *Me: A Book of Remembrance*. New York: Century, 1915.
Ellis, Mark. "America's Black Press." *History Today* 41 (September 1991):
    20–27.
————. " 'Closing Ranks' and 'Seeking Honors': W. E. B. Du Bois in
    World War I." *The Journal of American History* 79(1) (June 1992): 96–124.
————. "Federal Surveillance of Black Americans During the First World
    War." *Immigrants and Minorities* 12(1) (March 1993): 1–20.
————. "Joel Spingarn's 'Constructive Programme' and the Wartime Anti-
    lynching Bill of 1918." *Journal of Policy History* 4(2) (1992): 134–161.
————. "W. E. B. Du Bois and the Formation of Black Opinion in World
    War I: A Commentary on 'The Damnable Dilemma.' " *The Journal of
    American History*. March 1995: 1584–90.
Ewen, Elizabeth. *Immigrant Women in the Land of Dollars: Life and Culture on
    the Lower East Side, 1890–1925*. New York: Monthly Review P, 1985.
Fagin, N. Bryllion. "Writers of the Short Story." *The Jewish Tribune* (April
    15, 1927): 46, 68.
"Fannie Hurst, Popular Author of Romanitic Stories, Dies at 78." *New
    York Times* (February 24, 1968): 1, 29.
"Fannie Hurst's 'Lummox' " on "Our English Page." *Forward* (January 20,
    1924).
Fauset, Jessie Redmon. *The Chinaberry Tree and Selected Writings*. 1931.
    Boston: Northeastern UP, 1995.
————. *Comedy: American Style*. 1933. New York: Frederick Stokes; New
    York: G. K. Hall, 1995.
————. "The Enigma of the Sorbonne." *The Crisis* (March 1925): 216–19.
————. "Impressions of the Second Pan-African Congress." *The Crisis*
    (November 1921): 12–18.
————. "Nostalgia." *The Crisis* (August 1921): 154–158.
————. *Plum Bun: A Novel Without a Moral*. 1928. New York: Frederick A.
    Stokes; Boston: Pandora, 1985.
————. *There Is Confusion*. 1924. New York: Boni and Liveright; Boston:
    Northeastern UP, 1989.
————. "This Way to the Flea Market." *The Crisis* (February 1925): 161–63.
————. "Tracing Shadows." *The Crisis* (September 1915): 247–51.

————. "Yarrow Revisited." *The Crisis* (January 1925): 107–109.

Feingold, Harry L. *A Time for Searching: Entering the Mainstream: 1920–1945.*
Baltimore: Johns Hopkins UP, 1992.

Ferber, Edna. *Cimarron.* 1930. New York: Bantam, 1963.

————. *Emma McChesney & Co.* New York: Frederick A. Stokes, 1915.

————. *Fanny Herself.* New York: Frederick A. Stokes, 1917.

————. *The Girls.* New York: Doubleday, Page, 1921.

————. "The Girl Who Went Right." 1918. *America and I.* Ed. Joyce
Antler. Boston: Beacon P, 1990.

————. *A Peculiar Treasure.* New York: Literary Guild of America, 1939.

Ferraro, Thomas. *Ethnic Passages: Literary Immigrants in the Twentieth
Century.* Chicago: U of Chicago P, 1993.

Fisher, Dexter. "Introduction." *Cogewea: The Half-Blood.* Mourning Dove.
Lincoln: U of Nebraska P, 1981.

————. *The Transportation of Tradition: A Study of Zitkala-Sa and Mourning
Dove, Two Transitional American Indian Writers,* Ph.D. dissertation, City U
of New York, 1979.

————. "Zitkala-Sa: The Evolution of a Writer." *American Indian Quarterly*
5 (August 1979): 229–238.

Fishkin, Shelley Fisher. "Interrogating 'Whiteness,' Complicating 'Black-
ness': Remapping American Culture." Ed. Henry B. Wonham. *Criticism
and the Color Line: Desegregating American Literary Studies.* New
Brunswick: Rutgers UP, 1996: 251–290.

Forman, Frieda et al., eds. *Found Treasures: Stories by Yiddish Women Writers.*
Toronto: Second Story P, 1994.

Frank, Florence Kiper. "A Letter to a Young Liberal." *The Jewish Tribune*
(September 14, 1928): 38, 59.

Franken, Rose L. "Is the Modern Girl Different?" *The Jewish Woman* 5
(June 1925): 1–3.

Frederick, Antoinette. "Fannie Hurst." *Notable American Women.* Eds. Barbara Sicherman, Carol Hurd Green, et al. Cambridge: Belknap P of
Harvard UP, 1980: 359–61.

Gaines, Kevin K. *Uplifting the Race: Black Leadership, Politics, and Culture in
the 20th Century.* Chapel Hill: U of North Carolina P, 1996.

Gates, Henry Louis, Jr., director. *The Black Periodical Literature Project.*
Alexandria, Va.: Chadwyck-Healey, 1990.

Gatewood, Willard B. *Aristocrats of Color: The Black Elite, 1880–1920.* Bloomington: Indiana UP, 1993.

Giddings, Paula. *When and Where I Enter: The Impact of Black Women on Race
and Sex in America.* New York: Bantam, 1984.

Gilmore, Glenda Elizabeth. *Gender and Jim Crow: Women and the Politics of White Supremacy in North Carolina, 1896–1920.* Chapel Hill: U of North Carolina P, 1996.

"The Gist of the Story." *Forward* (January 20, 1924).

Gleason, Philip. *Speaking of Diversity: Language and Ethnicity in Twentieth-Century America.* Baltimore: Johns Hopkins UP, 1992.

Glenn, Lillian G. " 'My Success Recipe.' " *The Jewish Tribune* (April 6, 1928): 29.

———. "What's the Matter with Marriage?" *The Jewish Tribune* (February 1, 1929): 10.

Glenn, Susan A. *Daughters of the Shtetl: Life and Labor in the Immigrant Generation.* Ithaca: Cornell UP, 1990.

Goldman, Golda M. "A Chat with Edna Ferber: Author of 'So Big' Touches on Several Topics—Including Herself." *The American Hebrew* (February 6, 1925): 380, 414.

———. "Mrs. Emanie N. Sachs—Author of 'Talk.' " *The American Hebrew* (September 19, 1924): 492.

Goldstein, Israel. "Intermarriage Will Not Solve the Problem of the Jew." *The Jewish Tribune* (April 1, 1927): 7.

Gordon, Jane Zane. "Will Indians Give Up Tribal Independence for Newly [sic] American Citizenship." *Indian Tepee* (August 1924): 2–3.

Gordon, Linda. "Black and White Visions of Welfare: Women's Welfare Activism, 1890–1945." *The Journal of American History* (September 1991): 559–590.

Goren, Arthur A. "The Jewish Press." *The Ethnic Press in the United States: A Historical Analysis and Handbook.* Ed. Sally M. Miller. New York: Greenwood, 1987. 201–228.

Goulette, Emma Johnson. "Common School Education for the Indian Child." *Quarterly Journal of the Society of American Indians* 1 (1913): 302.

———. "The Returned Girl Student." *American Indian Magazine* 4 (1916): 135.

Green, Norma K. "Four Sisters: Daughters of Joseph La Flesche." *Nebraska History* 45 (June 1964): 165–176.

Gridley, Marion E. *Indians of Today.* Chicago: Lakeside P, 1936.

Guy-Sheftall, Beverly. *Daughters of Sorrow: Attitudes Toward Black Women, 1880–1920.* Brooklyn: Carlson, 1990.

"Hall of Fame: Anzia Yezierska." *The Jewish Tribune* (April 5, 1929): 29.

Harper, Phillip Brian. *Framing the Margins: The Social Logic of Postmodern Culture.* New York: Oxford UP, 1994.

Harris, William J. "Etiquette, Lynching, and Racial Boundaries in Southern History: A Mississippi Example." *American Historical Review* 100 (1–2) (April 1995): 387–410.

Hauptman, Laurence M. "Designing Woman: Minnie Kellogg, Iroquois Leader." *Indian Lives: Essays on Nineteenth and Twentieth Century Native American Leaders.* Eds. L. G. Moses and Raymond Wilson. Albuquerque: U of New Mexico P, 1985: 159–188.

Heller, Adele and Lois Rudnick, eds. *1915, The Cultural Moment: The New Politics, The New Woman, The New Psychology, The New Art, and The New Theater in America.* New Brunswick: Rutgers UP, 1991.

Hemenway, Robert E. *Zora Neale Hurston: A Literary Biography.* Chicago: U of Illinois P, 1977.

Henriksen, Louise Levitas. *Anzia Yezierska: A Writer's Life.* New Brunswick: Rutgers UP, 1988.

Hertzberg, Hazel W. *The Search for an American Indian Identity: Modern Pan-Indian Movements.* Syracuse: Syracuse UP, 1971.

Higginbotham, Evelyn Brooks. *Righteous Discontent: The Women's Movement in the Black Baptist Church, 1880–1920.* Cambridge: Harvard UP, 1993.

Higham, John. *Strangers in the Land: Patterns of American Nativism, 1860–1925.* New Brunswick: Rutgers UP, 1955.

Hine, Darlene Clark, ed. *Black Women in American History: The Twentieth Century.* 4 vols. New York: Carlson, 1990.

Horowitz, Steven P. and Miriam J. Landsman. "The Americanization of Edna: A Study of Ms. Ferber's Jewish American Identity." *Studies in American Jewish Literature* 2 (1982): 69–80.

Hoxie, Frederick E. *A Final Promise: The Campaign to Assimilate the Indians, 1880–1920.* Lincoln: U of Nebraska P, 1984.

Hubler, Angela Elizabeth. " 'From Home to Market': Private Emotion and Political Engagement in the Work of Emma Goldman, Jessie Fauset, and Josephine Herbst." Ph.D. dissertation, Duke U, 1992.

Hughes, C. Alvin. "The Negro Sanhedrin Movement." *Journal of Negro History* 69(1) (1984): 1–13.

Hull, Gloria T. *Color, Sex, and Poetry: Three Women Writers of the Harlem Renaissance.* Bloomington: Indiana UP, 1987.

Hull, Gloria T., ed. *Give Us Each Day: The Diary of Alice Dunbar-Nelson.* New York: Norton, 1984.

———. *The Works of Alice Dunbar-Nelson.* 3 vols. New York: Oxford UP, 1988.

Hunter, Lucy. "The Value and Necessity of Higher Academic Training for the Indian Student." *Quarterly Journal of the Society of American Indians* 3 (1915): 11–15.

Hunter, Tera. "The Correct Thing: Charlotte Hawkins Brown and the Palmer Institute." *Black Women in American History.* Ed. Darlene Clark Hine. 3: 695–710.

Hunton, Addie W. and Kathryn M. Johnson. *Two Colored Women with the American Expeditionary Forces.* 1920. Ed. Henry Louis Gates Jr. New York: G. K. Hall, 1997.

Hurst, Fannie. *Anatomy of Me: A Wonderer in Search of Herself.* Garden City: Doubleday, 1958.

———. "Foreword." *Three Outstanding Women: Mary Fels, Rebekah Kohut, Annie Nathan Meyer.* Ed. Dora Askowith. New York: New York Bloch, 1941.

———. "How I Write My Stories." *The American Hebrew* (July 27, 1923): 219, 234.

———. *Imitation of Life.* 1933. New York: Harper; San Bernadino, Calif.: Borgo P, 1992.

———. "The Jewish Mother." *The Jewish Tribune* (Sept. 22, 1922): 9.

———. *Lummox.* 1923. New York: Harper; New York: Penguin, 1989.

———. "My Prophetic Soul." *The American Hebrew* (Sept. 26, 1924): 546.

———. "Roulette." *The Vertical City.* New York: Harper, 1922: 221–281.

———. "When the Pogrom Came to Vodna." *The Jewish Tribune* (April 7, 1922): 1, 20.

———. "Zora Hurston: A Personality Sketch." *Yale University Library Gazette* (1961): 17–22.

Hurston, Zora Neale. "Fannie Hurst: By Her Ex-Amanuensis." *Saturday Review of Literature* 16 (October 1937): 15–16.

Hutchinson, George. *The Harlem Renaissance in Black and White.* Cambridge: Belknap of Harvard UP, 1995.

Hyman, Paula E. *Gender and Assimilation in Modern Jewish History: The Roles and Representation of Women.* Seattle: U of Washington P, 1995.

"Ida B. Wells-Barnett." *Beyond the Home Front: Women's Autobiographical Writing of the Two World Wars.* Ed. Yvonne M. Klein. New York: New York UP, 1997: 99–102.

"Indian Leadership." *The Southern Workman* 41 (March 1912): 131- 133.

"Indian Suffragettes." *The Indian's Friend* 25 (March 1913): 11.

Iverson, Peter. *Carlos Montezuma and the Changing World of American Indians.* Albuquerque: U of New Mexico P, 1982.

Jenkins, Wilbert. "Jessie Fauset: A Modern Apostle of Black Racial Pride." *The Zora Neale Hurston Forum* 1(1) (Fall 1986): 14–24.

Johnson, David L. and Raymond Wilson. "Gertrude Simmons Bonnin, 1876–1938: 'Americanize the First American.'" *American Indian Quarterly* 7 (Winter 1988): 27–40.

Johnson, E. Pauline. *The Moccasin Maker*. Tucson: U of Arizona P, 1987.

Johnson, James Weldon. "The Larger Success." *The Southern Workman* 52 (September 1923): 427–436.

Jones, Beverly W. "Mary Church Terrell and the National Association of Colored Women, 1896–1901." *Journal of Negro History* 67 (1982): 20–33.

Jordan, William. " 'The Damnable Dilemma': African-American Accommodation and Protest during World War I." *The Journal of American History* 81(4) (March 1995): 1562–1583.

"Journalism." *Encyclopedia Judaica*. 10 Jerusalem: Keter Publishing House, 1971.

Karger, Howard Jacob Karger. *The Sentinels of Order: A Study of Social Control and the Minneapolis Settlement House Movement, 1915–1950*. Lanham: UP of America, 1987.

Kellogg, Laura Cornelius. "She Likes Indian Public Opinion." *Red Man and Helper* (October 1902): 1.

———. "Some Facts and Figures on Indian Education." *Quarterly Journal of the Society of American Indians* 1 (1913): 36–46.

Kleeman, Belle C. "The Evolution of the Modern Jewish Women (sic)." *The Jewish Woman* 6 (January 1926): 8–10.

Klein, Laura F. and Lillian A. Ackerman, eds. *Women and Power in Native North America*. Norman: U of Oklahoma P, 1995.

Klepfisz, Irena. "Introduction." *Found Treasures: Stories by Yiddish Women Writers*. Eds. Frieda Forman, Ethel Raicus, Sarah Silberstein Swartz, and Margie Wolfe. Toronto: Second Story P, 1994.

Koppleman, Susan. "The Education of Fannie Hurst." *Women's Studies International Forum* 10 (1987): 503–516.

Korelitz, Seth. " 'A Magnificent Piece of Work': The Americanization Work of the National Council of Jewish Women." *American Jewish History* 83 (June 1995): 177–204.

Kornweibel, Theodore, Jr. "Apathy and Dissent: Black America's Negative Responses to World War I." *South Atlantic Quarterly* 80 (1981): 322–338.

Kosmider, Alexia. " 'What the Curious Want to Know': Cherokee Writer, Ora Eddleman Reed Writes Back to the Empire." *Literature and Psychology* 41(4) (1995): 51–72.

Kuzmack, Linda Gordon. *Woman's Cause: The Jewish Woman's Movement in England and the U.S. 1881–1933.* Columbus: Ohio State UP, 1990.

Larson, Charles R. *American Indian Fiction.* Albuquerque: U of New Mexico P, 1978.

Lasch-Quinn, Elisabeth. *Black Neighbors: Race and the Limits of Reform in the American Settlement House Movement, 1890–1945.* Chapel Hill: U of North Carolina P, 1993.

Lasker, Florina. "Native and Newcomer." *The Immigrant* 3 (December 1923): 6–8.

———. "A Reply to Willa Cather." *The Immigrant* 4 (March 1925): 1–4.

Lasker, Florina et al. *Care and Treatment of the Jewish Blind in the City of New York.* New York: Bureau of Philanthropic Research, 1918.

Lawson, Roberta Campbell. "Indian Music Saved." *General Federation of Women's Clubs Official Report.* Ed. Mrs. James E. Hays. Washington: General Federation of Women's Clubs, 1924: 447–449.

"Lawson, Roberta Campbell." *American Women* 2 (1937–1938): 388.

"Lawson, Roberta E. Campbell." *Who's Who in America* (1938-1939): 1495.

"Legislative Notes." *The Immigrant* 1 (Mid-Summer 1921): 11.

Lehman, Mrs. Irving. "Immigrant Aid as a Factor in Americanism." *The Immigrant* 1 (March 1922): 6–7.

Lerner, Gerda, ed. *Black Women in White America: A Documentary History.* New York: Vintage, 1972.

———. "Early Community Work of Black Club Women." *Black Women in American History.* Ed. Darlene Clark Hine. 3: 855–865.

Lerner, Elinor. "Jewish Involvement in the New York City Woman Suffrage Movement." *American Jewish History* 70(4) (June 1981): 442–461.

Levinger, Elma Ehrlich. "Is the Jewish Home a Myth?: Our Sabbath Schools and Young Peoples' Societies Must Compensate for Mah Jong Mothers." *The American Hebrew* (October 3, 1924): 615, 656.

———. "It's All For a Good Cause." *The American Hebrew* (June 27, 1924): 213, 218.

———. "The Jewish Woman as Author." *The Jewish Woman* 2 (September 1922): 7–8.

———. "The Jewish Woman as Author." *The Jewish Tribune* 40 (October 13, 1922): 12.

———. "The New Jew in Fiction." *The American Hebrew* (January 2, 1925): 247, 262.

Lewis, David Levering. *W. E. B. Du Bois: Biography of a Race, 1868–1919.* New York: Holt, 1993.

Lewis, Vashti Crutcher. "Mulatto Hegemony in the Novels of Jessie Redmon Fauset." *CLA Journal* 35(4) (June 1992): 375–386.

Lichtenstein, Diane. "Fannie Hurst and Her Nineteenth-Century Predecessors." *Studies in American Jewish Literature* 7 (1988): 26–39.

———. *Writing Their Nations: The Tradition of Nineteenth-Century American Jewish Women Writers.* Bloomington: Indiana UP, 1992.

Littlefield, Daniel F., Jr. and James W. Parins, eds. *A Biobibliography of Native American Writers, 1772–1924.* Metuchen: Scarecrow P, 1981.

———. *A Biobibliography of Native American Writers, 1772–1924, A Supplement.* Metuchen: Scarecrow P, 1985.

Loeb, Therese M. "The Lucretia Mott Amendment: Pro and Con." *The Jewish Woman* 4 (February 1924): 3–4, 27.

Logan, Shirley. "Rhetorical Strategies in Ida B. Wells' *Southern Horrors: Lynch Law in All Its Phases.*" *Sage* 8 (1991–94): 3–9.

Lomawaima, K. Tsianina. *They Called It Prairie Light: The Story of Chilocco Indian School.* Lincoln: U of Nebraska P, 1994.

"The Looking Glass." *The Crisis* (August 1918): 178–179, 180, 182; (September 1918): 230–231, 232; (October 1918): 279; (November 1918): 23, 25, 27; (December 1918): 79, 80, 81; (January 1919): 127, 129; (February 1919): 186, 187, 190; (April 1919): 288–292.

Lorde, Audre. "The Master's Tools Will Never Dismantle the Master's House." Eds. Cherrie Moraga and Gloria Anzaldua. *This Bridge Called My Back.* New York: Kitchen Table: Women of Color P, 1981.

Lupton, Mary Jane. "Black Women and Survival in *Comedy American Style* and *Their Eyes Were Watching God.*" *The Zora Neale Hurston Forum* 1(1) (Fall 1986): 38–44.

———. "Bad Blood in Jersey: Jessie Fauset's *The Chinaberry Tree.*" *CLA Journal* 27(4) (June 1984): 383–392.

MacLean, J. P. "McWhorter, Friend of the Yakimas." *American Indian Magazine* 5 (1917): 154–159.

McAnulty, Sarah. "Angel DeCora: American Indian Artist and Educator." *Nebraska History* 57 (1976): 143–199.

McCoy, Beth A. " 'Is This Really What You Wanted Me To Be?': The Daughter's Disintegration in Jessie Redmon Fauset's *There is Confusion.*" *Modern Fiction Studies* 40(1) (Spring 1994): 101–117.

McDowell, Deborah. "The Neglected Dimension of Jessie Redmon Fauset." Eds. Marjorie Pryse and Hortense J. Spillers. *Conjuring: Black Women, Fiction, and Literary Tradition.* Bloomington: Indiana UP, 1985.

McLendon, Jacquelyn Y. *The Politics of Color in the Fiction of Jessie Fauset and Nella Larsen.* Charlottesville: UP of Virginia, 1995.

McLester, Thelma Cornelius. "Oneida Women Leaders." *The Oneida Indian Experience: Two Perspectives*. Eds. Jack Campisi and Laurence M. Hauptman. Syracuse: Syracuse UP, 1988: 109–111.

Mandel, Irving Aaron. "Attitude of the American Jewish Community Toward East-European Immigration." *American Jewish Archives* 3 (June 1950): 11–36.

Marcus, Jacob R. *The American Jewish Woman: A Documentary History*. New York: KTAV Publishing, 1981.

Martin, Tony, ed. *African Fundamentalism: A Literary and Cultural Anthology of Garvey's Harlem Renaissance*. Dover: Majority P, 1983.

"The Massacre of East St. Louis." *The Crisis* 14 (September 1917): 215–216.

Mathews, John Joseph. *Sundown*. New York: Longman, Green, 1934; Norman: U of Oklahoma P, 1988.

Matthews, Mark D. " 'Our Women and What They Think': Amy Jacques Garvey and the *Negro World*." *Black Women in American History*. Ed. Darlene Clark Hine. 3: 866–878.

Meisenheimer, D. K., Jr. "Regionalist Bodies/Embodied Regions: Sarah Orne Jewett and Zitkala-Sa." *Breaking Boundaries: New Perspectives on Women's Regional Writing*. Eds., Sherrie A. Inness and Diana Royer. Iowa City: U of Iowa P, 1997: 109–123.

Mena, Maria Cristina. "Birth of the God of War." *Century Magazine* 88 (May 1914): 45.

———. "The Vine Leaf." *Century Magazine* 89 (December 1914): 289–292

Metzker, Isaac. *A Bintel Brief: Sixty Years of Letters from the Lower East Side to the "Jewish Daily Forward."* New York: Schocken, 1971.

Miller, Jay. "Introduction." Ed. *Mourning Dove: A Salishan Autobiography*. Lincoln: U of Nebraska P, 1990.

———. "Mourning Dove: The Author as Cultural Mediator." *Being and Becoming Indian: Biographical Studies of North American Frontiers*. Ed. James A. Clifton. Chicago: Dorsey P, 1989.

Moore, Deborah Dash. *At Home in America: Second Generation of New York Jews*. New York: Columbia UP, 1981.

Morrison, Daryl. "Twin Territories: The Indian Magazine." *Chronicles of Oklahoma* 60 (1982–83): 136–166.

Morton, Leah. *I Am a Woman and a Jew*. 1926. New York: Arno P, 1969.

———. "I Am a Woman—and a Jew." *The Jewish Tribune* (February 4, 1927): 16.

Mourning Dove. *Mourning Dove: A Salishan Autobiography*. Ed. Jay Miller. Lincoln: U of Nebraska P, 1990.

————. *Cogewea: The Half-Blood.* 1927. Boston: Four Seas; Lincoln: U of Nebraska P, 1981.

————. *Coyote Stories.* 1933. Idaho: Caxton Printers; Lincoln: U of Nebraska P, 1990.

Mueller-Cohen, Anita. "The World of the New Woman." *The Jewish Woman* 6 (October 1926): 1–3.

Murphy, James E. and Sharon M. Murphy. *Let My People Know: American Indian Journalism.* Norman: U of Oklahoma P, 1981.

Nakano, Mei. *Japanese American Women: Three Generations 1890–1990.* Berkeley: Mina P Publishing, 1990.

Nalty, Bernard C. *Strength for the Fight: A History of Black Americans in the Military.* New York: Free P, 1986.

"The National Association of Colored Women." *The Southern Workman* 45 (September 1916): 492–493.

Neverdon-Morton, Cynthia. *Afro-American Women of the South and the Advancement of the Race, 1895–1925.* Knoxville: U of Tennessee P, 1989.

North, Michael. *The Dialect of Modernism: Race, Language, and Twentieth-Century Literature.* New York: Oxford UP, 1994.

O'Brien, Sharon. *American Indian Tribal Governments.* Norman: U of Oklahoma P, 1989.

Omi, Michael and Howard Winant. *Racial Formations in the US: From the 1960s to the 1990s.* 1986. New York: Routledge, 1994.

"On the Bookshelf." *The Crisis* 22–23 (1921–22): 60–64.

Otis, D. S. *The Dawes Act and the Allotment of Indian Lands.* Ed. Francis Paul Prucha. Norman: U of Oklahoma P, 1973.

"Our Prize Essay Contest." *The Immigrant* (October 1923): 1–11.

"Our Second Prize Essay Contest." *The Immigrant* (October 1924): 1–11.

Owens, Louis. *Other Destinies: Understanding the American Indian Novel.* Norman: U of Oklahoma P, 1992.

Park, Marlene. "Lynching and Antilynching: Art and Politics in the 1930s." *Prospects* 18 (1993): 311–365.

Parker, Arthur C. "The American Indian in the World War." *The Southern Workman* 47 (February 1918): 61–63.

Patton, Gerald W. *War and Race: The Black Officer in the American Military, 1915–1941.* Westport, Conn.: Greenwood, 1982.

Peiss, Kathy. *Cheap Amusements: Working Women and Leisure in Turn-of-the-Century New York.* Philadelphia: Temple UP, 1986.

Perkins, Kathy A. *"Strange Fruit": Plays on Lynching by American Women.* Bloomington: Indiana UP, 1998.

Peterson, Carla L. *"Doers of the Word": African American Women Speakers and Writers in the North (1830–1880)*. New York: Oxford UP, 1995.

Peyer, Bernd C., ed. *The Singing Spirit: Early Short Stories by North American Indians*. Tucson: U of Arizona P, 1989.

Picotte, Agnes. "Biographical Sketch of the Author." *Waterlily*. By Ella Cara Deloria. Lincoln: U of Nebraska P, 1988.

Pierce, Evelyn. "The Value of Higher Academic Training for the Indian Student." *Quarterly Journal of the Society of American Indians* 3 (1915): 107–109.

Pike, Elvira. "Public Schools For Indians." *Quarterly Journal of the Society of American Indians* 1 (1913): 59–60.

———. "The Right Spirit for the Indian Student and How to Get It." *Quarterly Journal of the Society of American Indians* 1 (1913): 401–403.

Plant, Deborah G. *Every Tub Must Sit on Its Own Bottom: The Philosophy and Politics of Zora Neale Hurston*. Chicago: U of Illinois P, 1995.

Pratt, Norma Fain. "Culture and Radical Politics: Yiddish Women Writers in America 1890–1940." *Women of the Word: Jewish Women and Jewish Writing*. Ed. Judith Baskin. Detroit: Wayne State UP, 1994.

"A Premium on Bigamy." *The Immigrant* 4 (September 1924): 1–2.

"Problems in Adjustment." *The Immigrant* 6 (May 1927): 4–16.

Prucha, Francis Paul. *The Great Father: The United States Government and the American Indians*. Lincoln: U of Nebraska P, 1984.

Rampersad, Arnold. *The Art and Imagination of W. E. B. Du Bois*. Boston: The President and Fellows of Harvard College, 1976.

Ranson, Naomi. "Proposed National Marriage and Divorce Legislation." *The Jewish Woman* 7 (July-September 1927): 1–3.

Razovsky, Cecilia. "National Conference of Social Work Stresses Immigration Problems." Papers of Cecilia Razovsky, Box 1, American Jewish Historical Society, Waltham, Mass.

———. "The Relation of Nationality to Income." *The Immigrant* 7 (April 1927): 8–9.

———. *What Every Woman Should Know About Citizenship*. National Council of Jewish Women, 1926.

Reed, Barbara Straus. *"Pioneer Jewish Journalism." Outsiders in 19th-Century Press History*. Eds. Frankie Hutton and Barbara Straus Reed. Bowling Green: Bowling Green State U Popular P, 1995: 21–54.

Reichwein, Jeffrey C. *Emergence of Native American Nationalism in the Columbia Plateau*. New York: Garland, 1990.

Reis, Nannie A. "Council 'Thou Shalt Nots'—." *The Jewish Woman* (April-June 1929): 6–7.

———. "In the World of Jewish Womankind: Women and the Political Questions." *The Reform Advocate* (June 28, 1924): 778–779.

———. "The Modern Esther." *The Jewish Woman*. 8 (January-March 1928): 4–5.

Rischin, Moses. "Germans Versus Russians." *The American Jewish Experience*. Ed. Jonathan Sarna. New York: Holmes and Meier, 1986: 120–134.

"Roberta Campbell Lawson." *Tushka Homan* (September 24, 1935).

Rogow, Faith. *Gone to Another Meeting: The National Council of Jewish Women, 1893–1993*. Tuscaloosa: U of Alabama P, 1993.

Ruby, Robert H. and John A. Brown. *The Spokane Indians: Children of the Sun*. Norman: U of Oklahoma P, 1970.

Rudnick, Lois. "The New Woman." *1915, The Cultural Moment*. Eds. Adele Heller and Lois Rudnick. New Brunswick: Rutgers UP, 1991: 69–81.

Ruoff, A. LaVonne-Brown. "Justice for Indians and Women: The Protest Fiction of Alice Callahan and Pauline Johnson." *World Literature Today: A Literary Quarterly* 66(2) (Spring 1992): 249–255.

Sachs, Emanie. "The Small Town in Fiction." *The American Hebrew* (October 3, 1924): 631.

Salem, Dorothy. *To Better Our World: Black Women in Organized Reform, 1890–1920*. Brooklyn: Carlson, 1990.

Samuels, Shirley, ed. *The Culture of Sentiment: Race, Gender, and Sentimentality in Nineteenth-Century America*. New York: Oxford UP, 1992.

Sarna, Jonathan D. " 'The Greatest Jew in the World Since Jesus Christ': The Jewish Legacy of Louis D. Brandeis." *American Jewish History* 81 (Spring-Summer 1994): 346–364.

Schniderman, Harry, ed. *American Jewish Yearbook* 24. Philadelphia: JPSA, 1922.

Schniderman, Harry and Itzhak J. Carmin, eds. *Who's Who in World Jewry*. New York: Who's Who in World Jewry Inc., 1955.

Schoen, Carol B. *Anzia Yezierska*. Boston: Twayne, 1982.

Schreier, Barbara A. *Becoming American Women: Clothing and the Jewish Immigrant Experience, 1880–1920*. Chicago: Chicago Historical Society, 1994.

Scott, Anne Firor. *Natural Allies: Women's Associations in American History*. Urbana: U of Illinois P, 1991.

Scott, Emmett J. *Scott's Official History of the American Negro in the World War*. Chicago: Homewood P, 1919.

Seller, Maxine S. "World of Our Mothers: The Women's Page of the *Jewish Daily Forward* Foreword." *The Journal of Ethnic Studies* 16 (Summer 1988): 95–118.

Shepherd, Naomi. *A Price Below Rubies: Jewish Women as Rebels and Radicals*. Cambridge: Harvard UP, 1993.

Shoemaker, Nancy, ed. *Negotiators of Change: Historical Perspectives on Native American Women*. New York: Routledge, 1995.

Simon, Rita and Susan H. Alexander. *The Ambivalent Welcome: Print Media, Public Opinion, and Immigration*. Westport: Praeger, 1993.

Singerman, Robert. "The American Jewish Press, 1823–1983: A Bibliographic Survey of Research and Studies." *American Jewish History* 73(4) (June 1984): 422–444.

Sinkoff, Nancy B. "Educating for 'Proper' Jewish Womanhood: A Case Study in Domesticity and Vocational Training, 1897–1926." *American Jewish History* 77 (June 1988): 572–599.

Sochen, June. *Consecrate Every Day: The Public Lives of Jewish American Women, 1880–1980*. Albany: State U of New York P, 1981.

Solis-Cohen, Judith. "The Jewish Woman of Yesterday and Today." *The Jewish Woman* 7 (April 1927): 1–2.

Sollors, Werner. *Beyond Ethnicity: Consent and Descent in American Culture*. New York: Oxford UP, 1986.

Sorin, Gerald. "Mutual Contempt, Mutual Benefit: The Strained Encounter Between German and Eastern European Jews in America, 1880–1920." *American Jewish History* 81 (Autumn 1993): 34–59.

———. *A Time for Building: The Third Migration 1880–1920*. Baltimore: Johns Hopkins UP, 1992.

Stern, Elizabeth Gertrude. "The Job, the Home and Woman." *The Jewish Woman* 5 (March 1925): 6–8.

Sternberger, Estelle M. "The Birth of Democracy." *The Jewish Woman* 1 (March 1925): 9–10.

———. "Has Woman's Vote Improved Politics?" *The Jewish Woman* 5 (October 1925): 15–17.

———. "Racial Minorities." *The Immigrant* 2 (May 1922): 6–7.

———. "Sane Americanism." *The Jewish Woman* 4 (April 1924): 16.

Streitmatter, Rodger. *Raising Her Voice: African-American Women Journalists Who Changed History*. Lexington: UP of Kentucky, 1994.

Stubbs, Katherine. "Introduction." *Arrogant Beggar*. Durham: Duke UP, 1996: vii–xxxiv.

Sugimoto, Etsu Inagaki. *A Daughter of the Samurai*. 1926. Rutland, Vt.: Charles E. Tuttle, 1966.

Sylvander, Carolyn Wedin. *Jessie Redmon Fauset, Black American Writer*. Troy: Whitston, 1981.

Szasz, Margaret. *Education and the American Indian: The Road to Self-Determination, 1928–1973*. Albuquerque: U of New Mexico P, 1974.

Tate, Claudia. *Domestic Allegories of Political Desire: The Black Heroine's Text at the Turn of the Century.* New York: Oxford, 1992.

Terrell, Mary Church. *A Colored Woman in a White World.* Washington, D.C.: Ransdell, 1940.

Thompson, Mildred I. *Ida B. Wells-Barnett: An Exploratory Study of an American Black Woman, 1893–1930.* Brooklyn: Carlson, 1990.

Tolbert, Emory J. "Federal Surveillance of Marcus Garvey and the U.N.I.A." *The Journal of Ethnic Studies* 14(4) (Spring 1986; Winter 1987): 25–46.

Tompkins, Jane. *Sensational Designs: The Cultural Work of American Fiction, 1790–1860.* New York: Oxford UP, 1985.

Trennert, Robert A. "Educating Indian Girls at Nonreservation Boarding Schools." *The Western Historical Quarterly* (July 1982): 271–290.

Trolander, Judith. *Professionalism and Social Change: From Settlement House Movement to Neighborhood Centers, 1886 to the Present.* New York: Columbia UP, 1987.

"A True Daughter of Israel." *The Jewish Tribune* (April 7, 1922): 1, 20.

Tulsa Tribune. (December 31, 1940): 1–7.

Umansky, Ellen M. "Representations of Jewish Women in the Works and Life of Elizabeth Stern." *Modern Judaism* 13 (May 1993): 165–176.

Utley, Robert, ed. *Battlefield and Classroom: Four Decades with the American Indian, the Memoirs of Richard H. Pratt.* New Haven: Yale UP, 1964.

Viehmann, Martha L. " 'My people. . . my kind': Mourning Dove's *Cogewea, The Half-Blood* as a Narrative of Mixed Descent." *Early Native American Writing: New Critical Essays.* Ed. Helen Jaskoski. Cambridge: Cambridge UP, 1996: 204–222.

Wald, Priscilla. " 'Changed But Not Yet Fused': The Discourse of Becoming and the Narrative of Assimilation." Narrative: An International Conference, Gainsville, Fla., April 5, 1997.

———. *Constituting Americans: Cultural Anxiety and Narrative Form.* Durham: Duke UP, 1995.

Wall, Cheryl A. *Women of the Harlem Renaissance.* Bloomington: Indiana UP, 1995.

Wallach, Sidney. "A Novelist Who Refuses to Preach Sermons." *The Jewish Tribune* (July 22, 1927): 5.

Warrior, Robert Allen. *Tribal Secrets: Recovering American Indian Intellectual Traditions.* Minneapolis: U of Minnestota P, 1995.

Welch, Deborah Sue. *Zitkala-sa: An American Indian Leader, 1876–1938.* Ph.D. dissertation, U of Wyoming, 1985.

Wells-Barnett, Ida B. *Crusade for Justice: The Autobiography of Ida B. Wells.* Chicago: U of Chicago P, 1970.

————. *On Lynchings: Southern Horrors, A Red Record, Mob Rule in New Orleans.* 1892, 1895, 1900. New York: Arno P, 1969.

Wexler, Laura. "Looking at Yezierska." *Women of the Word: Jewish Women and Jewish Writing.* Ed. Judith R. Baskin. Detroit: Wayne State UP, 1994: 153–181.

————. "Tender Violence: Literary Eavesdropping, Domestic Fiction, and Educational Reform." *The Culture of Sentiment.* Ed. Shirley Samuels. New York: Oxford UP, 1992: 9–38.

" 'What the Public Wants': A Remarkable Symposium By Gifted Writers." *The Jewish Tribune* (Dec. 1, 1922): 9.

Whitfield, Stephen J. "The American Jew as Journalist." *Studies in Contemporary Jewry III.* New York: Oxford UP, 1987: 161–180.

Whiteman, Maxwell and Kenneth Libo. *A People in Print: Jewish Journalism in America.* Philadelphia: National Museum of American Jewish History, 1987.

"Who Are the Twelve Outstanding Jews?" *The Jewish Tribune* (July 21, 1922): 1.

"Who's Who in Literature—1924." *The American Hebrew* (December 5, 1924): 140, 144.

"Who's Who of Contributors." *The American Hebrew.* (September 26, 1924).

"Why the Temporary Committee on Naturalization." *The Immigrant* 5 (September 1925): 6–7, 12.

Wilentz, Gay. "Cultural Mediation and the Immigrant's Daughter: Anzia Yezierska's *Bread Givers.*" *MELUS* 17(3) (Fall 1991–92): 33–41.

————. "Introduction." *Salome of the Tenements.* Urbana: U of Illinois P, 1995: ix–xxvi.

————. "White Patron and Black Artist: The Correspondence of Fannie Hurst and Zora Neale Hurston." *Library Chronicle of the University of Texas* 35 (1986): 20–43.

Willard, William. "The First Amendment, Anglo-Conformity and American Indian Religious Freedom." *Wicazo-Sa Review* 7 (Spring 1991): 25–41.

————. "Zitkala-Sa: A Woman Who Would Be Heard." *Wicazo-Sa Review* 1 (Spring 1985): 11–16.

Williams, Lee E. *Post-War Riots in America 1919 and 1946: How the Pressures of War Exacerbated American Urban Tensions to the Breaking Point.* New York: Edwin Mellen P, 1991.

Williams, Walter L. "Twentieth Century Indian Leaders: Brokers and Providers." *Journal of the West* 23 (July 1984): 3–6.

Wilson, Christopher P. *White Collar Fictions: Class and Social Representations in American Literature, 1885–1925.* Athens: U of Georgia P, 1992.

Wise, Stephen S. "Booker Washington: American." *The Southern Workman* 45 (June 1916): 382–383.

Wolcott, Victoria Widgeon. "Remaking Respectability: African-American Women and the Politics of Identity in Inter-War Detroit." Ph.D. dissertation, U of Michigan, 1995.

"Women in Social Service—1924." *American Hebrew* (December 5, 1924): 91.

"Women in the World's News." *The Jewish Woman* 9 (October—December, 1929): 47.

"Women Who Do Things." *The Jewish Tribune* (August 18, 1922): 15.

Wynn, Neil A. *From Progressivism to Prosperity: World War I and American Society.* New York: Holmes and Meier, 1986.

Yezierska, Anzia. *All I Could Never Be.* New York: Brewer, Warren, and Putnam, 1932.

———. *Arrogant Beggar.* 1927. New York: Doubleday; Durham: Duke UP, 1996.

———. *Bread Givers.* 1925. New York: Doubleday; New York: Persea Books, 1975.

———. *Hungry Hearts and Other Stories.* 1920. New York: Doubleday; New York: Persea Books, 1985.

———. "'The Lost Beautifulness': The Story of a Seeker After Beauty in the Ghetto." *The Jewish Tribune* (September 22, 1922): 26, 45.

———. *Salome of the Tenements.* 1923. New York: Boni and Liveright; Urbana: U of Illinois P, 1995.

Yung, Judy. "The Social Awakening of Chinese American Women as Reported in *Chung Sai Yat Po*, 1900–1911." *Unequal Sisters: A Multicultural Reader in U.S. Women's History.* Eds. Ellen Carol DuBois and Vicki L. Ruiz. New York: Routledge, 1990: 195–207.

Zierler, Wendy Ilene. "Border Crossings: The Emergence of Jewish Women's Writing in Israel and America and the Immigrant Experience." Ph.D. dissertation, Princeton U, 1995.

Zitkala-Sa. "America, Home of the Red Man." *American Indian Magazine* 6 (July-September, 1918): 165–167.

———. *American Indian Stories.* 1921. Washington D.C.: Hayworth; Lincoln: U of Nebraska P, 1979.

————. "The Black Hills Council." *American Indian Magazine* 7 (Spring 1919): 5–7.

————. "Hope in the Returned Indian Soldier." *American Indian Magazine* 7 (Summer, 1919): 61–62.

————. "Indian Gifts to Civilized Man." *American Indian Magazine* 6 (July-September, 1918): 115–116.

————. *Old Indian Legends*. 1901. Boston: London Ginn and Co.; Lincoln: U of Nebraska P, 1985.

————. "A Protest Against the Abolition of the Indian Dance." *Red Man and Helper* 3 (August 22, 1902): 1, 4.

————. "The Ute Grazing Land." *American Indian Magazine* 7 (Spring 1919): 8–9.

————. "Why I Am a Pagan." *Atlantic* 90 (December 1902): 801–803.

Index

Abbot, Robert, 54, 57

Acculturation, 6, 7; *see also under* Jewish Americans

Addams, Jane, 92, 111, 124

Adler, Lillian, 109

African American press, 75, 88; women's periodical journalism, 4, 13, 146–47*n*1; World War I controversies in, 53–70

African Americans, 8, 9, 11, 89, 95, 99; American identity of, 60, 62, 64–65, 78; elites, 72, 82–83, 90, 156*n*22; family, 82–83, 87; and Jewish Americans, 5; migrants, 110; nationalism, 8, 64, 154*n*16; position in U.S. society, 48, 64–65, 71, 80–82, 89–90, 94, 148–49*n*7, 150*n*16; protest, 57, 61, 66, 70, 71, 80, 82; representations of, in Jewish women's fiction, 10, 112, 125, 128–29, 130, 133–34, 164*n*18; "respectability," 151*n*2

—women, 1, 2, 7, 8, 9, 10, 100, 116, 131–36; and domesticity, 6, 82–83, 105, 152*n*3; domestic service, 67–68, 90, 129, 130, 132, 156*n*23, periodical journalism, 4, 13, 146–47*n*1; social activism of, 150–51*n*22; wartime organizing, 31, 67–69; welfare workers, 151*n*52.

African American soldiers (World War I), 7, 13, 55, 61, 63–64, 65, 69, 72–77, 80, 81–82, 86, 148*n*6, 149*n*7; accused of rape, 152*n*7; and French society, 61, 69; returned from war, 63–64

Alba, Richard, 140*n*22

Allen, Paula Gunn, 44

Allotment, 15, 16, 32–33, 38, 40, 42–43, 52, 132, 133; critique of, 35, *see* General Allotment Act

American Friend's Inter-racial Peace Committee, 65

American Hebrew, The, 5, 109